International Joint Commission (waterways).: Hearings Before The Committee On Foreign Affairs, House Of Representatives, February 24, 1913, On H.r. 28607...

United States. Congress. House. Committee on Foreign Affairs, James A. Tawney, Allan Joseph McLaughlin

United States. Foreign Affairs
      Committee.   (House)

63 Cong.   1 Sess.

Hearings.   Miscellaneous.

1.   Diversion of water from the
          Niagara River.

2.   International Joint Commission
          (Waterways).

DIVERSION OF WATER FROM THE NIAGARA RIVER

HEARINGS

BEFORE THE

COMMITTEE ON FOREIGN AFFAIRS

HOUSE OF REPRESENTATIVES

JANUARY 23 AND 24, 1913

ON

BILL PROPOSED BY THE SUBCOMMITTEE ON NIAGARA
FALLS LEGISLATION, DATED JANUARY 15, 1913

WASHINGTON
GOVERNMENT PRINTING OFFICE
1913

COMMITTEE ON FOREIGN AFFAIRS.

HOUSE OF REPRESENTATIVES.

[Committee room, gallery floor, west corridor.   Telephone 230.   Meets on call.]

HENRY D. FLOOD, Virginia, *Chairman*.

JOHN N. GARNER, Texas.
GEORGE S. LEGARE, South Carolina.
WILLIAM G. SHARP, Ohio.
CYRUS CLINE, Indiana.
JEFFERSON M. LEVY, New York.
JAMES M. CURLEY, Massachusetts.
J. CHAS. LINTHICUM, Maryland.
ROBERT E. DIFENDERFER, Pennsylvania.
WILLIAM S. GOODWIN, Arkansas.
CHARLES M. STEDMAN, North Carolina.

EDWARD W. TOWNSEND, New Jersey.
BYRON P. HARRISON, Mississippi.
WILLIAM B. McKINLEY, Illinois.
HENRY A. COOPER, Wisconsin.
IRA W. WOOD, New Jersey.
RICHARD BARTHOLDT, Missouri.
GEORGE W. FAIRCHILD, New York.
N. E. KENDALL, Iowa.
J. HAMPTON MOORE, Pennsylvania.

FRANK S. CISNA, *Clerk*.
B. F. ODEN, *Assistant Clerk*.

II

DIVERSION OF WATER FROM THE NIAGARA RIVER.

COMMITTEE ON FOREIGN AFFAIRS,
HOUSE OF REPRESENTATIVES,
Wednesday, January 22, 1913.

The committee met at 10.30 o'clock a. m., Hon. Henry D. Flood (chairman) presiding.

The CHAIRMAN. The committee will come to order. The matter set for hearing this morning is on the bill proposed by the subcommittee, which is now printed and is now before the committee. Attorney General Carmody, of New York State, is here and we will be glad to hear you now, General.

Mr. DIFENDERFER. Mr. Chairman, is this supposed to be a hearing regarding this report?

The CHAIRMAN. Yes. At the last hearing, Mr. Difenderfer, the committee adopted a resolution, in response to a request from Gov. Sulzer and Attorney General Carmody, to have this hearing on this bill. That was all that the committee decided on at that time.

[Bill proposed by subcommittee on Niagara Falls legislation.]

A BILL For the control and regulation o fthe waters of the Niagara River in the State of New York for the preservation of Niagara Falls, and for other purposes.

Be it enacted by the Senate and House of Representatives of the United States of America in Congress assembled, That the diversion of waters from the Niagara River in the State of New York is hereby prohibited, except with the consent of the Secretary of War, as herein authorized by this act: *Provided,* That this prohibition shall not be interpreted as forbidding the diversion of water of the Great Lakes or of Niagara River for public use for sanitary or domestic purposes, or for navigation, the amount of which, except that needed for the navigation of the Erie Canal, may be fixed from time to time by the Congress of the United States, or by the Secretary of War under its direction.

SEC. 2. That the Secretary of War is hereby authorized to grant for the public benefit of the State of New York and other States into which electrical power may be transmitted revocable permits for the diversion of water in the United States from said Niagara River above the Falls to an aggregate amount stated in said permits not exceeding in daily diversion at any one time the amount of fifteen thousand six hundred cubic feet of water per second: *Provided,* That whenever the Secretary of War shall determine that the diversions of water herein authorized in connection with the amount of water diverted on the Canadian side of the river interferes with the navigable capacity of said river, or its proper volume as a boundary stream, or its efficiency as a means of national defense, or the scenic grandeur of Niagara Falls, or that the waters diverted for the development of electrical power are not being utilized to their full or proper standard of efficiency, or that the public interests are not being conserved or protected in the use, transmission, or sale of electrical power generated therefrom, he shall revoke any permit granted after giving five years' notice to the said parties holding the said revocable permits and to the Congress of the United States of his intention to make such revocation.

SEC. 3. That the Secretary of War is hereby authorized to issue permits for the diversion of water below the Falls.

SEC. 4. That in granting a revocable permit for the diversion of waters from the Niagara River above the Falls under the conditions of this act the Secretary of War shall have due regard for those investments which have already been made in the construction of power plants under permits issued by the State of New York and the Federal Government and shall give preference in the issuing of such permits to companies, corporations, or bodies now lawfully organized and holding permits and now diverting water under said permits and generating electrical power for the use of cities, towns, manufacturing plants, and other corporate bodies under long-time contracts or leases over any and all other companies and corporations not now having fixed investments for the development of such electrical power: *Provided further*, That the Secretary of War shall certify a copy of any and all revocable permits to the governor of the State or States in which such permits authorize the operation of the company holding the permits.

SEC. 5. That all persons, companies, or corporate bodies now holding permits for the diversion of water from Niagara River for the purpose of creating electrical energy shall, if necessary, reconstruct the plants they are now operating within five years after notice by the Secretary of War that such plant is not constructed so as to utilize the water at its full or proper standard of efficiency in the production of electrical power, and that standard shall be determined by the Secretary of War.

SEC. 6. That the Secretary of War is hereby authorized to grant permits for the transmission of electrical power from the Dominion of Canada into the United States, and the Secretary of War may specify the companies, corporations, or bodies legally organized therefor by whom the same shall be transmitted and the companies, corporations, or bodies to whom the same shall be delivered: *Provided*, That no such transmission permit or delivery of power shall be given by the Secretary of War without the approval of the governor of the State or States into which said power is to be transmitted or delivered: *And provided further*, That the companies, corporations, or bodies receiving such permits for the transmission or delivery shall be governed and regulated as to rates and otherwise as the public service commission of such State, and if no such public service commission exists, then as the governor of such State or States may determine: *And provided further*, That whenever the Secretary of War shall determine that electrical power transmitted from Canada under permits heretofore or hereafter granted is not being utilized, distributed, or sold with due regard to the public interest, or that the right granted under the permit has not been reasonably exercised to its full power or proper capacity, he shall revoke said permit or any part thereof: *And provided further*, That the quantity of electrical power which may be transmitted from Canada into the United States under this act shall not exceed two hundred thousand horsepower.

SEC. 7. That any person, company, or corporation diverting water from the Niagara River or its tributaries or transmitting electrical power into States from Canada, except as herein stated, or violating any of the provisions of this act, shall be deemed guilty of a misdemeanor, and upon conviction thereof shall be punished by a fine not exceeding $2,000 nor less than $500 for each and every day on which such violation occurred or is committed, or by imprisonment (in case of a natural person) not exceeding one year, or both of such punishments in the discretion of the court: *Provided*, That the removal of any structure or parts of structures erected in violation of this act or any construction incidental to or used for such diversion of water or transmission of power as herein prohibited, as well as any diversion of water or transmission of power in violation thereof, may be enjoined or enforced by a suit in the United States in any district court having jurisdiction in any district in which same may be located, and proper proceedings to this end may be instituted under the direction of the Attorney General of the United States.

SEC. 8. That nothing in this act contained shall be construed to validate or confirm any grant heretofore made by the State of New York of any rights or privileges heretofore made directly or indirectly by the said State of New York for the diversion of the waters of Niagara River or of rights in or title to land under the waters thereof, nor shall the grantee under any such grant, or their heirs, representatives, successors, or assigns of such grantees, be deemed by virtue of this act entitled to divert or continue to divert the waters of said river.

SEC. 9. That the provisions of this act shall remain in force and effect during the life of the treaty with reference to the use of boundary waters entered into between the United States and Great Britain and proclaimed on the thirteenth day of May, nineteen hundred and ten.

SEC. 10. That for the accomplishment of the purposes detailed in this act the sum of $10,000, or so much thereof as may be necessary, is hereby appropriated from any moneys in the Treasury not otherwise appropriated.

SEC. 11. That all laws in conflict with this act are hereby repealed.

STATEMENT OF HON. THOMAS CARMODY, ATTORNEY GENERAL OF THE STATE OF NEW YORK.

Mr. CARMODY. Mr. Chairman and gentlemen of the committee, I desire, first, to thank you for the courtesy of being again permitted to appear in behalf of the State of New York, especially as this matter has been before this committee such a length of time that I presume that there is a settled position in the minds of the members of the committee as to the principle which will dominate in the legislation. I am authorized by Gov. Sulzer in what I have to say here, to express his views also in regard to this matter, and for him to thank the committee for the courtesy of being permitted to do so.

The State of New York has not changed its position in regard to the principle of this measure from what it was stated to be in the hearing that we had about a year ago. In that hearing, as I will do now, I stated our position to be this: That we claim that the State of New York is entitled to control, after the Government has decided how much water may be diverted from the Niagara River, the diversion of the water, and to decide the parties to whom it shall go. I announced that principle, not only as what I believe to be the constitutional right of the State of New York, but, what is more concrete, even more important, the property rights of the State and of the citizens of the State. This bill in its title expresses the proposition that the Federal Government has the right to control and regulate the diversion of water from the Niagara River and to preserve the Falls. The two purposes expressed in the title of the bill are in absolute antagonism, it seems to me, to the constitutional rights of the Federal Government in dealing with this proposition. The Federal Government has, without doubt, the right to determine the quantity of water that may be diverted from a boundary stream in the exercise of its constitutional rights to control navigation, but that power is exercised pursuant to that constitutional right only for the purpose of regulating and controlling navigation, and for no other purpose. I have never heard of the regulation proposition——

The CHAIRMAN (interposing). But this is a boundary stream.

Mr. CARMODY. Yes; it is a boundary stream, and it is of such a stream that I am speaking, and in regard to such a stream there is no different principle involved when the boundary line has been determined and the expense to which the territory of the State goes. There is no different principle involved in the regulation of commerce in a boundary stream and in any other navigable stream.

The CHAIRMAN. Except that the Government may insist on controlling that stream as a matter of national defense.

Mr. CARMODY. That, of course, is true; of course in so far as that prerogative of the Federal Government may be involved. There is no such purpose, however, of preserving national defense expressed in this bill. Now, then, this bill is undoubtedly pursuant to the provisions of the treaty between this Government and Canada, and pursuant to that treaty it has been decided that there may be diverted from the Niagara River not to exceed 20,000 cubic feet of water per second.

Mr. DIFENDERFER. That would naturally lead us to the opinion that this is still an international stream in the control of the United States.

Mr. CARMODY. Not necessarily so.

Mr. DIFENDERFER. And as an international boundary it is an international stream.

Mr. CARMODY. I do not understand what an international stream is, in the purview of this question, at all. There is no such thing as an international stream so far as riparian rights are concerned in this country. For instance, the St. Lawrence and Niagara Rivers are boundary streams, the boundaries between this country and its neighbor being defined in terms of law. The boundary of the Niagara River is defined by law and all courts, the courts of the State of New York, have decided that the riparian rights of those who live upon the shores of the Niagara River are precisely the same up to the boundary line as they are on the Mohawk River or the Hudson River. Once having established that boundary line the riparian rights follow and are fixed, not only pursuant to the decisions of the State courts, but pursuant to the decisions of your Federal court, and I make bold to say that there is no decision of the United States Supreme Court that questions this principle, that in respect to a boundary stream, when the boundary of the States has been fixed, then the riparian rights go to the State and are regulated by State laws and not by Federal authority. If there is such a decision I would like to have my attention called to it.

Mr. GARNER. May I ask you a question in that connection?

Mr. CARMODY. With pleasure.

Mr. GARNER. Would the Federal Government have authority to say what degree, or in what portion, you could use this water after you acquire riparian rights?

Mr. CARMODY. Unquestionably not.

The CHAIRMAN. Before you start again there is a question I would like to ask. This was a boundary stream and the Government has right to use this stream in such a way as it saw fit to protect the country in the general defense of the country, and they might want the water at one point in this stream high and at another point low, and the right of general defense would give them the right to control the waters of this boundary stream?

Mr. CARMODY. That is a very interesting question, but not necessarily involved in the principle of this bill. We start in, Mr. Chairman, with the concession on the part of the Federal Government, expressed through this treaty, that there may be diverted from this stream not to exceed 20,000 cubic feet of water per second. Now, the Federal Government has released all Federal control over that amount of water in that river.

The CHAIRMAN. Not necessarily.

Mr. KENDALL. By that treaty was that release effected?

Mr. CARMODY. By that treaty it recognized that this amount of water may be diverted, as the Canadian Government recognizes that a certain amount may be diverted.

Mr. KENDALL. You do not construe that treaty to mean that the Government permitted that water to be diverted, do you?

Mr. CARMODY. No; but that having been determined by the high contracting parties it relieved Federal control and Canadian control from that amount of water from the river and the riparian rights became immediately invoked on that portion of the water.

Mr. KENDALL. On the contrary, didn't the treaty by its express terms reserve to the contracting parties the right to dispose of that much water and place an effectual limitation thereon?

Mr. CARMODY. Did the treaty do that?

Mr. KENDALL. Yes, the treaty consituted a contract between the two countries that no additional water save that provided by the treaty should be so diverted.

Mr. CARMODY. We are not questioning that amount, that 20,000 cubic feet. I am not questioning the principle of the treaty; I am questioning the principle of this bill. You start in with the concession of the water, but you undertake to say in the bill how that 20,000 cubic feet, which belongs to riparian owners, shall be disposed of. The Federal Government has released its control and authority from the amount of water that it permits to be diverted.

Mr. KENDALL. If I understand your contention, it is this, that after the boundary line is established, then the rights of the riparian owners automatically attach, to which the United States Government would have no right; they would have no right to interfere with the disposition of the water?

Mr. CARMODY. I did not mean to be so understood, because I stated before I advanced that proposition that the Federal Government had the right to decide in conjunction with Canada or independently how much water might be diverted from the river, but having so decided, the riparian rights attached to that portion of the water. That is the principle I intended to state here, and not the denial of the power of the Federal Government to limit the amount that may be diverted.

Mr. GOODWIN. Why should the Federal Government reserve 20,000 cubic feet of water per second and then forfeit its control to the disposition of that water, after reserving it?

Mr. CARMODY. Simply because the functions of the Federal Government are twofold. First, in respect to navigation; second, in respect to military defense. Now, having decided that 20,000 cubic feet, or 15,600 cubic feet per second, may be diverted, they have decided that the diversion of that much water does not interfere with the function of military defense. Secondly, the Federal Government has exercised the only power it has when it has decided that that much water shall be diverted, and, having done so, the riparian rights attach to that water at once.

Mr. CLINE. Have you any authority where the Federal Government divides its jurisdiction with the State over any stream that it assumes to have jurisdiction of?

Mr. CARMODY. That might be stated, perhaps, in the language of the Constitution itself, which provides by the tenth amendment that the Federal Government has such powers as are reserved to it by the Constitution, and I ask where in the Constitution has the Federal Government any right to say to the riparian owners, "You shall, or you shall not enjoy your riparian rights to certain streams."

Mr. CLINE. But you are not answering my question.

Mr. CARMODY. If you will make it specific.

Mr. CLINE. I am making it specific. Here is the proposition, that the Federal Government assumes jurisdiction of a navigable stream; it ousts the jurisdiction of the State completely, the riparian owner.

Mr. CARMODY. I do not concede that.

Mr. CLINE. It is so stated in the case of St. Anthony Falls Power Co. *v*. Minneapolis. When the Federal Government assumes jurisdiction over a stream it ousts completely the State government, the riparian owner.

Mr. CARMODY. I do not concede that the court has ever decided that directly. I do not know of any court who has ever decided that way.

Mr. CLINE. Now, let me call your attention to this question. It has been decided over and over again that the Government has the right to issue a license or permit, and it also has the right to limit the use. There is no question about that.

Mr. CARMODY. Yes.

Mr. CLINE. Now, do you assume that there is any conflict between the constitutional power of the bodies entering into this treaty and the treaty itself? Is the treaty principle in harmony with the powers granted by the Constitution?

Mr. CARMODY. I do not question that.

Mr. CLINE. I want to call the attention of the gentleman to Article V of the treaty on page 13:

> The high contracting parties agree that it is expedient to limit the diversion of water from the Niagara River so that the level of Lake Erie and the flow of the stream shall not be appreciably affected. It is the desire of both parties to accomplish this object with the least possible injury to investments which have already been made in the construction of power plants on the United States side of the river under grants of authority from the State of New York, and on the Canadian side of the river under licenses authorized by the Dominion of Canada and the Province of Ontario.

Now, if the treaty is invested with that power it must be invested with power to protect these power plants, and in that is involved the limitations connected with the diversion of this water. That, it seems to me, is a fairly deductible sequence of the treaty.

Mr. CARMODY. I prefer to answer you in the language of the United States Supreme Court. This principle has been announced so often, and I find it nowhere questioned, that it seems to me this is one question that has been settled as well as any question that has ever come before the courts. This is the case of Martin *v*. Williams (16 Peters, 307). The principle there held was that when the American Revolution was won, the people of these States became themselves sovereign, and in that character held the absolute right to all their navigable waters and the soils under them for their own common use, except only the rights of the United States surrendered by the Constitution to the General Government. That is a principle of law that has been often repeated and it is in absolute antagonism to the principle of this bill. I do not question the rights of the Federal Government to decide how much water may be diverted. We go further, I think, than our rights should justify us in conceding that principle, but we do concede it. We say you have decided, you have decided by treaty, that 20,000 cubic feet may be diverted without interfering with navigation or without interfering with the flow of this stream. Now, having done that, you have exercised the only prerogative that the Federal Government has to exercise. That is a principle that has never been questioned until recently, but I am aware of the fact that recently the policy of the Federal Government has been to overturn this line of decisions and overturn not only what seems to me to be the constitutional rights of the States, but the rights of property in the

States, and there is presented now not merely the question of State rights, but the question of property rights. The man living along the banks of the Niagara River has a right to the water that flows by his banks, and when you have decided how much of this water is needed for military purposes or navigation purposes you interfere when you undertake to regulate the distribution of the remainder of the water—you invade the property rights of those riparian owners, according to our court decisions, according to the decisions of the United States Supreme Court.

Mr. GARNER. May I ask you a question, General? I understand your position to be that there is no difference between an internal stream and a boundary stream, and after Congress has decided what amount of water can be taken for any purpose that does not injure navigation it has no right to fix the distribution of that water?

Mr. CARMODY. That is my proposition.

Mr. GARNER. Therefore, in this instance, Congress having determined by treaty, which is equal to, if not superior to, an act of Congress itself, that 20,000 cubic feet may be taken on the American side, your contention is that the people of New York are entitled to this water by virtue of riparian rights?

Mr. CARMODY. Yes, sir.

Mr. GARNER. Therefore there is no necessity for any act of Congress in the premises whatever?

Mr. CARMODY. I do not think there is any necessity if we concede that they have exercised by that treaty——

Mr. GARNER (interposing). One step further; I understood you to say awhile ago that you thought, for instance, in the State of New York that the Federal Government did not have absolute control of the navigable streams to the exclusion of riparian rights. Is that correct?

Mr. CARMODY. Yes, sir.

Mr. GARNER. I do not understand the logic of your argument in these boundary propositions. In one statement you contend that Congress has determined how much water may be taken; then we have no right to say how it shall be used. Another time you say Congress has no right to take or determine the amount of water.

Mr. CARMODY. In an internal stream.

Mr. GARNER. An internal stream?

Mr. CARMODY. Certainly not, because there is no interstate commerce involved there.

Mr. GARNER. Well, it has been the settled rule in Congress, and has not been disputed so far as I know, that the Federal Government has the right, after it has once declared a stream to be navigable, to prohibit the taking of the waters that would destroy the navigability of the stream. Otherwise there would be no use of appropriating money for making these streams navigable if they could not protect them after they had made them navigable.

Mr. CARMODY. I do not concede the right of the Federal Government, so far as the internal stream is concerned, but that is not the question. I am stating the principles of our State courts. This is the law that has been settled in our State by our State courts. Now, I do not want to waste any great amount of time of this committee, but I want our position to be known and it is this: That you have the right to say how much water may be diverted from the Niagara River. You have said that. Now, having said that, the control of it belongs to the State and to the riparian owners.

Mr. CLINE. Then you do not give any effect to the declaration of the contracting parties in this fifth provision of the treaty?

Mr. CARMODY. I do not question the treaty. I concede what the treaty has done. I concede what Congress has done, but the point I am trying to make is that the Secretary of War has no power whatever, no right after the Federal Government has released a certain amount of water to decide who shall have it, or how it shall be distributed.

Mr. KENDALL. How do you claim that the Federal Government released the 20,000 cubic feet of water?

Mr. CARMODY. The Federal Government has not, except by treaty, and under the Burton Act.

Mr. KENDALL. I direct your attention to these words in the treaty: "The United States may authorize or permit the diversion."

Mr. CARMODY. Well, I do not think the United States has authorized the diversion of the full amount. It has authorized the diversion of 15,600 cubic feet.

Mr. KENDALL. But your contention is that by entering into that treaty for that 20,000 cubic feet of water per second that the United States released that amount of water.

Mr. CARMODY. Congress has authorized the diversion of 15,600 cubic feet, and I believe that Congress should authorize the diversion of the full 20,000 cubic feet. But I am not here to argue that question. Now, I say that, having authorized the diversion of 15,600 cubic feet of water, its power over that amount of water, and the use of it, belongs to the riparian owners and to the State of New York. That is what I say, and that is all I contend for here.

Mr. DIFENDERFER. Do you believe that they have the right to exclude the rights of the generating companies?

Mr. CARMODY. The public service is here represented by its counsel, and in the division of topics here I would rather leave that question to them. I simply want to confine myself in the brief time that I shall take up here to this one question which I have advanced, that having decided that we are entitled or that there may be diverted from that stream certain quantities of water, your power ceases and you should not further provide that these permits must be granted by the Secretary of War. I believe that the reservation of that power to the Federal Government is not justified by the Federal Constitution. I believe it is an invasion of our property rights. I believe it is an invasion of the sovereign authority of the State of New York, that, with its citizens, owns the bed of this stream to its center and owns the water that passes over it; owns the power generated from any water diverted from the stream, and you interfere with our property rights when you say the Secretary of War may grant the right to that water or decide who shall have it.

The CHAIRMAN. Will you file the authorities you have on these questions with the stenographer?

Mr. CARMODY I will be very glad to do so.

[NOTE.—These data not received at time of sending to press. Will be printed in a later edition.]

Mr. CLINE. Will you tell how the Government can accomplish that if your theory is correct?

Mr. CARMODY. I say the Government has nothing to do with it so far as the investment—so far as the investments have been made. Under permit that has been heretofore granted, property rights have been fixed that are absolutely under the control of the laws of the State of New York, and not the Federal Government. The Federal Government has no power to interfere with or to regulate or administer or create any property rights in the State of New York growing out of this diversion. If the Federal Government has any such power I want to know where it gets it. It must be in the Constitution. It is not in the Constitution and, consequently, they do not have it. Now, there is another question, and that is in regard to the transmission into the State of New York of electric power. I do not want to criticize this bill, but there are two interests that are entirely different, so far as character of function is concerned, and so far as the question involved is concerned, but I do say with respect to that that the Federal Government has no right to say how much power shall come into the State of New York, nor what shall be done with it.

Mr. CLINE. It does have the right to say from a foreign country how much shall come into this country?

Mr. CARMODY. It does——

Mr. HARRISON (interposing). Does the gentleman remember the embargo act passed in Jefferson's administration?

Mr. CARMODY. That was a military act.

Mr. HARRISON. It had the power to pass that act.

Mr. CARMODY. Sometimes the Government has the right to exercise special powers under special conditions. They have the right to suspend the writ of habeas corpus under certain circumstances, in time of war.

Mr. HARRISON. There was no war at this time; it was at a time of profound peace.

Mr. CARMODY. Let me ask a question or two: In what law does the Federal Government reserve to itself, or in what provision of the Constitution does it reserve to itself, the right to say how many bushels of wheat, for instance, shall come in from Canada? The Federal Government does not undertake to regulate the price or amount of imports from Canada, but here you undertake to regulate the amount of electric power that will come into the State of New York. We have the right to regulate the operation of foreign companies, to say what company shall do business in the State of New York and under what regulation they shall do it; we have the right to say how much capitalization they shall have and how their business shall be conducted. We have all power in that respect that the Federal Government has now.

Mr. KENDALL. Indirectly the Federal Government would have the right to exclude the transmission of power by levying a tax upon it so heavy that it would amount to excluding it.

Mr. CARMODY. Yes; it has that power.

Mr. KENDALL. That is simply attaining the same end in another way.

Mr. CARMODY. It is under that provision of the Constitution, apparently, that this bill is drawn, that the Federal Government has authority to levy tax on imposts. It may levy a tax large enough to exclude them, but it can not say "You can bring in a certain amount of horsepower and no more."

Mr. KENDALL. It seems to me to be only the difference between tweedledum and tweedledee, because it all amounts to the same thing. Now, taking into account the fact that this bill is enacted as the result of. the negotiations entered into between this country and Great Britain with reference to the diversion of water, how does that affect the situation in your mind?

Mr. CARMODY. Not at all. It all comes back to the original proposition that the Government, having decided how much shall be diverted, the Government has nothing further to say as to what shall be done with it.

Mr. KENDALL. If your position is correct on that, of course your contention is entirely correct.

Mr. CARMODY. I am basing my position on a decision of the United States Supreme Court. In a controversy between Arkansas and Colorado, in which the Government sought to intervene to stop the diversion of water from the Arkansas River in Colorado, and the Supreme Court decided that the Federal Government had nothing to do about the diversion of the water from that stream, that it was entirely a State right.

Mr. KENDALL. So long as navigability was not affected.

Mr. CARMODY. It even went further than that and excluded the United States entirely from the question.

Mr. CLINE. That was for the purpose of stopping the State from appropriating that water for irrigation purposes under the acts and did not turn upon the proposition that you cite at all. It turned upon the question, the decision that you cite, 206 U. S., upon the question as to whether the Federal Government had the right to intervene and prohibit the State from diverting water for irrigation purposes, and this question was not involved at all.

Mr. CARMODY. It involved the same question as to whether the Federal Government has control of navigable streams.

Mr. GARNER. As a matter of fact, if Congress wanted to pass such a provision as is contained in this bill, a limitation to the power coming in from Canada, they could say that 200,000 horsepower, or 100,000 horsepower, as the case might be, should come in free, and all power over that should be $1 a kilowatt, and accomplish the same thing in that way.

Mr. CARMODY. I do not think you could do that.

Mr. GARNER. And be within the Constitution?

Mr. CARMODY. No; no more than you could say that a certain quantity of tobacco should come in free and beyond that it should be taxed.

Mr. KENDALL. In some of our tariff laws we have that very discrimination now.

Mr. CARMODY. Not directly.

Mr. KENDALL. In the same way as was suggested by Mr. Garner.

Mr. LEVY. Your contention is that the Federal Government can only exercise authority over an interstate or boundary stream so far as it affects the navigation. Of course, if you include in that sanitation and irrigation and all those things—of course it has very general powers over them—but that is another function of the Government not involved here.

Mr. CARMODY. No. It has police powers, and they do a great many things that concern the public health that are not involved here.

The CHAIRMAN. But the Federal Government can do what it pleases with this stream if it is used for public defense.

Mr. CARMODY. Yes, sir.

Mr. KENDALL. Suppose that we had not entered into any treaty with Great Britain at all by which the diversion was limited as it is by this treaty, what would have been the situation then?

Mr. CARMODY. If the water were used from the Niagara River, the Federal Government could, upon saying that navigation was interfered with, prevent it.

Mr. KENDALL. And the Federal Government could assert at any time that, in its opinion, navigation was being interfered with, and make the prohibition, and that would be final because it could not be impeached.

Mr. CARMODY. I do not think its decision could be impeached.

Mr. COOPER. Have you read the Smith decision?

Mr. CARMODY. Yes.

Mr. COOPER. Under the arrangement, whose duty is it to issue permits for power?

Mr. CARMODY. It involves the issuance of permits by the Secretary of War.

Mr. COOPER. Has that been attacked before?

Mr. CARMODY. Not previous to this administration.

The CHAIRMAN. Have you read the Simmons bill?

Mr. CARMODY. I have read only the bill presented by the minority committee, Mr. Smith's bill.

Mr. LEVY. Under our public-service laws, as they exist in New York, all the public interests would be conserved and protected under our guardianship just as much as they would be under the National Government, would they not?

Mr. CARMODY. Much better, because we have the right to do it and the Federal Government has not.

Mr. CLINE. We are not inveigling that right in this bill.

Mr. CARMODY. The only purpose of this bill is to protect the scenic beauty of Niagara Falls, and you are invading it there. Can you provide, for instance, for preserving the scenic beauty of the Adirondack forest in New York?

Mr. CLINE. We have provided for the conservation of navigable streams by buying lands and reforesting them for that very purpose, and that is one of the enlarged powers of the Federal Government that is in happy accord with what we are trying to do here.

Mr. CARMODY. You may do that with any lands owned by the Government, but not with any lands owned by the State.

Mr. LEVY. And the fact is we would be in a better position than the United States to protect the interests and the scenic beauty of our State.

Mr. CARMODY. We are doing it now. We are policing it, we are policing our parks and protecting and preserving them by a commission. We are taking care of the Adirondacks, we are taking care of Niagara Falls in the State of New York and preserving their beauty. We are taking care of all the scenic beauties in the State of New York better than could be done by anyone else.

Mr. KENDALL. You spoke a while ago about the inviolability of private property rights there. We had before us sometime ago the representative of those interests, who advanced the principle that they had the right to divert all the water, even to the extent of obliterating the Falls. Of course, you do not acquiesce in a proposition of that sort?

Mr. CARMODY. No; I do not. The State of New York would prohibit such a thing.

Mr. CLINE. Isn't is a fact that when the State of New York issued these grants to power companies that they issued them for more than the Federal Government proposed to permit to be taken out of the Falls?

Mr. CARMODY. Do you mean in regard to permitting the use of the water of Niagara Falls?

Mr. CLINE. Yes.

Mr. CARMODY. I do not understand——

Mr. CLINE (interposing). You were not conserving the scenic beauty of Niagara Falls very much in that respect were you? You authorized over 200,000 cubic feet per second to be taken out of Niagara River, didn't you?

Mr. CARMODY. I am not defending anything that was done by the legislature in the past. I am simply talking about the concrete proposition of this bill. I want you people to understand that we oppose the question of Federal control.

The CHAIRMAN. Mr. Smith would like to ask you a question.

Mr. SMITH. I wanted to ask you whether the Federal Government has any right to protect the scenic beauty of the Falls?

Mr. CARMODY. In this bill?

Mr. SMITH. In any bill.

Mr. CARMODY. No; I do not think it is one of the functions of the Federal Government.

Mr. SMITH. Then that provision in the Burton law is unconstitutional?

Mr. CARMODY. I do not want to pass on that. I want to confine what I have to say to the principle involved in this bill.

[Bill proposed by Attorney General Carmody.]

A BILL To give effect to the fifth article of the treaty between the United States and Great Britain, signed January 11, 1909.

Be it enacted by the Senate and House of Representatives of the United States of America in Congress assembled, That in order to give effect to the fifth article of the treaty between the United States and Great Britain, signed January 11, 1909, the United States hereby authorizes and permits the diversion within the State of New York of the waters of Niagara River above the Falls of Niagara, for power purposes, not exceeding in the aggregate a daily diversion at the rate of 20,000 cubic feet of water per second: *Provided, however,* That no water shall be diverted from said river at said point for power purposes except pursuant to written permits signed by the Secretary of War, who is hereby authorized and directed to issue such permits for the making of such diversion to said amount only to the State of New York, and upon application made therefor by its officials, thereunto duly authorized.

The CHAIRMAN. Senator O'Gorman, we will hear you now.

STATEMENT OF HON. JAMES A. O'GORMAN, UNITED STATES SENATOR FROM THE STATE OF NEW YORK.

Mr. O'GORMAN. Mr. Chairman and gentlemen of the committee, I appear here as a citizen of the State of New York in support of the views generally advanced by Attorney General Carmody. There is a fundamental question involved in this legislation, which, if correctly understood, will remove much of the difficulty in determining what the Congress should do with respect to the Niagara River. This is a question that is receiving a great deal of attention from members in both branches of Congress. There may be want of harmony at the present time as to the correct legal view, and I think it may aid us in appreciating the rights of the State and of the nation if we remember that at the close of the Revolution each of the 13 States became possessed of every right theretofore enjoyed by the King of England. Taking the State of New York as one of the 13 States for purposes of illustration, the people of the State of New York became the owners of every navigable stream within their State and the soil underneath. The State of New York became possessed of a part, at least, of Niagara River, as it did of the Hudson River, the Mohawk River, and other rivers within the State, and if these rights remain to-day as they were then, we would have the rights insisted upon by Attorney General Carmody.

Now, when the various States, for the purpose of forming a more complete Union, adopted the Constitution, which was simply their agreement, it was provided among other things, that the States would grant to the Federal Government, first, the right to make treaties with foreign powers, because up to that time each one of the separate States could make a treaty with a foreign power. The value of that provision, of course, will be appreciated by everybody. You could not have a perfect Union if every one of the 13 States had had the power to enter into a treaty with a foreign power, and therefore they agreed that the Federal Government should have the treaty-making right. Then there was that provision of the Constitution with which you are all familiar, known as the commerce clause, which, as construed by the Supreme Court of the United States, means that the Federal Government may, for the purpose of promoting the navigability of any stream, in any part of the country, do whatever it deems proper for that purpose only. Now, the right of the Federal Government to enter a State for the purpose of improving the navigability of a stream is a naked right. It confers no property right upon the Federal Government. I am aware, as you gentlemen are, that for some years past the practice of the Federal Government has been to take complete charge of a stream, ignoring all the rights of the State, and to undertake to sell the excess water, sometimes produced as result of Federal improvements. Personally, I have no doubt in mind as to the absolute illegality and invalidity of every act of the Federal Government where it attempts to traffic in the water that belongs to the State. When I speak of the State, I speak of the State as a body and the rights of its people.

Mr GOODWIN. You are speaking of an intrastate river alone, are you?

Mr. O'GORMAN. No; I am speaking of all streams, practically, because they come within this limited power of the Federal Government with respect to interstate commerce and commerce between the States and foreign powers.

Mr. CLINE. Senator, do you concede the constitutionality of the general dam act of June, 1906?

Mr. O'GORMAN. I do not concede the legality of any act by which the Federal Government assumes to treat the water of a river, which is really the property of the State, as its own. In another branch of Congress we are considering that matter and have been considering it for a year or more. And I might add to what I have said that the practice has grown up with the Federal Government, if it erects a dam or makes an improvement in a navigable stream for the purpose of aiding commerce, it has in some instances undertaken to lease and sell the surplus water. That water, before it reaches the dam, is the water of the State of New York—taking New York as an illustration—and it continues to be the water, the possession, of the State after it passes over the dam. There is nothing in the Constitution that grants to the Federal Government the property right, but the privilege—the naked, narrow privilege—is confided to the National Government to go into any stream to improve its navigability. When it does that its function ceases, and when it attempts, as the present administration has, and as, perhaps, previous administrations have, to say, "We will only make an improvement in a certain stream provided the Federal Government is permitted to go and lease that surplus water and in that way secure revenue which may to a certain extent defray the expense of making the improvements," the Federal Government, in my judgment, is attempting to do something without warrant of law, because the Constitution prescribes the only way in which the Government shall raise revenue necessary for the purpose of carrying on the Government, and that is by taxation.

Mr. KENDALL. So far as this proposed legislation is predicated upon the policies to which you refer?

Mr. O'GORMAN. Yes, sir. The dam act was passed in 1906 and has been acquiesced in ever since that time without attack in any court anywhere, and hasn't the right for the purposes of this legislation become the settled policy of the Government?

Mr. O'GORMAN. No; I am quite sure that no member of this committee, or any Member of Congress, will feel that his judgment is foreclosed, if, upon reflection and study he concludes that the statutes passed some years ago was in contravention of the rights of the States. This matter has been taken up with the present administration and attempt has been made to impress upon the administration the principles that I am now bringing to the attention of the committee.

Mr. CLINE. But the administration is not in harmony with your ideas, is it?

Mr. O'GORMAN. Not at the present time, but I am in hopes that the coming administration will have a sufficient appreciation of the limitations of the Constitution as to recognize it. [Laughter.] Now we will go back to the third point, which more closely touches the question before your committee. Besides giving to the Federal Government the authority to regulate interstate commerce, and, as we have said, under that language the Congress has said that they can go into any stream to promote its navigability or to improve its navigability, there is that other provision, the specific limited powers conferred upon the Federal Government, the power to make treaties. Now, of course, the power to make treaties impliedly carried with it everything essential to the performance of their duty. New York, for instance, could not enter into a treaty with Great Britain. If New York should find, for one reason or another, that its relations were not pleasant with Canada, we could not undertake to make an agreement, but the Federal Government could, and really as the agent of the State of New York, would represent the State in the negotiations with the foreign power, and any act, any engagement, any treaty, entered into by the United States with a foreign power would of course be binding on the State of New York, and every other State in the Union.

But once the treaty is made and the United States, the Federal Government, assumes certain international relations with respect to the foreign power its function with respect to the State, the individual State, ceases, except in so far as the Federal Government has the right to say that the engagement made by the Federal Government with the foreign government will not be interfered with by any one of the States. So it seems to me, and I think it is reasonable and the only logical view, that once the Federal Government takes up a matter peculiarly affecting one or more of the States, and the negotiations result in a treaty, that the only function reserved to the Federal Government from that time on is to see that no provision of the treaty is offended by any act of the State. Subject to that provision the State comes into its own property and continues to use it as its right as a sovereign should permit it to use its property as a citizen. Now, therefore, I urge that the State of New York be permitted to make such disposition as the people of that State care to make of this water within the limitations fixed in the treaty, and that the only right reserved, the only right that should be exercised by the Federal Government, is to so supervise the use of that water afterwards that the treaty entered into between the Federal Government and Great Britain shall not be violated.

Mr. DIFENDERFER. You believe that the State of New York should fix the limitations upon which importations should be shipped into this country from Canada?

Mr. O'GORMAN. Until such time as the Federal Government should impose a duty or tax. There is no power, and I defy any member of this committee to point to any provision in the Constitution to the contrary—there is no power in the Federal Government under the Constitution to positively exclude power from Canada, to prevent it from coming into the United States. It has a right to impose, and of course it might impose such a tax as would amount to exclusion, but I have no doubt that if any such legislation was passed and it was clearly and unequivocally shown that the purpose of the tax was to exclude, the Supreme Court of the United States would hold it to be unconstitutional.

The CHAIRMAN. It has the right to provide for the public defense, has it not?

Mr. O'GORMAN. Where is the provision with respect to that?

The CHAIRMAN. The Constitution provides that this Government can provide for the defense of this country.

Mr. O'GORMAN. Yes; but there is considerable difference of opinion as to that. Are you speaking of the general-welfare clause?

18   DIVERSION OF WATER FROM THE NIAGARA RIVER.

The CHAIRMAN. Yes.

Mr. O'GORMAN. I think you will find that all the text-writers on the Constitution and the decisions of the Supreme Court are to the effect that the so-called general-welfare clause of the Constitution simply means that taxes may be raised to pay the debts and to promote the general welfare. What may be done, as a matter of fact, to promote the general welfare by the General Government must be found in other sections of the Constitution. That is no general omnibus provision that the Federal Government may do anything it sees fit to promote the general welfare. I repeat, that that provision as to the general welfare must be associated with the words which precede it, which are that the Federal Government may raise taxes to pay debts and to promote the general welfare.

Mr. TOWNSEND. To raise taxes to promote the general welfare?

Mr. O'GORMAN. I have it here in a memorandum. These are the words: "Congress shall have the power to levy and collect taxes, duties, and imposts necessary to pay the debts and to provide for the common defense and general welfare of the United States." As I say, you will find, I think without an exception, that in every text-book on the Constitution and every decision of the Supreme Court of the United States it is held that—with the exception of Storey— Storey was disposed to take what in those days was regarded as the Hamiltonian theory of the constitutional government generally, and their interpretation was that Congress had almost unlimited power to do anything it saw fit in promotion of the general welfare—but with the exception of Storey they indicate the purposes for which taxes may be raised and what Congress may do.

Mr. COOPER. Here, it seems to me, is a clause that would confront you on that argument: "Congress has power to regulate commerce with foreign nations and among the several States and with the Indian tribes."

Mr. O'GORMAN. Yes.

Mr. COOPER. Now, Congress, so far as the regulation of commerce with the Indian tribes is concerned, has absolute jurisdiction to prohibit anybody from buying or selling to the Indians. That is all under the same clause of the Constitution. Under that it was held to be constitutional that the Congress of the United States could prohibit the importation of any goods into the United States, as it did do by the Embargo act. That went to one of the Federal courts—not the Supreme Court—and it was held to be constitutional. Now, there is an unrestricted, unqualified, absolute conferring upon Congress of the power to regulate commerce with foreign nations. That is, to regulate it in its discretion, to stop the coming over here of a single kilowatt of electric power from anybody or any country if it desires to do so. That is the same power which it has to regulate commerce with the Indian tribes, and it is in the same clause of the Constitution.

Mr. O'GORMAN. I can not well understand how the power to regulate embraces the power to absolutely prohibit. It may well be argued, and I think justly, when you confer the power to regulate, there is impliedly an agreement, an understanding that the thing, whatever it may be, will exist that is to be regulated. If you destroy the thing you have nothing to regulate, and naturally your statute would become nugatory.

Mr. Cooper. Chief Justice Marshall in a famous decision put the power of Congress as to taxation in these words: "The power to tax is the power to destroy." So you see, that the power to regulate would comprehend the power to destroy.

Mr. O'Gorman. I have not put it precisely that way.

Mr. Cooper. So we never need to pay taxes if Congress has not the power to tax or to destroy it.

Mr. O'Gorman. I think the opinion, to get to a concrete proposition, the opinion is very generally entertained that if, for instance, a protective tariff bill comes before the Supreme Court of the United States, and it was admitted and conceded that the sole purpose of the act in question was to protect certain interests it would be held to be unconstitutional because no such power has been confided to Congress. Congress has the power to collect taxes, and if, under cover of that conceded power it seeks to do something else, it is exceeding the power conferred upon it. I only offer that in passing.

The Chairman. The Federal Government has the right to provide for the general defense; that is conceded, isn't it?

Mr. O'Gorman. Yes, sir.

The Chairman. Now, it has the right to use this river in any way it may see fit in providing for the general defense. Isn't that sound doctrine?

Mr. O'Gorman. Has it any more right to use that river than it would have to use the eastern coast of New York State?

The Chairman. Not if it saw fit to use the coast of New York State, but if it sees fit to use this river for the purpose of public delic defense, isn't it a sound proposition that it has the right to use it as the discretion of the Federal Government directs it should be used?

Mr. O'Gorman. Has it any more right in that respect than it would have to use and sell the property of the State?

The Chairman. Is there any authority in the world that can question its right?

Mr. O'Gorman. I would like to have the chairman point to any specific section of the Constitution that gives it that right.

The Chairman. The one you read awhile ago.

Mr. O'Gorman. That has been declared not to give any such right.

The Chairman. That provision in reference to the general defense?

Mr. O'Gorman. The general welfare.

The Chairman. I am talking about that specific language in there that authorizes Congress to provide for the common defense. I would like to know what page that language has been construed in to deny that right to Congress?

Mr. O'Gorman. I think if you will read Willoughby on the Constitution, Foster on the Constitution, or Cooley on the Constitution, you will find that thoroughly discussed?

The Chairman. I thought there was a case.

Mr. O'Gorman. I am quite sure the Supreme Court has decided in harmony with those ideas, but I can probably get a case on that.

The Chairman. I would like very much to have it. That, it seems to me, is the provision of the Constitution that gives Congress power over that river.

Mr. O'Gorman. To the exclusion of the rights of the State?

The Chairman. To the exclusion of the rights of the State and everybody else. If Congress has got the right to provide for the general defense of this country and it decides that this boundary stream there is one of the means of providing for it, and at one place they want the water high and at another place they want it low, Congress has the right to use that water for that purpose in any way it sees fit. There is no doubt of that, and I do not see how anyone can question it.

Mr. GARNER. May I ask you a question there, so as to get your position clearly in my mind. Your position is that under the commerce clause Congress has the right to declare a stream navigable?

Mr. O'GORMAN. Yes; it has more than that. It can go into one of the sources of the stream where there is no navigation, if it can in that way promote navigation.

Mr. GARNER. It has the right to declare any water within the boundaries of the United States to be necessary for navigation?

Mr. O'GORMAN. Yes, sir.

Mr. GARNER. After it has declared the amount of water necessary for navigation, Congress has power over the balance of the water running down that stream. Do you claim that it has not the right, then, under the commerce clause of the Constitution, to either collect revenue on the surplus water or in any way control it?

Mr. O'GORMAN. Right there, if you will allow me, the only provision of the Constitution which permits the Government of the United States to collect rent is that provision which authorizes the Congress to dispose of its own lands and properties. If property was abandoned, they might acquire title to it in that way and sell it.

Mr. GARNER. I was speaking about the joint streams and riparian rights owned by individuals or by the State.

Mr. COOPER. Now, take this surplus water. Could the United States Government use it for the purpose of generating electric power to run an arsenal, for instance?

Mr. GARNER. Speaking for myself, I know of no power by which the Federal Government could take that water and use it, unless it was for the aid of navigation.

Mr. COOPER. The United States has spent on some dams millions of dollars to promote slack-water navigation. I have in mind a case where the Government has spent $3,000,000 in the construction of a dam in one State where we have an arsenal, and it has been found that electricity could be used for the arsenal if generated from the water which flows over the dam. The result of this $3,000,000 expended of the money of the people, of all the people of the States, not the people of any particular State, has been to make this power available. Now, the United States Government would have the right to go right to the end of that dam in that State and condemn property for the arsenal. Can it use that possible electric power which this $3,000,000 taken from the Public Treasury has made possible to run its own arsenal, condemn the water rights, and condemn the property?

Mr. O'GORMAN. Of course it could condemn the water rights and use it.

Mr. COOPER. Now, then, if it has the right to use the water for its own purposes——

Mr. O'GORMAN (interposing). By deduction?

Mr. COOPER. Not by condemnation.

Mr. SHARP. Is it your contention that the Government of the United States may not exercise absolute discretion over the Falls and the Niagara River, or do you think they may do that? I was not here when the discussion began.

Mr. O'GORMAN. I stated that in its power to make treaties it may enter into any engagement the Government sees fit to make with Great Britain. It has the right thereunder to say that the State of New York, or any other State affected, will not do anything that offends the treaty provision, but subject to that the case in question is entitled by the exercise of the sovereign right to do what it sees fit with respect to its property.

Mr. GARNER. Unless, Senator, the Federal Government needed this water for navigation purposes.

Mr. O'GORMAN. Oh, surely.

Mr. GARNER. Now, may I ask one more question? Suppose that the Burton Act should lapse, which I understand it does, on the 4th of March, and Congress should not enact any legislation whatever upon this subject, would the rights of the State of New York and the people of New York be invoked under the common law as applied in connection with this treaty?

Mr. O'GORMAN. The treaty, as I understand it, would be the only law covering this subject, other than Federal statutes and State statutes, and the common law, as applied to riparian rights, would apply to the people living along this stream?

That would be substantially the situation.

Mr. KENDALL. You were referring to section 8 of the Constitution a while ago, the general welfare clause, and I understood you to announce it as your opinion that the power to provide for the common defense and the general welfare of the United States is limited to the laying and collecting of taxes, duties, and imposts?

Mr. O'GORMAN. For that purpose.

Mr. KENDALL. For that purpose?

Mr. O'GORMAN. Yes.

Mr. KENDALL. Well, I did not understand you to qualify it. I want to call your attention to another section and ask you what you think of that. The last section of Article I of the Constitution, "No State shall without the consent of the Congress lay any imposts or duties on imports or exports." What does that mean, in your judgment?

Mr. O'GORMAN. I presume it means just what it says, that no duties or imposts should be collected by the State authorities without the consent of Congress.

Mr. KENDALL. Does that have any effect on your proposition that the State of New York has the right to control the transmission of power in that State?

Mr. O'GORMAN. No; it does not effect that.

Mr. GARNER. Didn't the Supreme Court in its decision in an assessor case hold in construing that provision of the Constitution that the State did not have any right to levy a toll or to make regulations for the safety of the property?

Mr. O'GORMAN. Yes. But I wanted to speak, gentlemen, this morning, as to the right of the Federal Government to prohibit the Canadian power from coming into the State of New York. I do not consider that as vital as the fundamental questions that, subject to observations of the treaty obligations, subject, also, if you will, to such precautions as the Federal Government may have provided for the national defense—subject to those things—the State of New York is supreme with respect to this power and with respect to the water in the river. I might say that this question, as you doubtless know, is agitating some of our friends in the western country very much. There is a very sharp division as to whether the Federal Government has not been pursuing an erroneous policy for some years with respect to these river matters, and it is hoped one of these days that the matter may be definitely settled. I have a very strong opinion, amounting to conviction, that the rights of the States with respect to their rivers, and the soil under the river and the waters above, remain absolutely in their power and subject only to the exercise of those specific rights which the Constitution has conferred upon the Federal Government.

The CHAIRMAN. If we were agreed on that proposition we would still have this provision for the public defense to fall back on.

Mr. O'GORMAN. Except that it seems to me that when Congress satisfied itself as to the precise quantity of water which might be taken by the State from the river, it is not without limitation in the act which has been drafted here by Attorney General Carmody—I do not know whether he called it to your attention or not—that the disposition of the restricted quantity of water, whatever it may be, should be left to the decisions and the Federal Government should not intrude itself into the State in the exercise of a State function.

The CHAIRMAN. The National Government has the right to improve the navigation of a stream.

Mr. O'GORMAN. Yes, sir.

The CHAIRMAN. Then you would not contend that the National Government relinquished the right to improve that navigation?

Mr. O'GORMAN. That would be a part of the improvement. The situation is much like this: Is there any private owner of a piece of land who would give some other person the right to come upon that land for a specific purpose—to come upon that land for the purpose which you are permitted to perform, and permit that person to carry off any separate thing or incidental advantages which the owner of the land reaped from the exercise of the privilege which was conferred upon the other person? That is the situation between the United States and the State of New York.

Mr. CURLEY. And conservation of navigation can only be exercised indirectly through the State?

Mr. O'GORMAN. The Government has the right to go into any stream at any time it sees fit for the purpose of improving its navigability, subject only to the exercise of that right   The sovereign right of the State remains unimpaired.

Mr. BARTHOLDT. Before I permit the Federal Government to die of consumption, I should like to ask a question.

Mr. O'GORMAN. If it dies at all it will not die of consumption.

Mr. BARTHOLDT. Under the Constitution the Federal Government has control of all navigable rivers, has it not?

Mr. O'GORMAN. That is not the word. I do not think that word is in the Constitution, but it has the right to regulate.

Mr. BARTHOLDT. I understand; but it means the same thing as I have stated. Now, it has control, because if you want a navigable river, a river that is looked upon as navigable, declared nonnavigable, you have to come to Congress for a special act to declare it nonnavigable, which means the Federal Government has control of all navigable rivers, and doesn't that control carry with it the right of the Federal Government to prevent what might interfere with the navigability of rivers?

Mr. O'GORMAN. The result is correct, but not by the process by which you reached it. I can not concede that the Federal Government has control of any river. The Constitution does not give it such control. If it had control that would mean a violation of the absolute dominion of the people. The Constitution simply says that the Federal Government may regulate interstate and foreign commerce, and those words have been so construed and interpreted by Congress as to mean that the Federal Government may at any time go into any State and into any stream at any time for the purpose of promoting its navigability, but that is the only purpose. It has resulted in promoting the navigability and enhancing the use of the river, but it has no right to say, "You must pay the Federal Government for the improvement of the river," nor has it any right to say to any individual, "You must pay for the improvement of this river." That is my understanding of the result of the exercise of the right which the States voluntarily gave to the Federal Government.

Mr. COOPER. Has not the Government the right to limit the amount of power from other countries distributed in this country?

Mr. O'GORMAN. I have said all I care to say on that subject, I think. I am strongly of the view, first that the Government has not that right, and if it did have it could not exercise it. I am trying particularly to impress this idea upon the committee, namely, to recognize the fact that the State in its sovereign capacity remains the owner of all of its property, subject only to the exercise of all of those rights or provisions which the States voluntarily transferred to the Federal Government. For instance, to promote navigation, make treaties, and provide for the common defense.

Mr. HARRISON. This right exercised by the Federal Government under the Burton Act, with reference to the conservation and regulation of the Niagara River has never been previously attacked?

Mr. O'GORMAN. I do not know.

The CHAIRMAN. This meeting was specifically set apart to hear the gentlemen representing the State of New York. There are two others here, Mr. Van Kennen, president of the Conservation Commission, and Mr. Richards, attorney for the commission. It is nearly 12 o'clock now and I think we ought to hear them to-day, and I just want to ascertain from the committee whether we shall go on now.

Upon vote the committee decided to proceed.

The CHAIRMAN. Mr. Van Kennen, we will hear you now.

STATEMENT OF MR. GEORGE E. VAN KENNEN, PRESIDENT OF THE NEW YORK CONSERVATION COMMISSION.

Mr. VAN KENNEN. Mr. Chairman, I promise the committee that I will keep them but a very few moments in the discussion of this question. It has been very ably discussed, and it is perfectly clear that this committee is composed of a large number of eminent law-yers, and I will only discuss the question for the purpose of answering directly or indirectly a few questions that have been asked.

The function of the conservation commission of the State of New York is for the purpose of utilizing the natural resources of the State. In other words, we think that it is proper for the State of New York to utilize all the undeveloped water power of the State, and among the water powers of the State which we feel that the State owns is some of the water powers from the Niagara River, the water powers along the St. Lawrence, and the internal water powers that arise from the flow of the streams, such as the Hudson, the Racket, the Black, the Genesee, and others. Now, it seems to me that this question divides itself practically into three elements, so far as the provisions of this bill are concerned. The first is, Shall there be any diversion of water from the Niagara River for power pur-poses? If so, to whom shall this permit to divert be given? The third is, The purpose of that diversion? Now, it seems to me that it is clear, and I believe that we are substantially in accord upon this question, that the water of the Niagara River may be diverted to a limited degree, which has been expressed by a solemn treaty between the United States and Great Britain. They have limited that amount as I understand it, to the diversion of 20,000 cubic feet per second.

Now, it is undoubtedly the right of Congress to determine whether the whole of that 20,000 shall be diverted or not. They might say that they will not permit any diversion of any part of that water, because they have the paramount right over that river for the pur-poses of controlling navigation. However, the bill here proposes to divert, or to permit the diversion, of a certain portion of that 20,000 cubic feet, 15,600 cubic feet, which is the exact amount, as I under-stand it, that is already being diverted under permits from the Sec-retary of War. We think there ought to be a greater diversion and we believe that greater diversion is permissible without in the slight-est degree interfering with the scenic grandeur of the Niagara Falls, or in anywise destroying the beauties of the lower river.

The CHAIRMAN. Would you concede the right of Congress to limit that diversion?

Mr. VAN KENNEN. I concede the right of Congress to limit the diversion of 20,000 cubic feet, or any other number of cubic feet.

The CHAIRMAN. Or to limit to 15,000 cubic feet?

Mr. VAN KENNEN. Yes; I concede Congress would have that right. I believe that the treaty gives them that right according to its pro-visions. If the treaty had said that there might be diverted these 20,000 cubic feet, then another question would have arisen, but I believe that it intended that Congress should determine that question according to the provisions of the treaty itself. Now, then, that dis-poses of the first proposition, namely, Shall there be any diversion? Yes; Congress would doubtless have the right to say that there shall be a diversion to the full extent, and they might issue a permit that would be good for any length of time, and they might, in the interest of navigation, revoke that permit at any time that they saw fit.

When you go that far, however, I think that the powers of Con-gress terminate. At that point they are exhausted. I do not think that Congress has the right to say to whom that water shall be diverted, nor do I think that Congress has the right to say for what purpose that diversion shall be made; as, for instance, to illustrate: The State of New York has made two grants to power companies on the Niagara River. That was done before there was any question raised by the Federal Government in the way of limiting the amount of water that was diverted, and the Federal Government not having acted, I believe that it is sound law to say that the State of New York had the right to make these grants in the way in which they did it. Now, while it is in my mind, in that connection I want to say that some person has asked this: "What would be the effect if the so-called Burton Act should expire by limitation?" One of the members of the committee asked that question. Now, I do not pretend to be able to say definitely what would be the effect, but in my judgment it would be maintained by the persons that are now using that power under grant from the State of New York that they had the right to the use of the 20,000 cubic feet of water.

The CHAIRMAN. They already have the machinery installed to use it, haven't they?

Mr. VAN KENNEN. They have not, as I understand it.

Mr. GARNER. I asked the question, and for that reason I make bold to interrupt you. Do you mean to say that the additional 4,400 cubic feet, I believe it is—these people have already taken it—that they would have a legal right to that additional amount without the consent of the State of New York?

Mr. VAN KENNEN. I should say that in my judgment they would claim under their grants that the State of New York has already made that they are entitled to that amount, and the reason why I say that is because I do not believe that the grants to these people are definite enough as to the quantity of power, as to the quantity of water they may divert.

Mr. GARNER. I am not using the word "claims" now. They will claim everything. I never saw one that did not. But I asked you whether they would have the legal right, without the consent of the State of New York, to take the other 4,400 cubic feet?

Mr. VAN KENNEN. I wish I could answer that question positively as a member of the conservation commission. I would feel greatly relieved if I knew just what their legal rights were.

Mr. GOODWIN. Is the amount not specified in the grants?

Mr. VAN KENNEN. No, sir.

The CHAIRMAN. One of those companies is authorized to make 200,000 horse-power, isn't it?

Mr. VAN KENNEN. I think that is it.

The CHAIRMAN. They are now diverting 8,600 cubic feet of water per second, and making less than 100,000 horsepower, are they not?

Mr. VAN KENNEN. Yes, sir; but if they had utilized that water at the proper head they would now be making 200,000 horse power.

The CHAIRMAN. Under that grant could not they go ahead now and divert water enough to make that 200,000 horsepower but for this treaty?

Mr. HARRISON. That is, with their present plans?

Mr. VAN KENNEN. Well I think they could, possibly. Possibly they might do that.

Mr. CLINE. Haven't these water-power companies abandoned their rights under these grants? Did they not abandon them when they relinquished the rights to their New York grants? Did they not abandon that right when they took rights from the Federal Government? They could not go back now could they and take up other rights after the Burton Act expired?

Mr. Van Kennen. I think they have vested rights there. And particularly by the view expressed by the State of New York, I think they must have a grant from the State of New York, and in order to control the water they must operate within the limits imposed by the Federal legislation.

Mr. Sharp. You stated a while ago that before there was any Federal action whatever taken in reference to Niagara Falls, or Niagara River, the State of New York had years ago gone on there and granted certain rights to riparian owners, that the riparian owners themselves had exercised those rights, and now being in possession of those righsts it was extremely doubtful if the Government of the United States could exercise any authority to the extent of modifying them.

Mr. Van Kennen. That is not quite the way I wanted to be understood. I believe the Federal Government could say to-day, "There shall be no diversion of the Niagara River."

Mr. Sharp. And it is a fact that these men have without any express act of Congress taken that right?

Mr. Van Kennen. It is a fact that the State of New York has given the right to these people to divert that water.

Mr. Sharp. That is in keeping with the decisions the Supreme Court has made upon that?

Mr. Van Kennen. There is one view that I want to express in connection with that which might modify it. I believe that the State does have the right to do a certain act, but that the Federal Government has supreme power over that question; but provided the State acts, and there has been no inhibition placed upon it by the Federal Government, the State acquires some rights then.

Mr. Sharp. That assumes that the State has primarily the right to act.

Mr. Van Kennen. Yes; but it might go further. The individual, I believe, would not have the right to put down, for instance, a pier or a dock in waters over which the Federal Government has jurisdiction, in the interest of navigation, and if they did it before the Federal Government fixed the dock line I think they would acquire certain rights.

Mr. Sharp. That is in direct conflict with the decision of Justice Bradley, made 35 years ago in the Parkersburg case in regard to navigation on the Ohio River, in which the justice said that Congress had the right, in the face of absolute statutes, not only statutes of the State, but of the Nation, to cut down the height of chimneys and smokestacks, and remove bridges for the benefit of navigation; and so it would seem to me that the power of Congress in that respect was absolutely unlimited, so far as navigation is concerned.

Mr. Van Kennen. I think the idea I have expressed came up in a question where a private individual had put down piers in waters over which the Federal Government had jurisdiction, but had never established the dock lines.

Mr. Sharp. Now, one other question in regard to a point which was raised by Mr. Garner when Senator O'Gorman was speaking, a moment ago. I would like to get your views as to what would happen should the Burton act expire by limitation—what would be the rights of the State of New York or the present users of that power to go on and take up the full limit, especially with reference to what right, if any, the Government will have under the treaty, in the absence of any act of Congress to still control this diversion?

Mr. VAN KENNEN. If I understand you correctly, I believe that these present power owners would claim the right, and possibly legally claim the right, to use up to the 20,000 cubic feet.

Mr. SHARP. Would the Secretary of War under that treaty have any further rights?

Mr. VAN KENNEN. No; if there is any right lodged with anyone, it would be with the Joint High Commission. That is my view of it.

Mr. GARNER. Having expressed you view with reference to the policy of Congress in permitting New York to take 20,000 cubic feet, the full capacity, what is your view, as a conservationist, with reference to permitting the importation of power from Canada?

Mr. VAN KENNEN. I can not see any reason why there should be any limitation upon the importation of power from Canada.

Mr. GARNER. Then, you do believe that under the treaty the full limit of diversion both on the Canadian and American sides should be utilized?

Mr. VAN KENNEN. I believe, as a conservationist, that true conservation is to utilize the resources of the State and the Nation.

The CHAIRMAN. Mr. Van Kennen, if 36,000 cubic feet a second of water was used on the Canadian side, how much power would be made from that?

Mr. VAN KENNEN. Over 400,000 horsepower. It is something over 400,000 horsepower, as I understand it; but I am not an engineer.

The CHAIRMAN. Is there not a law in Canada that prohibits the exportation of more than half of the amount that is needed in Canada?

Mr. VAN KENNEN. I so understand, that there is a limitation of the amount of power that can be exported.

The CHAIRMAN. And 200,000 horsepower is about the amount that could be legally and properly imported into this country. You figure 200,000 horsepower is about half the horsepower that can be made from the water on the Canadian side?

Mr. VAN KENNEN. About that; yes; I should think that is about half of it.

Mr. GARNER. Is it not a fact, that improvements in machinery may be able to develop 600,000 horsepower on the Canadian side without using any more water, and if this bill limits it to 200,000, then you could not get the half that the Canadian Government would permit you to bring over.

Mr. VAN KENNEN. You are undoubtedly right about that. Undoubtedly there may be improvements in machinery that will increase the efficiency and increase the amount of power that can be derived. The head is the thing that they need in developing power.

The CHAIRMAN. And they can not get the head on the Canadian side that they get on the American side?

Mr. VAN KENNEN. I can not answer that question certainly, but we can not get a large head on the American side now. But, of course the plant contemplates extending the canal down farther in the lower regions of the Niagara. At present, of course, you can not increase the head any to those companies that are actually using power at the present time. That is fixed now and can not be increased.

The CHAIRMAN. You do not catch my point. On this side there is such a head that one of these companies has made 21 horsepower from 1 cubic foot.

Mr. VAN KENNEN. You have the right idea. One is producing a great deal more per cubic foot of water than the other.

The CHAIRMAN. And on this side one company, it has been testified here, was producing 21 horsepower to the cubic foot, and on the Canadian side the figures put it about 12 horsepower to the cubic foot.

Mr. VAN KENNEN. Well, I can not give you that exactly. It is safe for you to say, as I understand it, that 1 cubic foot of water per second, falling 11 feet, will produce a horsepower. Now, then, if you have got 40 feet, why you can figure out what each cubic foot per second will make. Of course, it is not perhaps absolutely true, but it is theoretically true. Friction, machinery, and other matters come in to affect it.

Mr. DIFENDERFER. Is it your opinion that the State of New York has the right to regulate the importation of electricity?

Mr. VAN KENNEN. I do not.

Mr. DIFENDERFER. Distribute it in the State?

Mr. VAN KENNEN. I do not; no, sir.

Mr. TOWNSEND. If it is a good thing, you think New York should get all of it?

Mr. VAN KENNEN. We possibly can; I believe so.

Mr. TOWNSEND. As a conservationist, of course, you ought to get more in Canada and less on this side.

Mr. VAN KENNEN. Yes. There is a great deal of difference of opinion. I understand that the diversion of the water permitted on the American side at the present time does not appreciably lower the water over the falls.

Mr. HARRISON. Does it on the Canadian side?

Mr. VAN KENNEN. Less than it did, so that nobody could discover it by looking at it.

Mr. SHARP. Is it not true that the report of the Government engineers states that there is quite an appreciable fall, amounting to about 9 inches?

The CHAIRMAN. Nine inches on the Canadian side of Horseshoe Falls.

Mr. VAN KENNEN. I want to say that as I understand it—I am not an engineer, nor have I examined carefully the statements made by engineers, so the engineers are better qualified to speak upon that question than I am, but I have heard that a wind from Lake Erie will affect the flow of water over the falls more than all the diversion permitted by Congress.

Mr. DIFENDERFER. What per cent of water is taken from the falls?

Mr. VAN KENNEN. I can not give you that.

Mr. DIFENDERFER. Is it not 27 per cent?

Mr. VAN KENNEN. No. I can not say absolutely, and I do not want to answer that without having definite knowledge.

The CHAIRMAN. We will now adjourn until 10.30 to-morrow morning.

COMMITTEE ON FOREIGN AFFAIRS,
HOUSE OF REPRESENTATIVES,
Washington, D. C., Thursday, January 23, 1913—10.30 a. m.

The committee this day met, Mr. Flood (chairman) presiding.

STATEMENT OF HON. GEORGE E. VAN KENNEN, OF NEW YORK.

The CHAIRMAN. Gentlemen, the committee will come to order. Mr. Van Kennen, you may proceed, sir.

Mr. VAN KENNEN. Gentlemen, I have practically concluded my remarks upon the first proposition, namely, the power or the paramount right of the Federal Government to control the question of the diversion of water from the Niagara River. I think it is practically settled, in the minds of most of us, that the Federal Government has the right to issue the permits, to limit the amount and to revoke the permits.

The next step will be the question as to whether it is within the province of the Federal Government, or within the right of the State of New York, to determine to whom these permits should be issued, and further to determine for what purpose this water might be used. This has been very ably discussed by Senator O'Gorman and by Attorney General Carmody, and I do not think I shall go into that branch of the subject further than to point out a few illustrations, which may be of some service. For instance, it is entirely feasible to divert the water from the Niagara River above the Falls for purposes of irrigation, as well as for purposes of power. While that is not contemplated, I am speaking of it as a matter of right.

Now a conflict between the State and the Federal Government would arise in an event where the Federal Government might issue such a permit for purposes of irrigation, and where the State Government, through its grants to various persons developing power, has issued grants for the purposes of the development of power.

Again, let us assume, for the sake of argument, that this bill should pass, which relates to the question of the diversion of 15,600 cubic feet of water. Under the provisions of the treaty, and I think it may be assumed that the Government has determined that without interfering with navigation, it is possible to divert 20,000 cubic feet, then we have 4,400 cubic feet of so-called surplus water; that is, in addition to the water that is now permitted to be diverted, by permits issued by the Secretary of War. Let us take an illustration, for the sake of argument, that the city of Detroit should come to the Secretary of War and ask for a permit to divert this 4,400 cubic feet of water for uses in the city of Detroit, and let us assume, for the sake of argument, that the Secretary of War, under the authority of this bill, issued a permit to the city of Detroit. Then you would have this situation: Water which the State of New York claims, within its borders, water that passes over lands that belong to the State of New York, diverted by the Federal Government to some municipality or corporation, in some foreign State, and they would have the right to the use of that water to the exclusion of the State of New York. I maintain that that would be inequitable at least, and I believe unlawful.

Now that is all I care to say upon that subject. I can see that the conflict of authority might raise some very serious questions, and if exercised improperly against what we claim to be the rights of the State of New York it certainly would lead to inequitable results. But the question that I want to discuss at this moment is the use of the surplus, or the 4,400 cubic feet of water.

Mr. GARNER. Would you let me ask you a question a moment?

Mr. VAN KENNEN. Yes, sir.

Mr. CLINE. Do you think that the fact that the Niagara River is an international boundary line and involves the right of the Government to prepare for national defense enlarges the powers of the Government over that stream as compared with an internal stream?

Mr. VAN KENNEN. I do not think there will be any difference of principle; that is my view. I concede that the Federal Government would have the right to use that water for navigation or for military defense or the land there the same as it would the land or water of any stream, but it must proceed in the same way; that is my view.

Mr. CLINE. Isn't it a fact that the conditions arising out of just that situation gave rise to the necessity for treaties between foreign powers and the United States so that those matters might be regulated to a larger degree than would be possible on internal streams?

Mr. VAN KENNEN. Why, I think, strictly speaking, than local internal streams; that is, so far as these streams have any relation to the boundary waters, such as the lakes or streams that cross the boundaries. I don't think that it would be the subject of treaty outside of that class of waters. I do not know that I have answered the question exactly, but I do not believe that the rights of the State differ on that principle simply because this is a boundary stream.

The CHAIRMAN. You will concede that the Government has the right to use that stream as a national defense?

Mr. VAN KENNEN. I think so.

The CHAIRMAN. And they could take all the water, if it was possible, that went over the Falls, or prohibit the taking of any of it, if it was necessary for national defense?

Mr. VAN KENNEN. I believe so.

The CHAIRMAN. Then would that not give them the right to say when and how and by whom this water should be taken?

Mr. VAN KENNEN. I think not. I do not think it would go to that extent; that is my view. It is very ably expressed by Senator O'Gorman, in which I concur entirely.

The CHAIRMAN. I do not think Senator O'Gorman dealt with that phase of the right of the Federal Government.

Mr. VAN KENNEN. I think the principles he enunciated cover that.

Mr. CLINE. When the Government made land grants out of its own property to the transcontinental railroads, it of course fixed certain limitations in connection with those grants; that is, the grants carried with them the power to determine under what conditions the grants should be used. Now, how does that case differ from this? In other words, does not the power to make the grant carry with it the limitations under which the grant may be appropriated?

Mr. VAN KENNEN. I think in case the Federal Government made a grant of land belonging to the Federal Government, it could impose limitations, but I do not think that that would apply in this case, because the property rights and the rights of the State of New York, by reason of the fact that the waters belong to the State of New

York and the bed of the stream belongs to the State of New York, would give them that right.

Mr. DIFENDERFER. Where does that right begin? On the boundary, does it not?

Mr. VAN KENNEN. Well, of course; it runs from the lake.

Mr. DIFENDERFER. Then Ohio may claim the same right, and Michigan may claim the same right?

Mr. VAN KENNEN. I think they did assert the same right, as far as I understand. This case was decided, as I understand it, at Chicago. The jurisdiction of the Federal Government was challenged there, in the case between the Illinois Railroad and others, and it was decided, as I understand it.

Mr. DIFENDERFER. Suppose Illinois was to divert all that water? Would you suppose that New York would enter a protest?

Mr. VAN KENNEN. I think they would have the right.

Mr. DIFENDERFER. Through whom would they enter that protest?

Mr. VAN KENNEN. I think through the State of New York, directly against the State of Illinois, or the City of Chicago.

Mr. DIFENDERFER. Would they not come to the National Government for redress?

Mr. VAN KENNEN. It seems to me that that question was decided in the Colorado-Kansas case, where it was held, as I understand it, that the Federal Government could not intervene even, and that the rights for the diversion of water for irrigation purposes there must be enforced by the persons who were injured, and they must demonstrate their injury, as I understand it.

Mr. DIFENDERFER. Can you give that decision?

Mr. CURLEY. Where is your decision? Read it to the committee.

Mr. VAN KENNEN. I am speaking generally of my conception; I am not asserting it; it is my opinion merely, on the question of law and what was decided there.

The CHAIRMAN. Proceed, Mr. Van Kennen.

Mr. VAN KENNEN. I will proceed upon the question of the use of that 4,400 cubic feet of water. I want to put myself on record, in behalf of the State of New York, that we do not want any legislation of any kind which will permit the existing power owners to get that additional water. I want to say that it is the present policy of the State of New York, so far as I know, to utilize all the undeveloped water power of the State of New York for the benefit of the people generally. Therefore I say that legislation, so far as the Federal Government has any control of it, should permit the State of New York to utilize that for its own purposes.

Mr. DIFENDERFER. What guaranty can you give that the State of New York would control that, and what guaranty have you to give us that they would not give it to existing power companies?

Mr. VAN KENNEN. I can only say that the present policy of the State of New York, as I understand it, expressed through our commission, by our reports to the legislature and by the bills which we have introduced in the legislature, contemplates that the State of New York is to develop all of its undeveloped water power for the benefit of the people. I can not go any further than that. I can only say that very recently the governor of the State of New York has recommended the repeal of the so-called Long Sault Development Co. charter upon the strength of the opinion of the Attorney

General, and the bills have been introduced in the legislature of the State of New York to repeal that, the view being that that should be left to the State of New York for development by the State of New York and energy transmitted to the various municipalities and distributed through the municipalities, the same as they do water, to the ultimate consumer. That, briefly speaking, I believe to be——

The CHAIRMAN. Mr. Van Kennen, 500 cubic feet of this water is taken, as I understand it, from the Erie Canal?

Mr. VAN KENNEN. Yes, sir.

The CHAIRMAN. What is your view as to whether that ought to be counted as a part of this 20,000 cubic feet that should be allowed to be taken?

Mr. VAN KENNEN. My view is that it should be counted.

The CHAIRMAN. It should?

Mr. VAN KENNEN. Should; yes, sir; should be included. Now I do not want to stand here and say that the power companies of Niagara Falls, who have relied upon their grants and who have made their investments, should be deprived of the water that they are now using. That is not my position. I am speaking of the undeveloped water.

The CHAIRMAN. I understand that.

Mr. VAN KENNEN. Now the same thing is true with reference to Lockport, where they are using 500 cubic feet for industrial purposes at that point, which we carry through the canal that has cost us practically $200,000,000.

The CHAIRMAN. What I want to get your view on is, it has been suggested here that that 500 cubic feet ought not to be included in this 20,000 cubic feet authorized by the treaty to be taken from above the Falls.

Mr. VAN KENNEN. I really do not see how you could exclude it, under the terms.

Mr. HARRISON. Mr. Chairman, I would like to ask a few questions.

The CHAIRMAN. Mr. Harrison.

Mr. HARRISON. Did I understand you to say that if Canada were to utilize all the power that under the treaty it was entitled to, and if the United States were to utilize all the power that it was entitled to, it would not affect the scenic beauty of the Falls? Was that your statement?

Mr. VAN KENNEN. I can not answer it that way. It would, to a degree, I suppose, lower the water of the Niagara River if that water was diverted. That is, it does not need the skill of an engineer to determine that question, but to what extent, or whether, it would appreciably interfere with the so-called scenic beauty of Niagara Falls I do not know. Now, I can not conceive of a situation which would at all affect the scenic beauty of that cataract if the water was a half inch, possibly 2 inches, or possibly 5 inches lower; it might; I don't know but that it would be more beautiful.

Mr. DIFENDERFER. Suppose it was lowered 9 inches, how about that?

Mr. VAN KENNEN. I am not sure but that it would be more beautiful then. I do not know what effect that would have. I think that is a matter about which every man can have his own opinion.

The CHAIRMAN. Suppose it was 20 inches?

Mr. VAN KENNEN. Well, if it was eliminated entirely, I presume we would not see any water flowing over the Falls.

Mr. DIFENDERFER. I suppose if it was eliminated entirely it would increase the scenic beauty?

Mr. VAN KENNEN. I do not think so; no, sir. Everyone has his personal impression; it is a matter of taste to a large extent. Below, in the gorge of the Niagara River, there is a possibility of developing a large amount of power by the construction of canals along the side of the stream, which would divert a certain amount of water from going through the regular channel. Now I can conceive the fact to be that if we damned the Niagara River below that there would be no turbulent condition of waters that attracts our people. That is what we pass along that section for, to see the turbulent condition of the waters and that is all the scenic beauty that I can see in the water.

Mr. DIFENDERFER. That is not what we are talking about.

Mr. VAN KENNEN. No; but I am getting to this point. If they diverted some of that water I am not sure but that the scenic beauty would be increased because it is a well-known fact that in most cases, where waters flow over rock ledges, the higher the water is the less is its turbulent condition, and consequently it is less beautiful.

Mr. DIFENDERFER. There is a drop of 82 feet, I understand, in about 9,000 feet there?

Mr. VAN KENNEN. I can not give you the exact figures.

Mr. HARRISON. This section 3 of the proposed bill reads as follows: "That the Secretary of War is hereby authorized to issue permits for the diversion of water below the Falls." Now, do you believe that that diversion of water below the Falls might affect the scenic beauty of the rapids?

Mr. VAN KENNEN. I think if you diverted it in a certain way it would increase the scenic beauty of the rapids.

Mr. HARRISON. Do you not believe that there should be some condition as to how much diversion should take place below the Falls?

Mr. VAN KENNEN. I certainly do, and as I understand it the joint high commission is clothed with the power of determining that question, and as I understand it this bill makes another tribunal altogether.

The CHAIRMAN. Mr. Van Kennen, your statement is that under the treaty the control of the water below the Falls is vested in the joint high commission?

Mr. VAN KENNEN. I think it is.

The CHAIRMAN. And therefore that section 3 of this bill is improper in creating another tribunal to control it, in contravention of the provisions of the treaty?

Mr. VAN KENNEN. That is my position.

Mr. HARRISON. If the treaty so states, it would have to get the permission of the joint high commission.

The CHAIRMAN. It seems to me that Mr. Harrison is right about that.

Mr. VAN KENNEN. It seems to me you are just creating two tribunals, if we wanted to divert water, and I am in favor of diverting the water for the development of power just so far as you can go practically without destroying the effect of the Niagara Falls or the beauty below Niagara Falls.

The CHAIRMAN. We would be creating a tribunal that would be in conflict with the supreme law of the land?

Mr. VAN KENNEN. I think so, in case that third section——

The CHAIRMAN. That was prepared hurriedly.

Mr. HARRISON. I want to ask you a question in that connection. Do you believe that under the existing treaty, without any further law on the proposition, you can go to this joint high commission and get permission to divert water below the Falls?

Mr. VAN KENNEN. I am of the opinion that we could, yes, sir. I am speaking now of the provisions of the treaty. The Burton Act, as I understand it, applies to all the Niagara River, both above and below; consequently there can be no diversion.

The CHAIRMAN. The Burton Act was enacted before the treaty.

Mr. VAN KENNEN. Yes; and its provisions have generally been carried on since that time. Until this question can be settled my view is that the provisions of the Burton Act ought to remain.

I am speaking of the fact that since we are legislating upon this question it seems to me that we should make provision not only for the 15,600 cubic feet that is now being used and for which there are outstanding permits, but we should also consider the 4,400 cubic feet which we claim should go to the State of New York for its development. Now, I do not care to go on at length in regard to the details of the plan of development, but I want to say, generally speaking, that in the State of New York to-day we have undeveloped 1,500,000 horsepower, including the power which we claim on the Niagara and on the St. Lawrence. In the main there is practically 400,000 horsepower that absolutely belongs to the State of New York. It comes from the Erie Canal, or the barge canal, and it also comes from the fact that the State of New York owns lands in the headwaters of many of these streams, owning both sides and the bed of the stream. Consequently we have, as I say, that enormous amount of undeveloped water power, amounting, in the right of the State itself, to 400,000 horsepower, and the only correct policy, as I believe, is to have the State of New York develop it for the benefit of its people. That is our position on that. In addition to that there is over 1,100,000 horsepower that is undeveloped throughout the State. I want you to understand that the State of New York is as rich in power-development possibility as any State in the Union, and we should adopt a plan that would safeguard the interests of the people, so that they could utilize that undeveloped resource. That is our position.

Our plan is simple: The development of this power by the State, or for the State, its transmission to various municipalities, its distribution through the agency of the municipalities to the ultimate consumer at practically the cost of its development.

Mr. DIFENDERFER. I do not think there is a man in Congress but would agree with you on that plan on that subject.

Mr. VAN KENNEN. I hope so.

Mr. DIFENDERFER. That is, that the State of New York will control that power and give the people the benefit, and not through the agency of corporations, who are usually banded together for the purpose of making the people pay all that it is possible to make them pay.

Mr. VAN KENNEN. Yes, sir; I find that is frequently so.

Mr. DIFENDERFER. That is the thing.

Mr. VAN KENNEN. And particularly so when it appears that no project of that kind can be financed without the permission of those people. That is the situation; we might as well face it as it is.

The CHAIRMAN. Mr. Van Kennen, there are companies up there that are not getting the best use from the water they have?

Mr. VAN KENNEN. That is true.

The CHAIRMAN. Do you think they ought to be allowed to continue to use this water, and develop the small quantity of power they are?

Mr. VAN KENNEN. That is a pretty hard question to answer. I am not in favor of destroying property, and I do not think it is necessary, but I want to say that engineers advise me that if this 20,000 cubic feet of water was utilized to the highest degree of efficiency, we could give all these companies that are now developing power all the power that they get, and we would have at least as much more besides.

Mr. HARRISON. If that is true, do you not think that the State of New York ought to do that?

Mr. VAN KENNEN. Well, I am afraid that if you insisted upon a provision of that kind, while it might be worked out equitably and honestly between the State and these people, I am afraid that there might be some difficulties in actually working it out, but I don't think we should give them any more.

Mr. DIFENDERFER. Isn't it a fact that those other companies who are not developing all that should be developed, still want more?

Mr. VAN KENNEN. Yes; they want this 4,400 cubic feet, and I am standing here to protest against it.

Mr. FAIRCHILD. Do you not think that those companies develop the power naturally, just as a business sequence, when they find out it is to their profit to do so?

Mr. VAN KENNEN. That is the natural business instinct.

Mr. HARRISON. They have pretty good business instinct, have they not?

Mr. VAN KENNEN. I have never heard them charged with failure in that respect.

Now I want to say, in answer to a question that was asked by one of the Congressmen yesterday with respect to this proposition, has the public service commission of the State of New York any jurisdiction over a purely generating company, that electricity must be generated, and therefore you can have a company that will generate electricity. In order to utilize it it must be transmitted ordinarily; therefore you might have a transmitting company; and besides that in practically all municipalities you must distribute it to the ultimate consumer, and therefore you can have a generating company, a transmitting company, and a distributing company. Now, so far as the distributing company is concerned, and the transmitting company, there is no question, as I understand it, but that the public service commission of the State of New York has jurisdiction; but when you come to the generating company alone, I find there is no authority, nor do I find that any authority can be given, to control the price that they may charge for their commodity.

Mr. LOVELACE. There has never been any contest on it, Mr. Van Kennen; we have always submitted to the public service commission.

Mr. VAN KENNEN. I think that if there is any provision made in this law it should be such a provision that when you grant a permit, the company to which the permit is granted must submit to the jurisdiction of the public service commission as to the price it charges. Otherwise you will find this condition: The generating company, by interlocking directorates with the transmitting and distributing companies, will charge any price that it sees fit for generating the current, and then the public service commission can not possibly reduce the prices; as, for instance, if the generating company charges $25 per horsepower to the transmitting company, when the public service commission is investigating the transmitting company they say, "There is our contract; we can not sell it for $20 per horsepower, we are paying $25."

Mr. DIFENDERFER. Is that not the condition existing to-day in Buffalo?

Mr. VAN KENNEN. That is exactly the condition, as I understand it, that exists in Buffalo to-day; and the city of Buffalo has paid, as I understand it, I don't know how many dollars, to consider and untangle that.

Mr. KENDALL. You spoke a moment ago about the permits?

Mr. VAN KENNEN. Yes, sir.

Mr. KENDALL. From what authority will they derive the permits?

Mr. VAN KENNEN. Well, the permits should come, under your view——

Mr. KENDALL. From the Federal Government.

Mr. VAN KENNEN. From the Federal Government.

Mr. KENDALL. Then you think the Federal Government ought to transfer to a commission of the State of New York the power to regulate prices?

Mr. VAN KENNEN. Yes, sir; I do think so. I think so, with the view of Federal Government that they have any control beyond the actual permit for the diversion of this amount of power. If that view is to obtain, then these permits ought to be issued only upon condition that the generating companies should submit themselves to the jurisdiction of some public tribunal like the public service commission.

Mr. KENDALL. Well, the public service commission is only a tribunal of the State of New York, not of the Federal Government.

Mr. VAN KENNEN. I understand that, but I think they could agree. For instance, I think they could agree to submit themselves to the public service commission.

Mr. LOVELACE. We do agree, right here.

Mr. HARRISON. Do you believe that these permits ought to be for a limited number of years?

Mr. VAN KENNEN. Yes; I think they should be.

Mr. HARRISON. Revocable at the will of the Government?

Mr. VAN KENNEN. Yes, sir, I do; but I think that this is the best proposition——

Mr. HARRISON. Why not a reasonable number of years?

Mr. VAN KENNEN. Well, it is the custom now to think that you ought to limit them.

Mr. DIFENDERFER Nine hundred and ninety-nine, isn't it?

Mr. VAN KENNEN. No; that you ought to limit them to, say, 20 to 30 years. But I think they should have longer.

Mr. GOODWIN. Well, at the end of the period you would be met with the usual vested-right theory, would you not?

DIVERSION OF WATER FROM THE NIAGARA RIVER.

Mr. VAN KENNEN. Yes, sir, I think you would; but that is not an unusual governmental function. The Provinces of Quebec and Ontario do the same thing with reference to their docking privileges. They retain the title, and men invest millions of dollars in equipment on the strength of the promise of the Federal Government to use that land for that purpose on the assurance that the Government will deal justly with its citizens. That is all the assurance they have.

Mr. HARRISON. Do you believe the Government ought to charge any toll for this?

Mr. VAN KENNEN. No; I think not; because any benefits should go in a case of this kind, of course, to the State of New York.

Mr. HARRISON. Do you think the State of New York ought to get the toll?

Mr. VAN KENNEN. Do you mean that they should charge?

Mr. DIFENDERFER. The tariff.

Mr. HARRISON. The tariff.

Mr. VAN KENNEN. You are speaking of the development of power from the water on the American side?

Mr. HARRISON. American and Canadian sides.

Mr. VAN KENNEN. Why, I think this, that the State of New York should have made some provision, if they are going to let private individuals develop it, by which those private individuals should pay a certain sum of money, which has not been the practice on our side excepting the infinitesimal matter of lighting the public park.

Mr. HARRISON. Well, is any toll now charged for this power?

Mr. LOVELACE. It amounts to about $6,000 a year, Mr. Van Kennen; the light and the water. It is small, of course.

Mr. VAN KENNEN. It is very small.

Mr. LOVELACE. We pay $3 a horsepower taxes a year. Our taxes aggregate $3 a horsepower per year to the State and municipalities.

Mr. HARRISON. What would be a reasonable rate should the Government charge any toll or tariff for this power?

Mr. VAN KENNEN. I want to be clear about the question you ask me. Do you mean tariff on imported power?

Mr. HARRISON. I mean on the imported power, and on that which is diverted on the American side, too, and utilized.

Mr. VAN KENNEN. That is a question which I do not think I am competent to answer. As I understand it, the Canadian Government charges practically $1 a horsepower a year. I do not think that is enough.

Mr. CLINE. That is an export duty, is it not?

Mr. VAN KENNEN. No, sir; as I understand it, that is the amount that they pay to the Federal Government.

Mr. LOVELACE. But the great quantity——

Mr. VAN KENNEN. Just one moment more, and I shall be through. Yesterday some one asked about the grants that had been given to these companies by the State of New York. Now, you must remember that when these grants were first given, for the diversion of the water from the Niagara River——

Mr. CLINE. Mr. Chairman, I am having difficulty in hearing Mr. Van Kennen.

The CHAIRMAN. Please come to order, gentlemen.

Mr. VAN KENNEN. I was about to state that when the grants were given to these companies on the Niagara River to divert this water originally, by the State, the art of electrical development had not advanced as far as it is to-day, and I believe in being fair with these people. They were the pioneers, they began the building up of this great work, and they demonstrated at their own expense, and I think at quite a considerable expense, the feasibility of developing electricity at that point, transmitting the same, and utilizing it for power purposes.

Mr. FAIRCHILD. And a great many people were skeptical at that time?

Mr. VAN KENNEN. Absolutely, sir, to be fair to these people, and they have demonstrated to the world that it can be done, and now it would not cost one-half as much money to develop and get the same amount of efficiency as it did those people that were pioneers in this business.

But that does not change my views in any way. We have given them these rights, such as they are, and they have gone to the limit. I think there should be a stop somewhere. Therefore I say that they should not be permitted to use that 4,400 additional cubic feet. Now, the grants have been made, and I will file this with you, because it may be of some use. To the Niagara Falls Power Co., the first was in 1886, and the limit under the State grant was 200,000 horsepower. They are using about 8,600 cubic feet per second, and are entitled to use that. Now, you can see how indefinite that grant was, showing clearly that nobody at that time had a clear conception of what they were doing. There is nothing said in that grant as to how they should utilize it, under what head they should utilize it, and under certain conditions it would take all the water of the Niagara River to make that 200,000 horsepower, while on the other hand, if they developed it to the highest degree of efficiency it would take practically half the amount that they now have permits for.

So I say that these grants are indefinite; for some reason or another the State didn't seem to understand it; they didn't seem to understand it themselves.

Mr. LOVELACE. There never had been a head of that extent used in the world up to that time for commercial purposes.

Mr. VAN KENNEN. Now, the Niagara County Irrigation Water Supply Co. have a grant by the State of New York, in 1891, and they are not developing any power; they are not utilizing any water. That is the situation there, but the grant is outstanding.

Mr. CURLEY. May I ask a question?

Mr. VAN KENNEN. Certainly.

Mr. CURLEY. You think that whatever grant is made should be utilized?

Mr. VAN KENNEN. Yes, absolutely.

M. CURLEY. Your idea is that whatever grant is made should be utilized to the highest efficiency?

Mr. VAN KENNEN. I think it should.

Mr. HARRISON. In that connection, suppose we should pass a bill here specifying that they should develop this power to its highest efficiency, what limit would you put on the time they should have to change their plants to meet that requirement?

Mr. VAN KENNEN. They should have all the time they need. The bill provides for five years, as I understand it, and that is none too much.

Mr. HARRISON. You do not think that is too long a time?

Mr. VAN KENNEN. No, sir; I do not, as I understand it. I am speaking as a layman, and not as a man who knows about the development of electricity.

Mr. FAIRCHILD. What would "highest efficiency" mean? How would you define it?

Mr. VAN KENNEN. That would be a difficult thing to define.

Mr. FAIRCHILD. It seems that is absolutely incomprehensible, because highest efficiency to-day may not be highest efficiency six months or a year from now.

Mr. VAN KENNEN. You can always make up your mind that a certain amount of water falling a certain distance will create a certain amount of energy or power.

Mr. FAIRCHILD. Under all conditions?

Mr. VAN KENNEN. Under all conditions; theoretically, of course, that is. Now, if your machinery is antiquated, then you will not get that high degree of efficiency as if you had up-to-date machinery, the best possible known, and these people of course have developed the best known up to the present time.

Mr. FAIRCHILD. Yes; but the machinery a year from now might develop a great deal more than the machinery of to-day?

Mr. VAN KENNEN. Well, they get up pretty well to the 80 or 85 per cent efficiency.

I was going a step further. Now, the Niagara Power & Development Co. have a charter outstanding, granted in 1893.

Mr. LOVELACE. Pardon me, that has no right to take water from the Niagara River. It is specifically excluded in the wording of the next to the last paragraph of the charter. It specifically excludes that right to the Niagara Power & Development Co.

Mr. VAN KENNEN. Well, we have the Niagara, Lockport & Ontario Power Co., with a charter in 1894, but there is no development under that charter. The Hydraulic Power Co.——

Mr. HARRISON. How much are they allowed?

Mr. VAN KENNEN. There is nothing in the provision of the law which states the limit of their power. They can take it under their charter. They could take it all.

Mr. DIFENDERFER. That is a charter granted by the State of New York?

Mr. VAN KENNEN. Yes, sir.

Mr. DIFENDERFER. And they have permitted these charters to remain in status quo?

Mr. VAN KENNEN. Yes.

Mr. DIFENDERFER. Then, is the State of New York responsible, do you think?

Mr. VAN KENNEN. Why, I think so. We are recommending that all these old charters——

Mr. DIFENDERFER. Will it be safe, then, to allow the State of New York to go further in this matter?

Mr. VAN KENNEN. Absolutely; yes, sir. They have come to the conclusion that that is the policy to adopt.

Mr. GOODWIN. Mr. Van Kennen, there was some talk as to the relationship subsisting between the generating company, the transmitting company, and the distributing company. The generating company is the company to whom the power was first granted, is it not—that is, the parent company?

Mr. VAN KENNEN. Yes.

Mr. GOODWIN. Now, is it not a fact that the transmitting company and the distributing company are subsidiary companies, practically, to the generating company?

Mr. VAN KENNEN. I so understand it.

Mr. GOODWIN. And that that is the necessity of interlocking directorates?

Mr. VAN KENNEN. I so understand it.

Mr. GOODWIN. And that when the ultimate consumer pays the freight, or receives the power from the distributing company, he is paying a dividend, so to speak, to three companies?

Mr. VAN KENNEN. Yes, sir.

Mr. GOODWIN. It is a wheel within a wheel?

Mr. VAN KENNEN. Absolutely.

Mr. GOODWIN. Interlocking directors?

Mr. VAN KENNEN. I understand so. That is why I say that in order to reach that question we must clothe some tribunal with the power to get at the parent company.

Mr. GOODWIN. And when a grant is made to the generating company, then we should prescribe that the public service commission of New York should have certain rights, or clothe that public service commission with authority to limit or prescribe the rate to be charged to the consumer?

Mr. VAN KENNEN. Or, putting it another way, the permittee should agree to come within the jurisdiction of the public service commission, so that the public service commission would have undisputed jurisdiction over it.

Mr. GOODWIN. Well, now, is there any such restriction incident to the grant?

Mr. VAN KENNEN. No, sir.

Mr. GOODWIN. Does the generating company come within the purview, or the dominion, or the control of the public service commission?

Mr. VAN KENNEN. I hold no. They tell me they are willing to submit to that.

Mr. LOVELACE. I would like to say now that the statute of the State of New York, the public service commission law of the State of New York, expressly provides that all electrical companies within that State come under the jurisdiction of the public service commission, and it gives them absolute jurisdiction as to the regulation of prices, and none of the generating companies have ever thought of contesting that provision of the law; and we report regularly, and we obey every mandate of the public service commission, and we have many of them.

Mr. SMITH. Mr. Lovelace, is it not a fact that within two weeks the Hydraulic Co. contested the right of the public service commission to interfere with the Hydraulic Co. in the regulation of prices in the Buffalo case?

Mr. LOVELACE. If Mr. Smith says so, very likely it is true; but I am speaking for the Niagara Falls Power Co., and I personally have charge of the relations of that company with the public service commission, make every report, and write every letter that is written to them, and we have never thought of contesting that provision.

Mr. VAN KENNEN. I want to say to you that I have no reason to doubt Mr. Lovelace's statement at all.

Mr. FAIRCHILD. I want to prosecute that inquiry a bit further. To what extent has the public service commission carried out its function, or the law with which it is clothed, in getting a tax from the generating company which goes to the behoof of the State of New York? In other words, has the public service commission been faithful in the discharge of its duty in making certain exactions in the way of tolls from the generating companies?

Mr. LOVELACE. It has no power to exact tolls, but it has power to regulate rates, and it has accepted and does give the public the benefit of those rates without the tolls. We have to pay tolls otherwise to other authorities of the State of New York, and in the case of our company it amounts to $3 per horsepower.

Mr. KENDALL. Has the public service commission reviewed your rates?

Mr. LOVELACE. They have never yet required us to reduce our rates. They have required us to file our rates with them and they require us to adhere to those rates, and there is a statutory provision of the State of New York which makes it a criminal offense to deviate from those rates—to increase or decrease them. There must be a uniform rate.

Mr. FAIRCHILD. What is the difference in the rate now that the ultimate consumer pays from the distributing company as compared with the rate provided by the contract subsisting between the generating company and the transmitting company? In other words, how much in excess do the people pay to the distributing company as compared with the charges by the generating company to the transmitting company?

Mr. LOVELACE. That is a difficult thing to answer offhand, because the power is sold and paid for in one manner to the distributing company and in another manner by the ultimate purchaser; but I can answer you generally. The rate paid by the Cataract Power & Conduit Co., which is the distributing company in Buffalo—our distributing company—to the parent company is $16 per horsepower per year. That is the rate, taken 24 hours in the day, every day in the year, per horsepower of electrical energy. It is the wholesale rate. They distribute it. Generally they have kilowatt-hour rates, and for the power houses they have a rate which, in most cases, amounts to practically $25 per horsepower per year. Now, of course, between the two, the $16 and the $25, you have to pay all the charges of transformation of the current, transformation up, its transmission to Buffalo and its transformation down, and distribution in Buffalo.

Mr. COOPER. Mr. Chairman, may I ask one question?

The CHAIRMAN. Mr. Cooper, yes.

Mr. COOPER. Is there any necessity for three corporations to get that power from the river to the consumer 30 miles away?

Mr. VAN KENNEN. I do not think so.

Mr. LOVELACE. It may not be necessary, perhaps, now, but there was a necessity at the time.

Mr. COOPER. I am speaking about it now. You said "perhaps." Is there any necessity for three corporations to get electrical power 30 miles to the consumer from Niagara Falls?

Mr. LOVELACE. Except for the fact that it now exists. The investments are made, the mortgages are made, and it is difficult now to separate them. That is the whole matter.

Mr. KENDALL. Are those corporations interlocked, Mr. Lovelace?

Mr. LOVELACE. Yes.

Mr. KENDALL. The same financial interests are supporting all three of them?

Mr. LOVELACE. We own one-half of the stock of the distributing company.

Mr. SMITH. Whom do you represent?

Mr. LOVELACE. The Niagara Falls Power Co.

Mr. KENDALL. You are the transmission company?

Mr. LOVELACE. Yes; of the pioneer generating company of New York.

Mr. KENDALL. You own half of the stock of the distributing company?

Mr. LOVELACE. Yes. It could not have been financed in any other way. In the day it was financed there was the greatest difficulty in the world to get men to take hold of any of them. They were offered the opportunity to take it, make their own backing, and finance it, and they fell down absolutely.

Mr. KENDALL. There is no impropriety in your generating it and transmitting it and distributing it?

Mr. LOVELACE. George Westinghouse said it could not be done.

Mr. KENDALL. There is no impropriety in your generating the power and transmitting it and distributing it? My question is as to the necessity of three distinct corporations.

Mr. LOVELACE. If we had to do it to-day, there would be but one.

Mr. KENDALL. Would it not be good business for you, and the consumer, so to revise your methods of business as to eliminate these other two corporations?

Mr. LOVELACE. We have had it under consideration.

Mr. KENDALL. How long have you been considering it?

Mr. LOVELACE. Ever since the matter has been agitated.

Mr. KENDALL. That is indefinite. A year, or two years?

Mr. LOVELACE. Perhaps a year, or over.

Mr. KENDALL. You own, do you, all of the stock of the conduit company?

Mr. LOVELACE. A half; a majority interest.

Mr. DIFENDERFER. How much money has been paid in as the sum total of all these three corporations?

Mr. LOVELACE. I can not speak for the other corporations, but the securities of the Niagara Falls Power Co. are practically bona fide investments at par to-day.

Mr. DIFENDERFER. No watered stock issued?

Mr. LOVELACE. Substantially none, sir. In the early days the securities were turned over to a contracting company at their par value, and the contractor had a fair margin of profit; that is all.

Mr. DIFENDERFER. Now, did the transmitting company issue any watered stock?

Mr. LOVELACE. It did issue two millions of stock for its franchises in the city of Buffalo and for the contract with the parent company, which at that time was considered a very advantageous contract.

Mr. DIFENDERFER. Has the transmitting company ever issued any watered stock?

Mr. LOVELACE. There is no transmitting company; the parent company transmits it.

Mr. DIFENDERFER. The service company then, the third company?

Mr. LOVELACE. I do not think so. That is a company in which we have absolutely no interest; there is no interlocking of directors.

Mr. HARRISON. What do you mean by watered stock? Do you mean stock relative to the generating of water power, or do you mean water power in the stock?

Mr. DIFENDERFER. Water power in the stock for public use.

Mr. LOVELACE. I didn't expect to add this. Perhaps the chairman will excuse me.

The CHAIRMAN. Certainly. Mr. Van Kennen, have you anything further?

Mr. SMITH. Perhaps he can go on later, and not interfere with Mr. Van Kennen.

Mr. HARRISON. Mr. Burden, in the other hearing, testified to practically all this.

Mr. VAN KENNEN. I want to ask Mr. Lovelace, if he knows, to tell us how much the Canadian company charges, the Hydro-Electric Commission of Canada, for energy, per horsepower?

The CHAIRMAN. I think that is in the record; we have that here.

Mr. LOVELACE. I know, and am willing to state.

Mr. VAN KENNEN. I thought that is a matter in this connection that ought to be brought up. It is practically $10 per horsepower, so that you can see the difference between the charges. He says that they charge the transmitting company or the distributing company $16 per horsepower, and there is this $9.40——

Mr. LOVELACE. Mr. Van Kennen, one is transmitted to Buffalo and the other is at the terminals of the transforming apparatus, practically at the power house.

The CHAIRMAN. We went into that very fully before, and we have no time to go into it now. The committee will come to order.

Mr. VAN KENNEN. I started to read here in connection with this. To the Hydraulic Power Co., of Niagara Falls, in 1896; the specifications in their charter are the capacity of a canal 100 feet wide and 14 feet deep. Well, now, I am not an engineer, but I don't understand that there is any engineer who can tell you what that amounts to.

Mr. HARRISON. Do they specify how much they shall use?

Mr. VAN KENNEN. No, sir; it depends altogether upon mechanical construction.

The CHAIRMAN. That is a pretty good argument against the recklessness of the New York Legislature in granting those charters.

Mr. VAN KENNEN. I am not here to defend those early grants at all, but I am here to say that I think the State of New York has now come to a point where they want to insist upon their rights and the distribution of this power upon equitable terms to the people of the State. That is what I want to say.

Mr. CLINE. Consider, Mr. Van Kennen. What additional power do you think the State of New York should be clothed with if in the past it has not required these people to conform to the law and has not regulated them as it should? Why should you clothe them with still more plenary power?

Mr. VAN KENNEN. I want to say that I believe the Public Service Commission of the State of New York is honestly endeavoring to administer the powers conferred upon it.

Mr. CLINE. Have been in the past?

Mr. VAN KENNEN. Yes, sir.

Mr. FAIRCHILD. There is a new order of things in New York State.

Mr. VAN KENNEN. The difficulty is this, as I understand it. They can not enforce jurisdiction over this generating company. Why? Because it is not a public service proposition at all. It is a private concern. They can not enforce that, any more than they can enforce a restriction on the amount that a man should charge for milk. That is the difficulty.

Mr. KENDALL. Where does the generating company derive its corporate authority from, the State of New York?

Mr. VAN KENNEN. Yes, sir.

Mr. KENDALL. Can not the State of New York impose such restrictions upon that as it desires?

Mr. VAN KENNEN. They haven't got a vote, even.

Mr. LOVELACE. Certainly they have, Mr. Van Kennen.

Mr. VAN KENNEN. I do not agree with the gentleman on that proposition.

Mr. KENDALL. I think Mr. Fairchild states that there is a new order of things in the Empire State to-day.

Mr. FAIRCHILD. It refers to the organization of the public service commission, because there is a new order of things as to corporations in the State of New York.

The CHAIRMAN. Mr. Van Kennen, how many of these franchises have been repealed by the State of New York?

Mr. VAN KENNEN. There is only one of them; that is the Lower Niagara River Power & Water Supply Co., with 200,000 horsepower below the Falls; not operated at all.

Mr. HARRISON. When was that granted?

Mr. VAN KENNEN. Granted in 1902.

The CHAIRMAN. Is it not a fact that there were 12 of them altogether?

Mr. VAN KENNEN. Not as I understand it; no, sir.

The CHAIRMAN. The franchises of all have been repealed except three; is that not correct?

Mr. VAN KENNEN. I think there are more than three; I think there are five outstanding, two of which are operating.

The CHAIRMAN. Two operating?

Mr. VAN KENNEN. Yes.

Mr. HARRISON. These are the five that you have read?

Mr. VAN KENNEN. Yes.

The CHAIRMAN. And the governor of New York has recommended to the legislature the repeal of the three that are not in operation?

Mr. VAN KENNEN. We have recommended that in our report to the legislature, asking the repeal of those three grants. A very grave question arises with reference to the repeal of a grant with respect to having operated under it, and when people have operated under them in good faith I am not standing here for the repeal of them without full compensation.

Mr. HARRISON. May I ask you how many persons compose the Public Service Commission of New York?

Mr. VAN KENNEN. We have two public service commissions.

Mr. HARRISON. The one that has jurisdiction of these?

Mr. VAN KENNEN. Five.

Mr. HARRISON. Are they elected or appointed?

Mr. VAN KENNEN. Appointed.

Mr. HARRISON. For how long?

Mr. VAN KENNEN. A five-year term, but when the law was originally passed there was one man appointed for one year, one man for two years, and so on. There will be a very material change under this new administration in the public service commissions law.

Mr. FAIRCHILD. There is a proposition to consolidate the two commissions in one.

Mr. VAN KENNEN. They will be changed, but I do not want to be misunderstood.

Mr. DIFENDERFER. The public service commission is improving upon its original methods, as well.

The CHAIRMAN. Please come to order. We can not talk across the table.

We are very much obliged to you, Mr. Van Kennen. We will now hear the counsel for the public service commission, Mr. Richards.

Mr. COOPER. Mr. Chairman, may I ask just one question? The gentleman here, Mr. Lovelace, as you sat down after testifying to the difference between the Canadian price and the American price, you said, "And Congress is responsible for that condition." What did you mean by that?

Mr. LOVELACE. From the fact that Congress has limited the amount of power that can come from Canada into the United States. They have glutted the Canadian market with power, that is all.

Mr. COOPER. But they sell it over there at a profit, do they not?

Mr. LOVELACE. I am not so sure of that, sir. I know that my company would not sell it for $5 a horsepower—no, I will not say that—for $4 a horsepower—more than they sell it for. My company was offered the same opportunity and refused to take it on the ground that they could not sell there at the price.

Mr. COOPER. The Canadians will still sell it.

Mr. LOVELACE. They have to, their plants are there. They would have an idle investment if they did not do it.

Mr. COOPER. I think Gen. Green testified, when he was here before the committee——

Mr. LOVELACE. His counsel is here, and very likely would say the same thing. I do not say they are not making a profit.

Mr. COOPER. I understood you to say that.

The CHAIRMAN. They make 17 horsepower to the cubic foot, and you make 10.

Mr. LOVELACE. We make about 11½, and they very nearly 17.

Mr. SMITH. Mr. Lovelace, I would like to ask you something about that.

Mr. LOVELACE. Perhaps I may be called later. I have slept with this thing from 1906, and there is not a thing about it I do not know.

The CHAIRMAN. Let us hear the gentleman who came over from New York, representing the public service commission.

STATEMENT OF HON. EUGENE RICHARDS, OF NEW YORK.

Mr. RICHARDS. I am counsel to the conservation commission, not the public service commission. Somebody has suggested that I represented the public service commission.

I want to say, in reference to some of these questions which our chairman was not able, or did not, answer in regard to this public service commission, that I agree with him that in the State of New York the public service commission is doing its full duty, but the trouble is that the public service commission was not established in the State of New York until after all these power grants that he has described here were made, not until several years after they were made, and that answers that proposition, more or less, as to their regulation.

On the question of the power to regulate their rates, I thoroughly concur with the chairman, that is, that at present, under the existing laws, or any law that can be framed, a generating company can not be forced by the public service commission act or any amendment thereto to regulate its rates by law, and the one thing that we ask for, and the very thing that we are going to ask for in an amendment to this bill, is that any permit that may hereafter be issued to anyone may be conditioned upon these very companies agreeing, as they can do, to waive their rights, to come under the public service commission, to submit to its jurisdiction, and to agree to abide by its rates and regulations.

I am going to take that up in detail. We have here a proposed amendment to this act, the bill that you have here before you, making such a provision as will give what we think is necessary for the protection of the people generally of the State of New York on that proposition.

The CHAIRMAN. What is the number of the conservation commission in New York?

Mr. RICHARDS. Three; three commissioners.

The CHAIRMAN. Mr. Van Kennen is the chairman?

Mr. RICHARDS. The chairman, and I am counsel for the conservation commission, and we have been together working up this question. Mr. Van Kennen, as I understand it, has largely taken up these questions of policy and power, and we are here to-day assuming that this committee is going to very largely insist upon the powers of the Federal Government. I may disagree with the committee on the question of the power of the Federal Government to do more than to issue and revoke permits, but in making these suggestions I am assuming that the committee will stand to the proposition that this act, in its essence, is an act which they are going to report, and it is on the basis of that that I have drawn here a memorandum, or rather a revised bill, with the eliminations and the amendments which we suggest.

Mr. HARRISON. In that connection, have you consulted with the Public Service Commission of New York in connection with this bill you have drawn?

Mr. RICHARDS. No; it is your bill; I mean an amendment to your bill.

Mr. HARRISON. That is what I am talking about.

Mr. RICHARDS. No. This matter has come along so fast that even after we got here we found there were some slight changes to be made.

Mr. CURLEY. Let me ask the gentleman to explain what the powers and duties of this commission are.

Mr. HARRISON. You have great faith in the Public Service Commission of New York, have you not?

Mr. RICHARDS. I have faith in their regulation, but I have not faith in their jurisdiction over a generating company, as a matter of law, unless the generating company can be forced in some way or other to agree to put itself in the category of an ordinary public service company; that is my point.

Mr. HARRISON. You do not answer the question that I asked you. You have faith in the public service commission in New York, that it is a sound and honorable and reliable body?

Mr. RICHARDS. Absolutely.

Mr. HARRISON. Then why have you not endeavored to get in touch with them, and have them consider this proposition that you submit here?

Mr. RICHARDS. Well, I think it will be safe to assume that they would be only too glad to have their powers extended, as I understand it, from practical application, that these companies do not yield to their jurisdiction, and this is for the purpose of giving them the power by way of these permits which, concededly, they have not got.

Mr. HARRISON. I assume that the proper functions of your conservation commission would be to work in conjunction with your public service commission over there?

Mr. RICHARDS. Yes, that is quite right.

Mr. HARRISON. But you apparently have not done it in this instance?

Mr. RICHARDS. Well, I do not know.

Mr. HARRISON. It is not because you haven't faith in them, is it?

Mr. RICHARDS. What do you mean, by working in conjunction with them?

Mr. HARRISON. You have not submitted to them this proposed amendment by which they are to exercise jurisdiction and authority, but you submit it for consideration, acceptance, or rejection by this committee without consulting the body that is going to have the administration of it?

Mr. RICHARDS. Yes, that is more or less true; but the fact is that the public service commission has not been able to find in the present act, or in any provision of law, power to regulate this very question. Now it may be that it would be more desirable to have them look over this proposed provision, but I am going to submit it for what it is worth.

Mr. HARRISON. You submit it without giving them an opportunity to approve it?

Mr. RICHARDS. I never saw a commission yet that did not want to have its powers enlarged.

The CHAIRMAN. Mr. Richards, Mr. Townsend wants to know the scope and power of your conservation commission, what its duties and powers are.

Mr. RICHARDS. The conservation commission has control and custody of the natural resources of the State of New York; that substantially covers it all; that is, their forest, their waters, whatever the State water powers may be, the control of their water supply for drinking purposes, the control of fish and game. In other words, as I say, it is all summed up in the control and custody of the natural resources of the State.

Mr. TOWNSEND. Let me get a clearer idea. Suppose you have a water power there, for the purpose of generating electricity?

Mr. RICHARDS. Yes.

Mr. TOWNSEND. Would your commission be the one that the applicants would go to for the right to use that?

Mr. RICHARDS. Yes.

Mr. TOWNSEND. And then having used it, having generated this power, the commission which would regulate its use or its price would be the public service commission?

Mr. RICHARDS. The public service commission.

Mr. TOWNSEND. Then you work for the State up to a certain point?

Mr. RICHARDS. Exactly.

Mr. TOWNSEND. And then, as a possible result of your work, the public service commission takes hold of it?

Mr. RICHARDS. Yes; exactly.

Mr. COOPER. I would like to ask a question that was suggested by your opening statement. You said you had faith in the good intentions of the commission, but you doubted the jurisdiction.

Mr. RICHARDS. Of this commission?

Mr. COOPER. The public service commission.

Mr. RICHARDS. The jurisdiction over this generating company.

Mr. COOPER. Exactly. Now, this generating company, you have generating companies for all of them?

Mr. RICHARDS. Yes; two of them.

Mr. COOPER. Well, now, they get their authority from the legislature of the State of New York?

Mr. RICHARDS. Yes, sir.

Mr. COOPER. Didn't that legislature reserve to itself the right to alter, amend, or repeal the charter?

Mr. RICHARDS. I see your idea. I have not examined every one of those charters, because there is generally that provision, but the courts hold that that provision is practically a nullity where the company has used and made its investments, if the amendment that you seek to put upon their charter would be in the nature of taking away their charter. It is all a question then of the constitutional vested rights of the company. That is, where they have started to operate.

Mr. COOPER. So you hold that, as a matter of law, if the Legislature of the State of New York grants a charter to a corporation, expressly reserving the right to alter, amend, or repeal, in its discretion, as quick as a company accepts that charter and invests its money the interests become vested, and the statutory reservation is repealed practically?

Mr. RICHARDS. No. This is what I say, that that is effective to this extent, that a repeal of that charter can be made provided a reasonable arrangement is made for compensation for the investments that have been made of property under the charter; and that is exactly the situation which we now confront the Long Sault Development Co. with.

Mr. COOPER. Suppose they simply wanted to amend it, but later it says, to confer upon this commission the right to require the company to charge reasonable rates. That would not be confiscatory; that would be simply regulative.

Mr. RICHARDS. Now, then, there is no such thing as compensating for property. You are not taking away property. Now, if that reservation is in their charter, you see the difficulty with making amendments of legislative provisions is this, that although you may make a legislative provision or amendment, if you get legislation it may not be valid legislation.

Mr. COOPER. What was the reason that that company objected to the requirements of your commission up there—that they were to do certain things?

Mr. RICHARDS. This was not my commission, sir—the public service commission.

Mr. COOPER. I mean the public service commission.

Mr. CURLEY. Actually, the public service commission has nothing to do with this matter that we are investigating at all?

Mr. RICHARDS. The public service commission had nothing whatever to do with it. The only way I am involved in it is the suggestion whereby the powers of the public service commission shall be sufficiently broadened to protect the interests of the people of the State, as we believe they can not be protected under existing laws without some such amendment as may be put in here, which will be a condition of their taking a permit.

Mr. COOPER. You are asking for a broadening of the powers of the public service commission?

Mr. CURLEY. He suggested——

Mr. COOPER. He just said he was asking for a broadening of the powers of the public service commission.

Mr. TOWNSEND. Mr. Cooper and I evidently misunderstand the relation of the commission this gentleman represents to the question that this committee is considering.

The CHAIRMAN. This gentleman represents the conservation commission.

Mr. TOWNSEND. What has that body to do with the point which this committee is investigating?

The CHAIRMAN. The powers he asks for are powers that go to the public service commission, and not to his commission.

Mr. CURLEY. He asked expressly for that.

Mr. RICHARDS. I have an amendment here suggesting an increase in the powers of the public service commission.

Mr. HARRISON. Mr. Curley tried to find out whether the public service commission asked this.

Mr. RICHARDS. I suppose it is pretty safe that the conservation commission, or myself, as a citizen of the State, will be glad to submit to the committee any proposition which gives protection to the ordinary, plain people of the State of New York in the way of regulation of public-service corporations or quasi public-service corporations, which will give us the rights we think we should have.

Mr. CURLEY. I did not want any question to rest in the minds of the committee here as to whom you represent. We heard a very distinguished citizen of New York yesterday, with great profit and pleasure, I am sure, and I do not think there is a disposition on the part of any committeeman to refuse you a hearing as a citizen of New York, but I did not want any confusion to remain in the minds of the committee as to what official right you had to address it. Now, as a citizen, we are, of course, charmed to have you address us.

Mr. RICHARDS. Now, then, if the conservation commission has authority to develop these waters let us go a step further. Would not the conservation commission, which I represent and which Mr. Van Kennen represents, have an interest to see that when the waters are developed the power is developed, the citizens of the State are protected after that development is made, and we believe that the proper body to have charge of that would be the public service commission, and we are making suggestions which are in the nature of a broadening of the powers of the public service commission, and in addition to what interest I may have as a citizen we have this direct interest. We consider that the first step. A direct charter of the flow of the water, and then the jurisdiction passes to this other board. We are in a position to take up these provisions as a whole, to make a suggestion to the committee for an amendment which would broaden the powers of the public service commission and make this thing effective.

Mr. COOPER. Do you think that Congress has any other jurisdiction over this water except to regulate the quantity which may be used?

Mr. RICHARDS. And issue permits and revoke permits.

Mr. COOPER. That is, simply for the amount of water that can be used, not anything as to rates?

Mr. RICHARDS. No; I do not think they have.

Mr. COOPER. Now, then, that is one thing. You think Congress has no such power, and you have the jurisdiction apparently of the Legislature of New York to confer upon a commission authority to do it, yet you have brought in an amendment to the law to confer authority upon that commission; but you can not do that, you say, except with the consent of the companies that would be regulated. You want them to agree to the terms of that instrument.

Mr. RICHARDS. That is true.

Mr. COOPER. Exactly. So then the law which shall be passed here must first be submitted to and meet with the approval of the companies that would be regulated. Now, then, analyzed closer, that is your position exactly?

Mr. RICHARDS. No.

Mr. COOPER. No one has any authority to say anything about rates. He doubts the jurisdiction of the commission, and of course they get their power from the State; he doubts the authority of the State to prescribe rates, and it leaves us remediless except for this statute which he proposes to enact, and we can only do anything after an agreement between the companies and the commission.

Mr. CLINE. I would like to ask the gentleman this question.

Mr. RICHARDS. I think the Congressman misunderstands me.

Mr. CLINE. Where does Congress get any authority to amend a charter issued by a State to a company doing purely a local business? That is what this amounts to.

The CHAIRMAN. Mr. Richards, as I understand it, is to offer a provision to amend this bill by which the Secretary of War is directed not to issue these permits until these people agree to submit themselves to the jurisdiction of the public service commission.

Mr. RICHARDS. That is it exactly. And this is the form that I wish to have put in, so that you can see exactly how far that proposition goes.

Mr. SMITH. Mr. Richards, if the public service commission has no authority to control water-power companies, what remedy will the people have?

Mr. RICHARDS. That was the question I was going to take up with the Congressman here. The public service commission has power to control the rates of certain companies—transmitting and delivering companies—but when it comes to these generating companies, which are the companies that are going to get the power, there being these three classes you can see with these interlocking directors, our idea is that the charge made to the ultimate consumer arises out of the relation between these three companies, the first of which is in no sense under the public service commission law a public-service corporation. It has one customer. It generates certain power and sells it to a transmitting company and there its functions end. And it is that one of the three classes of public-service corporations only that I say that the Public Service Commission of New York can not touch. That is the one we want to reach, if possible.

Mr. COOPER. Right there you come to the definition of a public service corporation. You say this generating company has a contract by which it confines its sales exclusively to one company, but has it not the option to sell it to other people? Could it not make contracts with 20 others?

Mr. RICHARDS. We are dealing with what it actually does.

Mr. COOPER. But that does not affect the character of the corporation. A public corporation might have only one customer, but it would be a public corporation, and the fact that this corporation has only one customer does not save it from being a public corporation, having received its charter from the State, and having the option to sell to as many people as it chooses.

Mr. KENDALL. Mr. Richards, may I ask for information, are you familiar with the operations of the company now which uses this power?

Mr. RICHARDS. So far as we learn it from the way it is being dealt with, as agreed by Mr. Lovelace.

Mr. KENDALL. You spoke a little while ago about an interlocking directorate with the different companies, the personnel being quite in common with the differenct companies.

Mr. RICHARDS. Practically, sir.

Mr. KENDALL. But there is practically no competition between the companies, on account of the similarity of directorates.

Mr. RICHARDS. There are three companies, the generating company and the transmitting company, and then the delivering company.

Mr. KENDALL. Practically one, except in name. As far as the real owners and the directors are concerned they are identical, are they not?

Mr. RICHARDS. Yes.

Mr. KENDALL. Now, carrying that inquiry a little further, is there any diversion of water for power below the Falls?

Mr. RICHARDS. None that has been developed. There was, in one of these grants here, one of these charters that have been issued, a grant of 200,000 horsepower below the Falls, but that has not been used or developed. With that exception there is not.

Mr. KENDALL. Is that to an independent company?

Mr. RICHARDS. That is to the Lower Niagara River Power & Water Supply Co., incorporated by special act in 1902, 11 years ago.

Mr. KENDALL. Do you know whether the identity of that is in any way connected with the other companies?

Mr. RICHARDS. I do not; no, sir.

Mr. KENDALL. You don't know anything about that?

Mr. RICHARDS. No, sir.

Mr. GARNER. I did not happen to be in here when you opened your remarks, but I gather from your remarks that there are three propositions that you would like to have this committee consider. First, you would like to have all the water that can be utilized on this side of the river.

Mr. RICHARDS. That is right, and Chairman Van Kennen has already stated that.

Mr. GARNER. And second, you would like, if Congress has the power to do so, to compel the companies to submit themselves to the jurisdiction of the controlling powers of the State of New York?

Mr. RICHARDS. Yes.

Mr. GARNER. And third, you would like to have Congress give that power in New York an opportunity to say what shall be done, and what price shall be given for this power after it comes into your State?

Mr. RICHARDS. Exactly, sir.

Mr. GARNER. That covers the three points that you favor, as I understand it?

Mr. RICHARDS. That is exactly my position; and the amendments that I submit here, except for some final changes, are practically amendments to carry out those suggestions. Now, in section 2—if you will follow me here I will go through these and see if my suggestions are not as I stated, simply for this purpose, that we shall have this property for the benefit of the people and for the good of the people, whether it comes through rates by the public-service commission or through the development of power under our control as a conservation commission; but what we want and desire is to develop the power for the benefit of the people themselves and not for private interests. Now, in section 2, I have a change here. The amendment is to strike out the words "at any one time the amount of fifteen thousand six hundred."

Mr. HARRISON. What line is that on, Mr. Richards?

Mr. RICHARDS. Line 9. Strike out "at any one time the amount of fifteen thousand six hundred," and place in lieu of that, "the rate of twenty thousand" cubic feet of water per second, which, in other words, covers our suggestion that now is the time when this additional 4,400 cubic feet should be granted. That power should be given to get that additional water supply; in other words, to take up the full 20,000 cubic feet. "Provided"—this is a further provision— "That no such permit shall be valid or effective until the same shall have been approved in writing by the governor of the State of New

York, who shall designate the persons, companies, corporate bodies, public bodies, or public officers to whom the same shall be granted." What we really want to do, if we can get the power from the legislature, we want to name, as far as this 4,400 cubic feet is concerned, the people of the State of New York to develop this power for the purposes of the people themselves; and it is for the purpose of giving that control to the State authorities, so that we can name and nominate the grantees of the permits.

Mr. GARNER. Would you lodge that power with the governor?

Mr. RICHARDS. Yes, sir; with the governor of the State, or to such—for the purpose of showing what we want, and the interest that the conservation commission has, as I suggested to the chairman, that is not a question of absolute desire for one particular person, it is a question of having the State of New York, the authorities who desire to have this power developed, and there could be put in place of that, if the committee so pleased, "such body or officers as may be charged with the custody and control of the water powers of the State of New York," which in this case would be the conservation commission.

Mr. GARNER. Now, let me ask you a further question. Do you not think that in granting and designating the parties who would be the beneficiaries of those rights, that they being already in possession and with their machinery in addition, and everything like that, there would be a very serious question as to who would get those very rights?

Mr. RICHARDS. That is just the proposition. What we want to do is to let them have what they have already been granted, because under the terms of your act you have to grant preferences to those who already have existing permits, for the power which has already been diverted, which is 15,600 cubic feet. For the 4,400 cubic feet there is absolutely no necessity, either in law or practicability, which would compel us to give the balance of the 4,400 cubic feet to these very same interests that have been developing this power, and which you are already in a later section endeavoring to govern the efficiency of and see that they develop enough power out of it.

Mr. GARNER. Now, as to the proposition of law, perhaps you are right; but as to being practical at all it seems to me that you err, because the people who are already in possession there and have their machinery and everything, ought to be in a very much better position to give cheaper power to the people than newcomers, had they not?

Mr. RICHARDS. It does not seem, from what we can learn from engineers, that the efficiency they have got out of the water they are already using, the number of cubic feet they are already using, is such as to show that they are going to do any better than the State of New York or a new corporation ought to do with an efficient plant and a higher head.

Mr. GARNER. That is the milk in the coconut. They have had no particular reason, up to the present time, for increasing their efficiency. They have had no competition. They are under no stress at all to do that. They have laid back on their oars, and if you threaten them with active competition don't you think they would increase the efficiency of that machinery?

Mr. RICHARDS. I think it would be a very good thing.

Mr. GARNER. Would they not have the advantage of everybody else on the outside?

The CHAIRMAN. Not as to the 4,400 cubic feet.

Mr. GARNER. Is that not so?

Mr. RICHARDS. If the State were to develop that 4,400 cubic feet I think it would have a very forcible effect upon the operations of those companies, make them give better and cheaper service.

Mr. GARNER. If they were to get the 4,400 feet.

Mr. RICHARDS. That would be up to us, to the attitude of the commission. The view of this commission is that it should be developed for public purposes and for public benefit; that the preference as to this 4,400 cubic feet shall not be to the existing companies, but to the State of New York, to be developed for the benefit of the whole State.

Mr. DIFENDERFER. How would it do to substitute the name of the Secretary of War instead of the governor of New York?

Mr. RICHARDS. Because, when you get that far, it comes back to the same proposition. I am not arguing on the question of law. I am arguing on the question of equity and fairness. What we wish, as far as diversion is concerned, is diversion for State use. We are better able to judge—I think I will put it this way—we are better able to judge at Albany, if we are doing our duty, as to how this should be developed and by whom, than the Secretary of War at Washington, having considered this thing and having taken up this matter in reference to a further State-wide development as described by the chairman.

The CHAIRMAN. The committee will please come to order. We will have to ask the questions so that the whole committee can hear them.

Mr. HARRISON. He said, "Not as reflected by past performances."

Mr. RICHARDS. I perfectly agree with him, and the best evidence, as I say, that its past performances are no longer going to be future performances are the protest of the conservation commission and the attitude of the legislature in repealing the Long Sault charter and the report of the commission that this power be developed for the benefit of the people.

Mr. SHARP. Mr. Richards, I may be wrong in getting the impression from what you say, but is it your plan that the State, in order to create this competition and give the people at large—the plain people, as you say—the benefit of these powers, as a State, would go into furnishing power, and so on?

Mr. RICHARDS. Exactly; just exactly that.

Mr. SHARP. Go into the business and deliver power?

Mr. RICHARDS. Exactly, as the municipalities and the State take charge of potable water. We think it has got to the point, as far as economics is concerned, where water power is just as much a public utility and a public service to the average citizen as water.

Mr. SHARP. Do you consider that those who already have this power have such vested rights as to keep it and maintain it in spite of any such action?

Mr. RICHARDS. You mean these other companies?

Mr. SHARP. Yes.

Mr. RICHARDS. In so far as the permits now existing to them are concerned, and covering such exact volume of water as they now have. In other words, that no permits shall be given by the Secretary of

War under this to the existing or present holders of permits except for the precise and limited amounts to which they have present permits.

Mr. SHARP. Then, if it is your intention and contention that you wish, through your commission, to have the State engage in this business, why not so word this amendment that you propose here, that instead of the governor designating the beneficiaries as to the new power, it shall rest in the State, and that they themselves shall use the power? Your amendment is in direct conflict.

Mr. RICHARDS. As I say, we have no opinion on the question of who the exact executive or legislative officer of the State of New York shall be who shall name the grantees, but it is for the purpose of having a New York officer charged with this duty, who will know what is the best way to develop these waters, whether it shall be used by the State and give the preference to the State or someone else.

Mr. SHARP. That is what I wanted to know, whether your plan was definite and certain to have the State do that work.

Mr. RICHARDS. We suggest the governor, because he is the chief executive.

Mr. SHARP. If it is planned to have the State itself control this, and give the power, and so on, then there would be no reason for inserting a provision giving the power to the governor to designate the beneficiary.

Mr. RICHARDS. The governor would either have to designate someone, or the conservation commission.

The CHAIRMAN. There has been a roll call going on down in the House. What is the pleasure of the committee?

Mr. HARRISON. Do I understand that the conservationists have taken a position in favor of using the entire 20,000 cubic feet?

Mr. RICHARDS. I say that the conservation commission has taken the position that any undeveloped water powers of the State of New York that the State itself can develop should be developed by the State and not turned over to private corporations or companies—should be developed and distributed to its citizens.

Mr. HARRISON. But you favor using up the balance of the 20,000 cubic feet?

Mr. RICHARDS. Yes; using that up as part of the undeveloped water.

Mr. HARRISON. I understood the last time the conservationists were here they said it would destroy the scenic beauty of the Falls?

Mr. RICHARDS. I am not a conservationist in that sense. I only take the evidence of your own committee here, that as far as the American side is concerned, the difference would be about five-eighths of an inch.

Mr. HARRISON. I move that we adjourn until to-morrow morning.

The CHAIRMAN. Mr. Harrison moves that this committee rise until to-morrow morning at 10.30.

Mr. SHARP. Mr. Chairman, before we pass upon that, the thought has occurred to me that we owe these gentlemen some courtesy here, they having come down from New York, and if we can accommodate them by extending the time to any here we ought to do so. I do not know how many of us can meet this afternoon, but it might be quite an accommodation to these gentlemen if we could meet this afternoon for several hours.

Mr. CURLEY. I would like to suggest that we meet at 8 o'clock to-night.

Mr. FAIRCHILD. May I ask a question in regard to that? As I understand it, so far as the State of New York is concerned, when Mr. Richards is through the State of New York is through. Now, if you intend to hear others outside, it may be that we should be here to hear what they have to say; if you do not intend to hear any others outside of the officers of the State of New York, why then of course we are through.

The CHAIRMAN. The original resolution was to hear only the officers of the State of New York, but I do not think it will be possible to confine the hearings to the officers of the State of New York.

Mr. VAN KENNEN. We do not want anything unfair.

Mr. CURLEY. I move that when the committee rises it rise to meet again to-night at 8 o'clock.

The CHAIRMAN. The committee can all be here then? The committee has heard the motion that we meet to-night at 8 o'clock. All in favor of that say ''aye.''

RESPONSE. ''Aye.''

Thereupon, at 12.10 o'clock p. m., the committee adjourned until 8 o'clock p. m., Thursday, January 23, 1913.

DIVERSION OF WATER FROM THE NIAGARA RIVER.

COMMITTEE ON FOREIGN AFFAIRS,
HOUSE OF REPRESENTATIVES,
Washington, D. C., Thursday, January 23, 1913.

The committee met, pursuant to the taking of recess, at 8 o'clock p. m., Hon. Henry D. Flood (chairman) presiding.

[Bill proposed by subcommittee on Niagara Falls legislation.]

A BILL For the control and regulation of the waters of the Niagara River in the State of New York, for the preservation of Niagara Falls, and for other purposes.

Be it enacted by the Senate and House of Representatives of the United States of America in Congress assembled, That the diversion of waters from the Niagara River in the State of New York is hereby prohibited, except with the consent of the Secretary of War, as herein authorized by this act: *Provided,* That this prohibition shall not be interpreted as forbidding the diversion of water of the Great Lakes or of Niagara River for public use for sanitary or domestic purposes, or for navigation, the amount of which, except that needed for the navigation of the Erie Canal, may be fixed from time to time by the Congress of the United States, or by the Secretary of War under its direction.

SEC. 2. That the Secretary of War is hereby authorized to grant for the public benefit of the State of New York and other States into which electrical power may be transmitted revocable permits for the diversion of water in the United States from said Niagara River above the Falls to an aggregate amount stated in said permits not exceeding in daily diversion at any one time the amount of fifteen thousand six hundred cubic feet of water per second: *Provided,* That whenever the Secretary of War shall determine that the diversions of water herein authorized in connection with the amount of water diverted on the Canadian side of the river interferes with the navigable capacity of said river, or its proper volume as a boundary stream, or its efficiency as a means of national defense, or the scenic grandeur of Niagara Falls, or that the waters diverted for the development of electrical power are not being utilized to their full or proper standard of efficiency, or that the public interests are not being conserved or protected in the use, transmission, or sale of electrical power generated therefrom, he shall revoke any permit granted, after giving five years' notice to the said parties holding the said revocable permits and to the Congress of the United States of his intention to make such revocation.

SEC. 3. That the Secretary of War is hereby authorized to issue permits for the diversion of water below the Falls.

SEC. 4. That in granting a revocable permit for the diversion of waters from the Niagara River above the Falls under the conditions of this act the Secretary of War shall have due regard for those investments which have already been made in the construction of power plants under permits issued by the State of New York and the Federal Government and shall give preference in the issuing of such permits to companies, corporations, or bodies now lawfully organized and holding permits and now diverting water under said permits and generating electrical power for the use of cities, towns, manufacturing plants, and other corporate bodies under long-time contracts or leases over any and all other companies and corporations not now having fixed investments for the development of such electrical power: *Provided further,* That the Secretary of War shall certify a copy of any and all revocable permits to the governor of the State or States in which such permits authorize the operation of the company holding the permits.

SEC. 5. That all persons, companies, or corporate bodies now holding permits for the diversion of water from Niagara River for the purpose of creating electrical energy shall, if necessary, reconstruct the plants they are now operating within five years after notice by the Secretary of War that such plant is not constructed so as to utilize the water at its full or proper standard of efficiency in the production of electrical power, and that standard shall be determined by the Secretary of War.

57

SEC. 6. That the Secretary of War is hereby authorized to grant permits for the transmission of electrical power from the Dominion of Canada into the United States, and the Secretary of War may specify the companies, corporations, or bodies legally organized therefor by whom the same shall be transmitted and the companies, corporations, or bodies to whom the same shall be delivered: *Provided*, That no such transmission permit or delivery of power shall be given by the Secretary of War without the approval of the governor of the State or States into which said power is to be transmitted or delivered: *And provided further*, That the companies, corporations, or bodies receiving such permits for the transmission or delivery shall be governed and regulated as to rates and otherwise as the public service commission of such State, and if no such public service commission exists, then as the governor of such State or States may determine: *And provided further*, That whenever the Secretary of War shall determine that electrical power transmitted from Canada under permits heretofore or hereafter granted is not being utilized, distributed, or sold with due regard to the public interest or that the right granted under the permit has not been reasonably exercised to its full power or proper capacity he shall revoke said permit or any part thereof: *And provided further*, That the quantity of electrical power which may be transmitted from Canada into the United States under this act shall not exceed two hundred thousand horsepower.

SEC. 7. That any person, company, or corporation diverting water from the Niagara River or its tributaries or transmitting electrical power into States from Canada, except as herein stated, or violating any of the provisions of this act shall be deemed guilty of a misdemeanor, and upon conviction thereof shall be punished by a fine not exceeding $2,000 nor less than $500 for each and every day on which such violation occurred or is committed, or by imprisonment (in case of a natural person) not exceeding one year or both of such punishments in the discretion of the court: *Provided*, That the removal of any structure or parts of structures erected in violation of this act or any construction incidental to or used for such diversion of water or transmission of power as herein prohibited as well as any diversion of water or transmission of power in violation thereof may be enjoined or enforced by a suit in the United States in any district court having jurisdiction in any district in which same may be located, and proper proceedings to this end may be instituted under the direction of the Attorney General of the United States.

SEC. 8. That nothing in this act contained shall be construed to validate or confirm any grant heretofore made by the State of New York of any rights or privileges heretofore made directly or indirectly by the said State of New York for the diversion of the waters of Niagara River or of rights in or title to land under the waters thereof, nor shall the grantee under any such grant, or their heirs, representatives, successors, or assigns of such grantees, be deemed by virtue of this act entitled to divert or continue to divert the waters of said river.

SEC. 9. That the provisions of this act shall remain in force and effect during the life of the treaty with reference to the use of boundary waters entered into between the United States and Great Britain and proclaimed on the thirteenth day of May, nineteen hundred and ten.

SEC. 10. That for the accomplishment of the purposes detailed in this act the sum of $10,000, or so much thereof as may be necessary, is hereby appropriated from any moneys in the Treasury not otherwise appropriated.

SEC. 11. That all laws in conflict with this act are hereby repealed.

The CHAIRMAN. Mr. Richards, we will hear you further now.

STATEMENT OF EUGENE L. RICHARDS, ESQ.

Mr. RICHARDS. Mr. Chairman, the first change which we suggest is in relation to the limitation, right straight through and the diversion of water from above the falls, and so in every case where reference has been made in the bill to that matter we have made that suggestion. We suggest an amendment on line 4, page 1, after the word "New York" to insert the words "above the Falls of Niagara."

The CHAIRMAN. That is, you mean that the bill shall be in keeping with the treaty, section 5?

Mr. RICHARDS. And also in keeping with our suggestion that this section, section 3, be dropped out.

Mr. CLINE. If section 3 is dropped out there is no necessity for this correction that is suggested here.

Mr. RICHARDS. It is only in order to make it entirely harmonious, because you have general provisions which provide for the diversion of water in the Niagara River without limitations, running all through the bill, and then you have a separate section in which you say the Secretary of War is authorized to issue permits for the diversion of water below the falls.

Mr. CLINE. If section 3 is dropped out will not the bill without your amendment be harmonious?

The CHAIRMAN. Let me suggest to you, Mr. Richards, that you observe the wording of the present bill in section 2 at the beginning of it, "that the Secretary of War is hereby authorized to grant for the public benefit of the State of New York, and other States in which electrical power may be transmitted, revocable permits for the diversion of water in the United States from said Niagara River above the falls to an aggregate amount stated in said permits, not exceeding in daily diversion at any one time the amount of 15,600 cubic feet of water per second," and later on you will find that is the only one in which that has been limited.

Section 2, line 7, the words "above the falls"——

Mr. RICHARDS. As it reads at present——

The CHAIRMAN (interposing). The reason you want this amendment in section 1 is because the treaty vests in the joint high commission the control of the water below the falls?

Mr. RICHARDS. Exactly. Then, in section 2, lines 4 and 5, we propose to strike out the words "and other States into which electrical power may be transmitted." The point of that is the course that Mr. Van Kennen argued and which I touched upon this morning, that is, whether we are right or wrong upon a question of law, we as representing the State of New York and the interests of its citizens, appeal to the equities of the case and ask that there shall not be any broad permit which would provide for the diversion of the water to other States than the State of New York; that is, the diversion of the water beyond our boundaries, because whatever there may be there, our waters are a boundary stream of the State of New York. That is conceded. So that in order to make that harmonious we think the amendment ought to be adopted.

Mr. KENDALL. I want to say that I had it in mind to offer an amendment to that section, beginning at the word "for," down to and including the word "transmitted."

The CHAIRMAN. The word "for" in line 4?

Mr. KENDALL. Yes; down to and including the word "transmitted" in line 5.

Mr. RICHARDS. Beginning with the words "for the public benefit"?

Mr. KENDALL. Yes; to strike it out.

Mr. RICHARDS. I think that that is substantially in line with my suggestion, except in so far as it takes——

Mr. KENDALL (interposing). I think it is not at all.

Mr. RICHARDS. Just to this extent, if you will accept the amendment which we follow with, with regard to having these permits issued upon approval by the governor of the State, who shall name the transmittees or grantees of the permits.

Suppose we take it up as a whole amendment, Mr. Kendall, and see if in the end we do not agree as to what I want to do and as to what the bill is.

We propose, first, in section 2, lines 4 and 5, to strike out the words "and other States into which electrical power may be transmitted"; and then, in lines 9 and 10, page 2, to strike out the words "any one time the amount of 15,600," and insert in place thereof the words "the rate of 20,000." That covers the question of the 4,400 additional diversion.

Then on line 10——

The CHAIRMAN (interposing). That covers more than that, Mr. Richards. The way this bill is framed they can not at any one second get more than 15,600 cubic feet; but according to your amendment, if they do not get out the amount provided for in one second or in one hour, they could make up the difference the next second or hour and get more water in the course of a given time.

Mr. KENDALL. Is that not the design of the amendment?

Mr. RICHARDS. Not at all.

The CHAIRMAN. That is the effect of it.

Mr. SMITH. It follows the wording of the treaty.

Mr. RICHARDS. The treaty contains that express language, and we simply conform it to the words of the treaty.

Then follows the section or the clause we ask to be inserted, namely:

Provided, That no such permit shall be valid or effective until the same shall have been approved in writing by the governor of the State of New York, who shall designate the persons. companies, corporate bodies, public bodies, or public officers to whom the same shall be granted.

That is the proposition. If Mr. Kendall's suggestion is made, as far as taking out the words "for the public benefit of the State of New York and other States into which electrical power may be transmitted," if our limitation is put in, it protects what we claim to be the equities of the State of New York; that is, that we should have, in substance, in preference under this permit that the Secretary of War is authorized to issue, a preference to the State of New York or to the State of New York's nominees.

In other words, that is the very language. I think Mr. Van Kennen argued at some length about whether or not it is fair and right and just for the State of New York to take water power from a boundary stream lying solely upon the boundaries of the State of New York and provide for the diversion of that water for the benefit of States other than the State of New York, unless the State of New York indicated or stated that they did not want it. We think that is a fair request on the part of the conservation commission, which is charged with the custody and control of the waters of the State. Is that not a natural and proper and equitable request for an amendment. so that we at least shall have a preference if it is deemed desirable that the general clause shall remain, and so that it might be reverted to other States, and that we should have in the first instance, the right to the use or the diversion of the water and the water power flowing therefrom in preference to other States or to the citizens of other States.

Now, the next amendment that we suggest is the striking out of section 3, which I have already discussed, and the next is in line 4, on page 3, after the word "River," insert the words "above the Falls of Niagara River," as was done before.

Mr. KENDALL. In section 4?

Mr. RICHARDS. Yes, sir.

Mr. KENDALL. What line do you propose to strike out?

Mr. RICHARDS. I am adding the words "above the Falls of Niagara River."

Then, in line 5, page 3, of section 4, after the words "Secretary of War," insert "and the governor of the State of New York." That is in regard to conditions to be imposed.

The CHAIRMAN. Why do you use the words "above the Falls of Niagara River"? My recollection is that the treaty contains the words "above the Falls of Niagara."

Mr. RICHARDS. I am not sure whether the word "river" is used.

Mr. SMITH. That is correct—"Falls of Niagara River."

Mr. RICHARDS. As I said, in line 5, page 3, in section 4, we suggest that it be amended by inserting, after the words "Secretary of War," the words "and governor of the State of New York," so that the governor, if the committee concede that either he or some one representing the State of New York shall have the power we suggest should be given under section 2, that by it the governor, or whoever it might happen to be, is bound to give preference to those already holding permits. In other words, the same protection which the committee has already proposed should be given to those who already have permits.

Then, with reference to those permits, in order that there shall be no construction which shall construe an increase of those permits in any way; that is, the increase of the rights under the permits, we ask that after the word "permits," in line 9 of section 5, the following words be inserted, "but to the extent only of existing permits for the diversion of water at the rate of 15,600 cubic feet per second." In other words, so that by no language of apparently a general provision giving the preference to the present companies, that if any claims should be made that in some way or other they have a little more than the permits for 15,600, which is all we claim that they have got, so that by no construction of this act will a permit under this act give them any more than they have under existing permits. We suggest it to add clearness, and to make sure that it is limited, for that reason we suggest that those words be inserted so that their permits shall be to the extent only of the amount which they are entitled to divert under their present permits.

Mr. DIFENDERFER. To those holding permits, whether operating or not?

Mr. RICHARDS. Well, I think it would be a very good idea, personally, to put in the words "holding and using or operating under permits." I do not pretend to have all the wisdom in the matter of the exact language which should be put in. We want to insure that under no guise of this further permit, or this additional permit, or blanket permit, something may be obtained for these companies more than they have already obtained.

The CHAIRMAN. I think Mr. Difenderfer is mistaken in saying that they have unused permits to develop water on this side.

There has been a permit granted to the Niagara Falls Power Co. for 8,600 and to the Hydraulic Power Co. for 6,500, and to the Lockport Co. for 500 feet, which makes the total of 15,600 feet.

Mr. KENDALL. All those parties holding permits are operating?

Mr. RICHARDS. All those parties holding permits are operating.

Mr. KENDALL. And there are others not holding permits which are not operating?

Mr. RICHARDS. Yes, sir; that is true.

Mr. KENDALL. That is where you got confused, I think.

Mr. RICHARDS. I can see and realize that there will be some claim that in some way or other, by practically obtaining a greater quantity of water than the 15,600 feet, that some of these companies may possibly lay claim that by being a user under these prior permits they have a little more water than we suggest that they shall be allowed to have. If you make it clear that their permits still stand at the exact amount which was allowed before, and only to that amount, so that this permit shall not in any way be a license to the further use or the diversion of further water, I think that would do. In other words, this permit might be considered as starting and legalizing some abuses. It is proposed that preference be given the companies holding these permits, and what I want to do is to limit it only to the extent of the permits which have hitherto been issued.

Mr. KENDALL. Have you considered the project of using the additional 4,400 for the conservation of public health up there, in the matter of a sanitary canal, at all?

Mr. RICHARDS. No; there has not been any such question raised at all. Of course, it could be raised, in a way, with our commission, but it would naturally be raised through the commissioner of health of the State of New York.

Mr. KENDALL. Have steps ever been taken to do that?

Mr. RICHARDS. There has been some talk about it, but there have been no complaints made to our commission, and, of course, if there were we would have to consider them because we are bound under the powers of the commission to consider that question as well as others. The commission, as I stated to the chairman in answer to a question, has charge, not only of the natural resources, but in a measure through certain sources, also the question of drainage and things of that kind that have more or less to do with the heal h of the communities of the State.   t

The next amendment we propose is on line 16 of the same section, page 3, after the word "power," that being the suggestion which was argued briefly this morning, that you asked me a question about, the public service commission, and with regard to whether it had been submitted to that and that provision, I believe as a lawyer, and the governor examined it, is a direct one; after the word "power" insert in section 4, line 16, page 3, insert the words:

Provided further, That the persons, companies, corporations, or bodies receiving such permits shall submit and agree to abide by the determinations of the public service commission of the State of New York as to prices, rates, and otherwise.

"Otherwise" is rather a broad term, but is meant to cover such questions as how they shall operate. That is the same sort of control that the public service commission has over street railways in the city of New York; that is, the regulating of the safety of passengers, regulating the way they shall operate their cars and their transit lines.

To that proposition there was some objection this morning. That was whether or not it was a proposition that was submitted without consideration or submitted to the public service commission. I do not believe for óne moment that any body which is desirous of doing its duty will object to having its powers enlarged, and that would be the case with the public service commission as far as this case is concerned. On the question of the method, there arises this question, which I discussed this morning; that is, the grave doubt that the generating company alone, a company that simply generates alone and delivers its power to another company, the transmission company, and then it is carried by the transmission company to another company, the distributing company—whether that first corporation can be, either by statute or in any way except some sort of consent and agreement on their part, held to be a public service corporation of the State, a public service corporation which would necessarily be compelled to abide by the decisions of the public service commission.

Mr. KENDALL. Have you never tested that question in New York?

Mr. RICHARDS. It has been tested in this way, but it has never gone through to a decision on this whole broad question. It has been tested in this way, that the public service commission has, at different times—I know of one or two instances where a company of similar character to this that had one customer, we will say, that does business with one person, that does not use the streets, but has some franchise from some municipality, or has some duty by reason of something they get from the municipality.

Mr. KENDALL. I think the analogy there is not very definite. Here is a case, if you please, where the generating company is really the transmitting company.

Mr. RICHARDS. Well, the fact would be, I think, unless you will make sure all these companies——

Mr. KENDALL (interposing). I am speaking of this particular company. That seems to be the case here, that the transmitting company is simply a subsidiary company to the generating company, and the distributing company is a third adjunct of those two.

Mr. RICHARDS. Yes.

Mr. KENDALL. Now, has the public-service commission of the State never asserted jurisdiction over the generating company; and, if not, why not?

Mr. RICHARDS. I think Mr. Riley, who knows that case in detail, can tell you about that.

Mr. KENDALL. Has it ever been disputed?

Mr. RICHARDS. They have practically avoided it. They have held substantially that they were not sure enough of their power so that they felt it worth while to proceed to try to enforce their regulations.

Mr. KENDALL. Has there been a recommendation to the Legislature of the State of New York, or an amendment to the law?

Mr. RICHARDS. No. There seems to be considerable discussion on the proposition of the law. When this law was first passed it was attacked on the ground of being unconstitutional.

Mr. KENDALL. It was sustained?

Mr. RICHARDS. It was sustained on the theory that they were a commission which had jurisdiction and control over corporations that were doing business with the public. In other words, the very thing that the generating company is not doing, except through two separate and distinct jumps or through two places.

Mr. KENDALL. Where the generating company is doing business with the public indirectly through these subordinàte channels as described here, is it not inferable that it is dealing with the public?

Mr. RICHARDS. As I say, I have only taken this position that our position is simply this, let us make sure that this can be done, and because it can be done in this particular way——

Mr. KENDALL (interposing). Do you think that Congress can confer any power on the public-service commission?

Mr. RICHARDS. Not at all; but these people, by accepting a permit and agreeing to take a permit under the conditions which the Secretary of War issues, can put themselves under a commission, and that is just what we want to have them do.

Mr. KENDALL. In doing that they put Congress and the State of New York in the attitude of saying that they have no control over these people unless they agree to it.

Mr. RICHARDS. I have great doubt as to whether it would.

Mr. KENDALL. I think it is your duty to test it in the State of New York.

Mr. RICHARDS. Yes; I think the public-service commission think it is their duty, and that is the embarrassment. If the public-service commission were brought into this matter, I think they would be very glad to have some such condition as this put upon the granting of these permits so that they would not have to carry on litigation through to the court of appeals to determine their powers over such a company as these in order that they would not have to wait two years.

Mr. KENDALL. Is the attorney general the legal representative of the public service commission?

Mr. RICHARDS. He is, in a way, I suppose.

Mr. KENDALL. Have they a general counsel?

Mr. RICHARDS. Yes; simply a solicitor, much the same kind of an official as you have in the departments of the Federal Government. These cases usually go to the solicitor.

I think there is one other suggestion of amendment, and that is at the end of section 6, and that relates to this importation of power from Canada, and as far as we are concerned, we are satisfied to put the limit at 200,000 horsepower; we believe that is the limit of power which will ultimately come to the United States, and there does not seem to us any particularly good reason why in this legislation we should really bind ourselves to say we will not take any more, because we believe that if our commission is able to carry out its plans for the general development of electrical power, and the distribution of that power in a way to send that power through the State, that there is not anywhere near enough to go around. It may be that under the conditions in Canada there may not be available under the terms of the Canadian—the rights of the Canadian power companies—more than 400,000 horsepower, half of which only they can transmit outside the Dominion.

The CHAIRMAN. Do you think they could possibly make more?

Mr. RICHARDS. I do not know; but there is the question of improvement in the case of water power, improved facilities, the question of taking the water and getting more force out of the water. If you looked at the improvement in the art in the last 10 years and see what advance has been made in the way of getting higher efficiency, and we are looking forward for, within five years, it seems to me, unless there is some reason——

The CHAIRMAN (interposing). If you were convinced that no law could get through Congress unless there was some limitation on that importation, would you not think it wise to put it there?

Mr. RICHARDS. As I understand it—I have not read all the testimony—there seems to be some question whether, even between the witnesses called on this subject—whether there was not at least 450,000 horsepower——

The CHAIRMAN (interposing). Suppose you put this at 225,000?

Mr. RICHARDS. All right; make it 225,000 or 250,000; we want to make it so that the State of New York shall get the right to get its legal proportion of any power which is transmitted from Canada.

Mr. CURLEY. What do you feel would be a proper standard of efficiency in the matter of development per foot?

Mr. RICHARDS. I am not an engineer, and I have not any opinion on the subject except what I hear from the engineers.

Mr. CURLEY. And you have not examined into the subject?

Mr. RICHARDS. I have not examined into the subject.

Mr. CURLEY. Have you not heard that phase of the subject discussed at all?

Mr. RICHARDS. No; I have not.

STATEMENT OF HON. EDWARD T. CAHILL, OF CHICAGO, ILL.

The CHAIRMAN. We will hear from you now, Mr. Cahill.

Mr. CAHILL. Mr. Chairman and gentlemen of the committee, I desire to say that I represent no interest save alone that of the public, and in appearing for the public interest I wish to state, as I did state before the Commerce Committee of the Senate, that I believe that I am not assuming to myself any prerogative that I am not justly entitled to, for the following reasons:

My first interest in the waterways of this Nation grew out of an official opinion which I rendered to the city of Chicago as a lawyer, concerning its rivers, as well also Lake Michigan.

Before the commencement of the litigation on the part of the State of Illinois to prevent the erection of a dam at Dresden Heights, in the Illinois River, I personally wrote Gov. Deneen and begged him not to commence a suit in the State court, alleging as a reason that the State court recognized riparian owners' interests to the center of the stream and not at the water's edge; that these decisions had been uniform and the public had no interest as against the riparian owner. My suggestion to him was not acted upon. This matter was tried in the State courts, first in the lower court, and my contentions of the law, that the court would be obliged to hold that the private owner owned to the middle of the stream, were supported. .

Feeling that I could serve the interests of the public and raise the ordinance of 1787, I then went to the State of Wisconsin and obtained from the governor of that State, as well, also, its attorney general, a joining with me in a petition addressed to the Supreme Court of the State of Illinois, in which we asserted that this body of water, owing to the fact that the waters of Lake Michigan passed through the same and there was a water route from Lake Michigan from thence through the Mississippi to the Gulf, it passed through various

States, and in consequence was international. The governor and
the attorney general of Wisconsin believed with me, and not only
joined me in my petition but also gave me a letters addressed to
Attorney General Wickersham, in which they advised that he join
with me together with the State of Wisconsin in the preservation of
this stream. I came to Washington here and interested in my
plea Senators Burton and La Follette. The Federal Government
at that time, through the advice of its Solicitor General, would not
join with us, but later on was obliged to start its own suit in the
United States Courts at Chicago, and this suit is still pending. I
have also fought for the preservation of the streams and lakes in the
State of Illinois, and received from the State legislature its public
acknowledgment and vote of thanks for my services in behalf of the
public interests of the inhabitants of the State of Illinois.

I have continued to fight for public interests from that hour to this,
and have fought not only these power companies now before you
but directly and indirectly every power company that has tried to
present a bill to Congress, and I am happy to state that I have been
successful in that no power grant has been made since my appearance before these various bodies of Congress. With these recitals
I trust you will not charge me with being interested for any private
corporation or interest.

DOCTRINE OF COMITY.

I desire to impress upon the minds of the lawyers of this committee
my real motive in interesting the State of Wisconsin and bringing it
as a sovereign power into the suit of the State of Illinois. As I have
already stated. the law of riparian ownership carried the center of the
stream. yet there was another and greater danger, viz: That the rules
concerning the submerged waters and the rights of riparian owners
as interpreted by many State courts, and here, should the State of
Illinois be defeated in its contentions and should appeal her suit to
the Supreme Court of the United States, that then. and in that case,
the Supreme Court would be obliged to follow the principle laid down
in the State court of Illinois under the doctrine of comity, which you
all know. To prevent this, I set forth the ordinance of 1787 and
further insisted that this stream was international, as I have stated.
That as against an international. should the State be about to improve
the same in the interests of navigation and commerce, it necessarily
had the right to remove obstructions therein, and in consequence of
it we could defeat the right of compensation claimed by the Economy
Light & Power Co. This company when it learned that the State
had appropriated the $20.000,000 mentioned for its improvement
immediately proceeded and did purchase 37,000 acres of land and
intended to build there the largest power plant in the world. This
litigation is still pending.

CONTENTIONS OF NEW YORK STATE.

I desire now to call your attention to the statements of the Hon.
Thomas Carmody, attorney general of the State of New York, and
to the Hon. James A. O'Gorman, United States Senator from the
same State. The attorney general was most strenuous in his denial
of the right of the Federal Government to control the Niagara River,

insisting that the State of New York is entitled to its control. That, what was more important, the property rights here are those of the State and of the citizens of the State; that there were two purposes expressed in the title of the bill, and are absolutely antagonistic to the constitutional rights of the Federal Government, in dealing with this proposition. The Federal Government might determine the right or quantity of water that might pass from the boundary stream, and had the right to control navigation, but beyond that it had no power. He further stated, in reply to a question of Mr. Difenderfer, that there is no such thing as an international stream, as far as riparian rights are concerned, in this country. And in reply to a question propounded to him by Judge Cline:

Mr. CLINE. Have you any authority where the Federal Government divides its jurisdiction with the State over any stream that it assumes to have jurisdiction of?

Mr. CARMODY. That might be stated, perhaps, in the language of the Constitution itself, which provides by the Tenth Amendment, that the Federal Government has such powers as are reserved to it by the Constitution, and I ask where in the Constitution has the Federal Government any right to say to the riparian owners, "You shall or you shall not enjoy your riparian rights into certain streams"?

He further stated that the treaty vested no power whatever in the Federal Government, and stated that the principles announced by him had been settled and it was beyond controversy. He cited the case of Martin v. Waddell, 16 Peters, 307.

The contentions of the attorney general of New York in his reliance upon the case of Martin v. Waddell must fall for want of proper application to the conditions of the Niagara River.

It will be noticed in the opinion I am about to cite to you that this case was, so far as the Supreme Court of the United States is concerned, but an application of the doctrine of comity, and later when the matter arose as to the title of the riparian owner in the submerged lands of the Potomac River in this city, the Supreme Court of the United States refused to follow this case and assigned as a reason that the reasoning of the court in the Waddell case concerned the application of the laws of New Jersey and in no way bound it.

If you will turn to this Morris case, 174 U. S., and read on page 228, you will find the court uses the following language:

In the argument of Martin v. Waddell the decision of the Supreme Court of New Jersey in the case of Arnold r. Mundy (6 N. J. L., 1), in which that court had laid down the rule as contended for by appellants, was cited as conclusive and as establishing a rule of property binding on the Federal courts.

In respect to this contention Mr. Chief Justice Taney says:

"The effect of this decision by the State court has been a good deal discussed at the bar. It is insisted by the plaintiffs in error that as the matter in dispute is local in its character, and the controversy concerns only fixed property within the limits of New Jersey, the decision of her tribunals ought to settle the construction of the charter, and that the courts of the United States are bound to follow."

It will be noticed in the language following that the Supreme Court refused to be governed by the Martin case. The reason for so doing is found in that the application of the principles that I have contended for in the matter of bringing Wisconsin into the suit of the State of Illinois against the Economy Light & Power Co. must govern. Here in this case of Morris v. United States the Potomac River was involved. If the doctrine of riparian ownership is interpreted in the New Jersey case, as now sought to be applied by the representatives of the State of New York, irrespective of any obligation due the Federal Government, then their contention would be true; but unfortunately for them the conditions are not the same. Here in the case of New York we have an international stream, nay, more, one regulated by treaty, and, as I shall show further, that by virtue of this treaty and the power possessed through the Federal Government in its inherent power of conservation is chargeable with the conservation and preservation of it, and for that purpose may destroy easements of all kinds, if need be the easements of these power companies, and that without compensation.

On page 241 the Supreme Court, after reviewing the various State decisions, say:

At the utmost such decisions can only be considered as affecting private rights and controversies between individuals. They may not be given effect to control the policy of the United States in dealing with property held by it under public trusts.

An examination of this elaborate opinion discloses the fact that the contention of the riparian owners here in the Potomac, like those on the Niagara River, failed, and the Federal Government was decreed to be the owner of the property in controversy and had a right to remove all obstructions in the Potomac River, as well as also have restored to it its water front.

NEW YORK DOES NOT OWN THIS WATER.

The attempt on the part of the State of New York in coming here and asserting its claim is not unlike that which was asserted in the case of Gibbons v. Ogden (9 Wheaton, 189–190) by the same State. There they have done precisely as they have done here in reference to these power companies now diverting water at the Falls of Niagara; only recently they gave them franchises covering a period of 999 years, a thing unheard of. Yet this same State, in the early days of navigation, granted absolutely to Livingstone and Fulton, the full control of the Hudson River.

This great suit called forth the efforts of Daniel Webster, and I beg pardon while I quote to you his argument applicable to-day as then, in our present contention. There he states, and I use it in reference to the language of Senator O'Gorman, wherein he states the objects of the original Constitution, and sought to limit the power of the Federal Government by virtue of the Confederation of the original 13 States. Webster says:

Few things are better known than the immediate cause which led to the adoption of the present Constitution and he thought nothing clearer than that the prevailing motive was to regulate commerce, to rescue it from the embarrassing and destructive consequences resulting from the legislation of so many different States, and to place it under the protection of uniform law. The great objects were commerce and revenue and they were the objects indissolubly connected.

In the history of the times it was accordingly found that the great topic urged on all occasions, as showing the necessity of a new and different Government, was the state of trade and commerce.

To benefit and improve these was of great object in itself, and it became greater when it was regarded as the only means of enabling the country to pay the public debt and to do justice to those who had effectually labored for its independence.

Mr. CAHILL. Now, kindly note the following as denying the concurrent power of the State:

NO CONCURRENT POWER ON MATTERS ON WHICH THE FEDERAL GOVERNMENT ALONE SHALL LEGISLATE.

What is it that is to be regulated? Not the commerce of the several States, respectively, but the commerce of the United States. Henceforth the commerce of the States was to be a unit, and the system by which it was to exist and be governed must necessarily be complete, entire, and uniform.

Its character was to be described in the flag which waved over it—E Pluribus Unum.

The doctrine laid down by Webster was followed in the Gibbons case and in the more recent case of In re Debs (158 U. S.), in which Justice Brewer used the following language, which I quote in reply to the contentions of the Senator, in speaking with reference to the commercial power and the right to remove obstructions even of land, as applied to the Pullman strikers:

The Government of the Union, then, is emphatically and truly a government of the people in form and, in substance. It emanates from them; its powers are granted by them and are to be exercised directly on them and for their benefit

Now, notice the unreasonableness of the position of the Senator from New York, as to State rights, as applied to the Constitution:

No trace is to be found in the Constitution of an intention to create a dependence of the Government of the Union on those of the States for the execution of the great powers assigned to it. Its means are adequate to its ends, and on those means alone was it expected to rely for the accomplishment of its ends. To impose on it the necessity of resorting to means which it can not control, which another government may furnish or withhold, would render its course precarious, the result of its measures uncertain, and create a dependency on other governments which might disappoint its most important designs, and is incompatible with the language of the Constitution.

Mr. CLINE. Senator, do you concede the constitutionality of the general dam act?

Mr. O'GORMAN. I do not concede the legality of any act by which the Federal Government assumes to treat the water of a river which is really the property of the State as its own.   •

We have here, then, the positive statement of the Senator from New York that the water flowing over the Falls of Niagara belongs absolutely to the State of New York. The first question which suggests itself here is, What is meant by ownership? Worcester's Dictionary defines it as "the right by which a thing belongs to some one in particular to the exclusion of all other persons." This puts the question to us direct. Under this definition the Federal Government has no power or control here at all, because the Constitution vests in the Federal Government the right of control of this stream.

I desire now to call your attention, in reply to the Senator, to the decision of the Supreme Court of the United States in the case of Scranton v. Wheeler (179 U. S.), wherein Justice Harlan says:

The Constitution invests Congress with the power to regulate commerce with foreign nations and among the several States. This power includes the power to prescribe the rule by which commerce is to be governed. It is complete in itself; may be exercised to its fullest extent and acknowledges no limitation other than are prescribed in the Constitution and comprehends navigation within the limits of every State in the Union. For this purpose they are the properties of the Nation and subject to all requisite legislation of Congress.

Here you have a public declaration that these waters are the property of the Nation. Clearly, the position assumed by the Senator can not be sustained. Again, Justice Harlan uses the following language:

It matters little whether the United States has or has not the theoretical ownership and dominion of the waters or the lands under them. It has more, the regulation and control of them for the purposes of commerce. So wise and extensive is the operation of this power that no State can place any obstruction upon any navigable water against the will of Congress and Congress may summarily remove such obstruction at its pleasure.

Running water is incapable of ownership, and neither the State nor the riparian owners have any title in it (Sweet v. Syracuse, 129 N. Y., 335; Syracuse v. Stacey, 169 N. Y., 246; Hudson County Water Co. v. McCarter, 209 U. S., 349; L. ed., 828.)

In connection with this matter, I desire to call your attention to the last above case of the Hudson County Water Co. v. McCarter, attorney general of the State of New Jersey, which was an appeal from the Supreme Court of New Jersey to the Supreme Court of the United States, and is reported in 209 United States, 349; first edition, 828. This was a company which desired to carry water from the State of New Jersey to the State of New York. The right to do so was terminated by an act of the Legislature of New Jersey, and it was contended that this riparian owner had a personal interest in this water and that under the Constitution he could not be deprived of his property without due process of law. It was further contended that the act of the legislature was an interference with interstate commerce.

Justice Holmes, who delivers the opinion of the court, says that the Court of Appeals of New Jersey and the Supreme Court of New Jersey pointed out—

That a riparian proprietor has no right to divert waters for more than a reasonable distance from the bed of the stream or for other than the well and ordinary uses, and even in that purpose he is limited in amount.

Continuing, he said:

It went on to infer that his only right in the bed of the stream is to have the flow outgoing, and that there is a residuum of public ownership in the State.

It reenforced the State's rights by the States' title to the body of the stream and concluded that it is against the rights of the riparian owners. The State was warranted in prohibiting the acquisition of the title to the water on a large scale.

The court further predicated its opinion upon the doctrine of public policy, that the State had a right to limit the height of a building under its police power, to protect the inhabitants in their health as well; also, the right to limit the use of water irrespective of any contractual relationship and notwithstanding the fourteenth amendment to the Constitution.

SENATOR O'GORMAN PLEADS FOR STRICT CONSTRUCTION.

Mr. O'GORMAN. I think you will find that all text writers on the Constitution and the decisions of the Supreme Court are to the effect that the so-called general welfare clause of the Constitution simply means that taxes may be raised to pay the debts and promote the general welfare. What may be done as a matter of fact to promote the general welfare by the General Government must be found in other sections of the Constitution. There is no general omnibus provision that the Federal Government may do anything it sees fit to promote the general welfare. (P. 19, pt. 1, hearing, Jan. 22–23, 1913.)

Senator O'Gorman continues further:

I can not concede that the Federal Government has control of any river. The Constitution does not give it such control. If it has control that would mean a violation of the absolute dominion of the people. The Constitution simply says that the Federal Government may regulate interstate and foreign commerce, and those words have been so construed and interpreted by Congress as to mean that the Federal Government may at any time go into any State and into any stream at any time for the purpose of promoting its navigability, but that is the only purpose. (P. 23, pt. 1, hearing, Jan. 22–23, 1913.)

This position, coming from the source it does, and with the further statement by him, in reply to a question of Judge Cline:

Mr. CLINE. But the administration is not in harmony with your ideas, is it?

Mr. O'GORMAN. Not at the present time, but I am in hopes that the coming administration will have a sufficient appreciation of the limitations of the Constitution as to recognize it.

Here is a danger fraught with most serious consequences. Have we been going forward or backward? Does a new crisis confront us? Shall State rights once more assail the citadel of the Union, or did we settle it in the War of the Rebellion?

Now, in reply to his contention, I call attention to the meaning of the words "strict construction," and let the Supreme Court, as it laid down the doctrine, not of strict construction, but that of elasticity, which yields and bends to the wishes of the people of the United States as it did in Gibbons v. Ogden, supra.

Has not the State of New York, by her franchises to these powerful power companies for 999 years, done precisely as she did in her grant to Livingstone and Fulton, giving them an exclusive monopoly by depriving her citizens and those of the States? She surely has. But a Webster will again arise and throw this powerful State, the State of monopolies, the State of interests, to the ground, and take from her hands her imperial banner and place it where it belongs, among the States, and she being no more than any other of the States, and the insignia "We are but one; but many in one," be a truth.

I quote the language of Chief Justice Marshall, rendering his decision upon the immortal argument of Webster, in speaking of the Constitution. He says in Gibbons v. Ogden:

This instrument (the Constitution) contains an enumeration of powers expressly granted by the people to their Government. It has been said that these powers ought to be construed strictly. But why ought they to be so construed? Is there one sentence in the Constitution which gives continence to this rule? In the list of enumerated powers, that which grants expressly the means for carrying all others into execution, Congress is authorized "to make all laws which shall be necessary and proper" for the purpose. But this limitation on the means which may be used is not extended to the powers which are conferred; nor is there one sentence in the Constitution which has been pointed out by the gentlemen of the bar or which we have been able to discern that prescribed this rule. We do not, therefore, think ourselves justified in adopting it. What do gentlemen mean by a strict construction? If they contend only against that enlarged construction which would extend words beyond their natural and obvious import, we might question the application of the term but should not controvert the principle. If they contend for that narrow construction which, in support of some theory not to be found in the Constitution, would deny to the Government those powers which the words of the grant, as usually understood, import, and which are consistent with the general views and objects of the instrument, for that narrow construction which would cripple the Government and render it unequal to the objects for which it is declared to be instituted, and to which the powers given, as fairly understood, render it competent, then we can not perceive the propriety of this strict construction nor adopt it as the rule by which the Constitution is to be expounded. As men whose intentions require no concealment generally employ the words which most directly and aptly express the ideas they intend to convey, the enlightened patriots who framed our Constitution, and the people who adopted it, must be understood to have employed words in their natural sense and to have intended what they have said. If from the imperfection of human language there should serious doubts arise respecting the extent of any given power it is a well-settled rule that the objects for which it was given, especially when those objects are expressed in the instrument itself, should have great influence in the construction. We know of no reason for excluding this rule from the present case.

The Hudson River runs within the limits of the State of New York. It is a navigable stream and a part of the navigable waters of the United States, so far at least as from Albany southward. One of the streams which flows into it and contributes to the volume of its waters is the Croton River, a nonnavigable stream.

The language already quoted, notwithstanding the statement of Senator O'Gorman that Marshall overdrew the power possessed by the Federal Government, in the case referred to, yet this same language is reiterated in the case he cites to you, viz, Kansas *v.* Colorado, wherein you will find that Justice Brewer uses the following language:

Let the end be legitimate; let it be within the scope of the Constitution, and all means which are appropriate, which are plainly adapted to that under which are not prohibited but consistent with the letter and spirit of the Constitution, are constitutional. (See 206 U. S., 88.)

KANSAS V. COLORADO (206 U. S., 41).

The Senator was quite positive that the Federal Government had no power in the premises, save as I have stated, with reference to navigation and the treaty-making power, and cited the case of Kansas *v.* Colorado (206 U. S., 41). An examination of this case, however, discloses the fact that his conclusions are clearly wrong. By turning to page 117 of that opinion, and looking at the summary of the court, you will find that the court uses this language:

We are of the opinion that the contention of Colorado of two streams can not be sustained; that the appropriation of the waters of the Arkansas by Colorado for the purposes of irrigation has diminished the flow of water into the State of Kansas; that the result of that appropriation has been the reclamation of large areas in Colorado, transforming thousands of acres into fertile fields. and rendering possible their occupation and cultivation when otherwise they would have continued barren and unoccupied; that while the influence of such diminution has been perceptible injury to portions of the Arkansas Valley in Kansas, particularly those portions closest to the Colorado line, yet to the great body of the valley it has worked little if any detriment; and regarding the interests of both States and the right of each to receive benefit through irrigation and in any other manner from the waters of this stream, we are not satisfied that Kansas has made out a case entitling it to a decree.

An examination of this case discloses the fact that this was a suit brought by Kansas against Colorado, and the original thereof will be found in 185 United States at page 125, where a demurrer was filed on the part of Colorado and the demurrer overruled. There it was asserted that the Arkansas River rises in the Rocky Mountains in the State of Colorado and flows through certain counties in that State, thence across the line of the State of Kansas, etc.; that the length of the river is approximately 280 miles, and that the drainage area of the river and its tributaries approximately is 22,000 square miles. Kansas desired to restrain the State of Colorado from the excessive use of the water for irrigating purposes, and in this latter case, as I have stated, a demurrer was filed by Colorado, which was overruled. An examination of that decision discloses the fact that the Federal power alone is supreme. There it was contended that the two sovereigns, being equal, no remedy could be had, yet the court said that the Federal court possessed the power and had the right to determine the issues, and overruled the demurrer. Following the decision of the State of Missouri *v.* Illinois, in 180 U. S., 208, reciting the doctrine:

Comity demands that navigable rivers should be free, and therefore the freedom of the Mississippi, the Rhine, the Scheldt, the Danube, the St. Lawrence, the Amazon, and other rivers has been at different times secured by treaty; but if a State of this Union deprives another State of its rights in a navigable stream, and Congress has not regulated the subject, as no treaty can be made between them, how is the matter to be adjusted?

Clearly they held they had jurisdiction, and ordered the case to issue, and from the language already quoted, there has been no decision that would for one moment sustain the position of the Senator from New York, but, on the contrary, it is opposed to his contention.

Now, if you will turn to the position of the Federal Government here, you will find in this case that a petition filed by the Government in nowise sought to interfere with the rights of the respective States, but claimed and asserted that—

It had large tracts of land; that the Government is itself the owner of many thousands of acres; that it has the right to make such legislative provisions as; in its judgment, is needed for the reclamation of all these arid lands, and for that purpose to appropriate accessible water.

The Government's position was sustained. The reclamation act of Congress was before the court in that case. They say, on page 92:

It does not follow from this that the National Government is entirely powerless in respect to this matter. These arid lands are largely within the Territories, and over them, by virtue of the second paragraph of section 3 of Article IV heretofore quoted, or by virtue of the power vested in the National Government to acquire territory by treaties, Congress has full power of legislation, subject to no restrictions other than those expressly named in the Constitution, and therefore it may legislate in respect to all arid lands within their limits.

It will be noticed here that under section 3 of Article IV of the Constitution they vest the Government with this power, and the question asked by Senator O'Gorman, where the Government gets this power, is answered in the language of the Supreme Court.

Now, if you will turn to the conclusion of this opinion, you will further find that the Federal Government was permitted to dismiss its suit without prejudice and to take such action in the future as it might deem necessary to preserve or improve the navigability of the Arkansas River. So that, under no circumstances, can this case be cited for the purposes mentioned by the distinguished Senator from New York.

Now, as to the State of Kansas. By turning to page 118 you will find that the court likewise dismissed the suit as against her without prejudice to her right to institute new proceedings—

whenever it shall appear that through a material increase in the depletion of the waters of the Arkansas by Colorado, its corporations, or citizens the substantial interests of Kansas are being injured to the extent of destroying the equitable apportionment of benefits between the two States resulting from the flow of the river.

Here, then, you have the substance of this case in all its bearings, and there is no language here which by any implication, save by an overdrawn construction, might have any tendency to justify the statements of the Senator.

RIPARIAN OWNERS AT NIAGARA FALLS CAN RECEIVE NO COMPENSATION.

I have already demonstrated by citations from the decisions of the Supreme Court of the United States that the Federal Government controls this passageway not only for commerce and navigation, but also is the owner of the waters passing through the same, burdened with the easement mentioned, revocable at any time, irrespective of any act of Congress. But we are not, however, forced to the position of the want of power or act of Congress in the premises, for Congress has already acted. It has spent in the improvement of the channel between Lakes Erie and Ontario over $700,000.

Not only has it improved these streams, but it has also entered into a solemn compact in the nature of a treaty between Great Britain and the United States, which was signed at Washington January 11, 1909, and the Congress of the United States prior to said treaty enacted the Burton Act, which limited the flow of water at Niagara; and we have also, in addition to these acts, the passage of the general dam act. All of these, in my judgment, positively divert whatever interest the State or the riparian owner may have had in the soil or the waters of this channel.

THE PURPORT OF OUR TREATY WITH GREAT BRITAIN IS TO PRESERVE THE WATERS OF LAKE ERIE.

The question arises, for what purpose the treaty was made between Great Britain and the United States. I call your attention to article 5 of said treaty, and there you will find that an emergency has already arisen whereby it was necessary to provide for the future safety of the level of Lake Erie. Article 5 is as follows:

The high contracting parties agree that it is expedient to limit the diversion of waters from the Niagara River, so that the level of Lake Erie and the flow of the stream shall not be appreciably affected.

Clearly under this language the State of New York can have, as against this article, no interest whatever, either in the soil or water over the same, and the same is subject hereafter to the action of the powers mentioned in the treaty.

In Rundle v. Delaware & Raritan Canal Co. (14 How., 80) this court held that by the law of Pennsylvania the Delaware River was a public navigable river, held by its joint sovereigns (the States bordering thereon) in trust for the public, that riparian owners in that State had no title to the river, or any right to divert its waters, unless by license from the States; that such license was revocable and in subjection to the superior right of the State to divert the water for public improvement, either by the State directly or by a corporation created for that purpose; and that the proviso and the provincial acts of Pennsylvania and New Jersey of 1771 did not operate as a grant of the usufruct of the waters of the river to Adam Hoops and his assigns, but only as a license or toleration of his dam.

I also call your attention to another power-site claim which was submitted from the Committee on Claims in the House of Representatives on the 17th day of February, 1905, under the Bowman Act, to the Court of Claims of the United States to ascertain what damages, if any, should be paid for a water mill, the property of the claimant, erected by him on the east side of the Monongahela River in West Virginia, Marion County. The mill was a substantial frame building, three stories high, and fully equipped with all the necessary appliances for a flour and grist mill. That said mill was connected with a dam extending entirely across said Monongahela River and located upon the land and property of the claimant and the same was constructed many years prior to the year 1903, when the United States Government for the purpose of improving the navigation of the Monongahela River began the construction across said river, about 2 miles below said dam, of a lock or dam, and completed the same in November of that year, from moneys appropriated by Congress.

That the construction and completion of the dam by the Government caused an accumulation and backing up of water to such an extent as to wholly destroy the water of said claimant. That such accumulations and backing up of said water rendered said dam and mill property wholly worthless.

There the Court of Claims held that he was entitled to no compensation. It reviews the earlier legislation of Virginia, as well also brings in the ordinance of 1787, as well also the various acts of Congress, recognizing the right of the Federal Government to improve its streams. The court say:

That the Virginia statute of 1776, citing Scott v. Lunt (7 Pet., 596), adopted the common law of England, and that the only waters recognized in England as navigable were the tide waters. That acts of Congress admitting the various States to the Union provide that the navigable waters should be common highways and forever free, although establishing jurisdiction and control over navigable waters.

Defendants (United States) concede that plaintiff owned the privilege of operating his mill with water power created by the ancient milldam extending across the river, by virtue of the permission granted by certain acts of the Virginia Assembly to build and maintain such dam in the bed of the river and the mill building over and above the stream.

It would seem, then, that inasmuch as the provisions of the Constitution for the regulation of commerce between the States had attached, any improvements authorized by the Virginia Assembly were done subject to the provisions of Federal Constitution.

A bridge across a navigable river of the United States is the subject of legislation by Congress. Such a bridge may be declared to be an unlawful structure by Federal authority, which the legislation of a State may not impair. So, when a river is capable of navigation and affords a channel for interstate commerce, it is open to the public and may be improved according to the directions of Congress. Again, oyster beds destroyed from the lawful action of the United States in dredging the channel of a river is not taking of private property for public use. While the State may grant the use of river beds to private citizens, such grants are subject to the obligation to suffer the consequences incident to the improvement of the navigation of the river under an act of Congress. (Richardson v. United States, 100 Fed. Rep., 774.)

Plaintiff's right as a riparian owner to the use of the stream on which his mill was located because of the ancient dam must be treated as a license. For these reasons plaintiff is not entitled to a judgment against the United States under the thirteenth section of the act of March 3, 1887 (24 Stat., 505).

(West Chicago Street Railway Co. v. Chicago, 201 U. S., 506; Union Bridge Co. v. United States, 204 U. S., 364; Monongahela Bridge Co. v. United States, 216 U. S., 177; Hannibal Bridge Co. v. United States, 221 U. S., 194.)

THE STATE OF NEW YORK, IN THE GRANTING OF NINE HUNDRED AND NINETY-NINE YEAR FRANCHISES, FORFEITED THE RESPECT OF THE GOVERNMENT, AND ITS ACTS IN SO DOING ARE ULTRA VIRES.

The State of New York nor any other State can pass an irrepealable act whereby it could release or relinquish its control of the water or the land underneath it. This power was clearly denied by Judge Field in the Illinois Central case, wherein he says:

The King, by virtue of his proprietary interest, could grant the soil so that it should become private property, but the grant was subject to the paramount right of the public use of navigable waters, which he could neither destroy nor abridge. In every such grant there was an implied reservation of the public right, and so far as it attempted to interfere with it, or to confer a right to impede or obstruct navigation, or to make an exclusive appropriation of the use of navigable waters, the grant was void. Supra, 146 U. S.)

This position is further shown in the case of Water Power Co. v. Water Commissioners (168 U. S., 371), wherein it was claimed on the part of the plaintiffs that, owing to their charter granted in 1856, they were granted the right to use and develop the water power of St. Anthonys Falls, and were authorized to complete such structures in and upon the river as would be necessary to develop that power.

The court held that this was not a contract.   It was a mere naked easement carrying with it no right to compensation should the waters be appropriated for other use, and the improvements built in the way of dams were denied any compensation whatsoever; and the court further held that the legislature could not bind future legislatures in dealing with these rights, and it predicated its opinion upon the Illinois Central case mentioned.   The court said:

If we should assume the validity of an act of the legislature of such a character (which, under the decisions of this court in the Illinois Central Railroad Co. *v.* Illinois (146 U. S., 387), it is at least doubtful), it is clear that we ought not to adopt a construction leading to that unless the legislative act be plain and beyond all doubt. We are of the opinion that these particular charters of the company are not to be construed so. "The right to build dams and the right to use such water as in the future and from time to time should flow down and through the dam" vested in these parties none of the rights claimed by them as to compensation. It is difficult to believe that a legislature would ever grant to individuals or companies rights of that nature, even if it be assumed that it had the power.

THE FEDERAL GOVERNMENT SHOULD PROTECT ITS INHABITANTS AS CANADA HAS DONE, AND FIX THE RATES FOR THE USE OF WATER POWER AT NIAGARA FALLS.

The Niagara River for the greater part of its length is navigable, and it is essential to the maintenance of its navigability not only to itself, but also to portions of the river and to Lakes Erie and Ontario. It is a boundary stream and belongs not alone to this Government, but also to the British Government, and by treaties from the earliest history, as such, is brought within the Federal power.   This is recognized in our treaty with Great Britain.

The present power companies at Niagara have already recognized this power and are estopped to-day to deny it.   I call attention to the present prohibitory acts on the part of the Canadian Government, which fixes a tax upon the exportation of any power into the United States.

The companies so recognizing this right are: Canadian Niagara Power Co., 42,351.60 horsepower per year; Electrical Development Co. of Ontario (Ltd.), 3,441.25 horsepower per year; Ontario Power Co. of Niagara Falls, 26,631.10 horsepower per year.   All these companies recognized the sovereignty of the Prince of Canada, and admit by the license granted by the Canadian Government and the permit of the Secretary of War of the United States, that they are subject not to State control, but to the control of the United States in its sovereign capacity, under the commercial clause of the Constitution, as well as its treaty-making powers, so that any statement that the State of New York has jurisdiction of the water flowing over Niagara is answered in the words of the great Premier of Canada, who, in speaking for Canada on April 19, 1905, said:

The water power at Niagara should be as free as air, and more than that, I say on behalf of the Government that the water powers all over this country shall not in future be made the sport and prey of capitalists, and shall not be treated as anything else but a valuable asset of the people of Ontario, whose trustees the Government of this people are.

Does not this language apply to-day, and are we not—the Government and the States—but mere trustees for the people here? Shall Canada surpass us? I answer, "No."   Because at a meeting of

60 representatives of all municipalities of Canada on March 23, 1906, the following resolution was passed:

Whereas power from the Niagara Falls is natural wealth, and as such should be enjoyed by the largest possible number; and

Whereas cheap power is essential to the success of factories and industries of almost any kind, particularly in Ontario, where coal is expensive; and

Whereas experience has shown that this great national and natural asset would be practically worthless if controlled by private companies; and

Whereas there is in our opinion no regulation sufficiently effective whereby power can be obtained from the owners of existing franchises at reasonable rates: Therefore be it

Resolved, That this gathering of municipalities urgently desire and respectfully ask the government of Ontario to at once themselves establish a power plant at Niagara Falls or secure the power produced under existing franchises for distribution to reachable municipalities of Ontario.

Here, then, you have the first protest of an outraged public, the people of Canada in arms against these power trusts—these purported "vested rights"—"riparian ownership." Can we not do as Canada has done? Are these "private interests" above the public demand? Shall these vast ramifications of purported rights for 999 years stand between the people of the United States and their inalienable rights—rights and privileges that can not be parted with even the sanction of the State or Nation? I answer "No."

I have already shown you that the State of New York nor its riparian owners has any easement as against the Government in the waters mentioned, and I shall close this feature of the case by calling your attention to the case of Green Bay Co. *v.* Patten Co. (172 U. S., 58), where you will find under the positive language of the Supreme Court of the United States that the Government has the power not only to regulate, but also to fix charges here. There it was contended that certain parties claimed riparian interests, but the court say as follows, with reference to the right of unusual diversion there:

If the riparian owners were allowed to tap the pond at different places and draw off the water for their own use, serious consequences might arise not only in connection with the public domain for the purposes of navigation, but between the riparian owners themselves as to the proper proportion each was entitled to withdraw—controversies which could only be avoided by the State reserving to itself the immediate supervision of the entire supply.

The court, after speaking of the acts of the State of Wisconsin, October 13, 1856, granting to the Fox and Wisconsin Improvement Co. all rights, etc., including the water powers created thereby for the purpose of making this improvement, say:

The legal effect and import of the sale and conveyance by the canal company was to vest absolute ownership in the improvements and the appurtenances in the United States, which property rights thereby become added to the jurisdiction and control that the United States possessed over the Fox River as a navigable water.

After speaking of the control of these water powers by reason of the purchase from the United States, the court said:

And we think it equally plain that the mode and extent of the use and enjoyment of such property by the canal company fell within the sole control of the United States. At what points in the dam and canal the water for power may be withdrawn and the quantity which may be treated as surplus, with due regard to navigation, must be determined by the authority which owns and controls that navigation. In such matters there can be no divided empire.

This aspect of the subject was before us in Wisconsin *v.* Duluth (40 U. S , 379), where the State of Wisconsin sought, by an original bill in this court, to restrain the city of Duluth from changing the current of the —— River, and make other improvements in the city harbor, to the detriment, as was claimed, of the harbor of Superior City, within the jurisdiction of Wisconsin. It, however, was disclosed that Congress had made large appropriations for the work complained of, and that the executive department had taken exclusive charge of it. The court dismissed the bill, and in its opinion, per Mr. Justice Miller, said:

"Nor can there be any doubt that such action is within the constitutional power of Congress. It is a power which has been exercised ever since the Government was organized. The only question ever raised has been how far and under what circumstances the exercise of the power is exclusive of its exercise by the State. And while this court has maintained in many cases the right of the States to authorize structures in and over navigable waters of the States, which may either impede or improve their navigation in the absence of any action of the General Government in the same, the doctrine has been laid down with unvarying uniformity that when Congress had, by an expression of its will, occupied the field, the action was conclusive of any right to the contrary asserted under State authority."

I have already called your attention to the river and harbor act of 1899, which changed the conditions applicable to the Federal power and control of the rivers prior to its passage. By virtue of the passage of that act there can be no question but what the Federal Government is alone supreme, because there it provides that no dam or dike shall be placed in any navigable water of the United States without the consent of Congress; that no breakwater shall be placed therein of any kind; removes obstructions in the way of bridges, no matter when built, or how built, or by what authority. If the same obstructs or impedes the navigation of any stream, they must be removed.

Here, then, we have the complete power vested in the Federal Government, as to surplus waters not needed for navigation, and under the various citations of the decisions mentioned, the acts of Congress, the treaty between the United States and Great Britain. I draw the conclusion, without limitation, that it is the duty of the Federal Government to fix the charges here, without any cooperation on the part of the State of New York; that the duty here concerns not the State of New York in its official capacity, but does concern the inhabitants there of the United States. We should do as Canada has done. We should harness these waters and dispose of the same to the inhabitants not only in the State of New York, but in all the States bordering upon the Great Lakes to which electricity can be carried. The method of determining the charges to be made or exacted should be left to the Secretary of War or his agencies, and there should be a primary use for this hydroelectric power, in that it might be used for the illumination of the various harbors and those portions of the lake to which the Government might deem it necessary in the interests of navigation to illuminate it to make it more safe for navigation purposes.

I desire to extend personally my thanks to the chairman here, as well also to Judge Cline and his associates of the subcommittee, who were so kind as to strike out from this proposed act that clause providing for compensation to companies who shall have made improvements under the permit issued by the Government. The acknowledgment of this vested interest would, in my judgment, put the Government of the United States to an expense of not less than from seventy to ninety millions, which would arise by reason of the withdrawal of the permits issued to existing companies.

Mr. CURLEY. What is your opinion as to the value of the conservation commission? Have they made any recommendations that should be taken up by this committee?

Mr. CAHILL. I will state that, with due respect to the conservation commission of New York, I have failed to see that they have in any manner served the interests either of the inhabitants of New York or the State of New York in its official capacity, in any manner whatsoever.

I have been more than surprised by the conduct of these parties as shown in this hearing, as well also the conduct of the public-utilities corporation as brought out and appears in the testimony of the former hearings in this matter before this committee. The first duty, as I understand it, of conservation means the preservation and the passage of such laws as will preserve for future generations the public lands, forests, mines, waters, and other natural resources of the State, not only for the present, but also for future generations. I have examined here and looked in vain for any act of this body that would commend itself to me. These agencies, as demonstrated, have not been able to perform the functions for which they were created. I have examined this record and was in hopes to find in some place some act or thing done by either the conservation or the public-utilities commissioners, and recall none save the perfidious acts of the State of New York, extending the franchises of these companies for the period of 999 years. I also failed to find that they have ever sought or tried to lower the rates which are admitted to be from three to ten times as large as those charged in Canada; a condition unparalleled.

As to any recommendations that they have made here, I fail to see that. The Government of the United States was prompted in the passage of the Burton Act to prevent from the devastating acts of the power companies the destruction of the scenic beauty of Niagara Falls. These gentlemen have done nothing to cooperate with the Government nor with the recommendations of the engineers in this matter, but come here now to unite their forces with all these power companies and ask that the flow of water be further extended to the amount of 4,600 cubic feet per second, regardless of its effect upon the scenic beauty of Niagara. Gentlemen, I have never either heard or read of such perfidious acts in all my life, and had I the power, and sitting as you are sitting for the purpose of being informed as to what action you should take in the premises, I have no hesitation in saying that if these gentlemen appeared before me I would kindly take their petition and hand it back to them with the request, by showing them the door, not to call again, as I think their mission is not public, but private. I would throw them and their documents out of the door and ask that they never darken it again.

I thank you kindly, gentlemen, for the time you have given me and I sincerely trust I have made myself plain, and I believe that you gentlemen are prompted by the public interest and will give due consideration to the suggestions I have offered.

STATEMENT OF J. BOARDMAN SCOVELL, ESQ., OF NIAGARA FALLS, NEW YORK.

Mr. SCOVELL. Mr. Chairman and gentlemen of the Committee on Foreign Affairs, this afternoon, in order that this might be presented very quickly I took the time to go down to the Supreme Court library and write out what I wished to say, so that it might be very definite, and while some of it may seem to be taking an undue amount of time, it all leads up to a definite conclusion, which may be stated briefly, so that I will not take a great amount of time.

Yesterday morning your committee listened to a very able and lucid presentation by the attorney general of the State of New York, and by junior United States Senator O'Gorman, of New York, of principles of constitutional and common law bearing in a general way upon the matters before you, but the discussion soon assumed a purely academic character which was as applicable to the relative merits of a tariff whether for revenue or for protection as to the legislation pending before you, thus degenerating into a restatement in glittering generalities of the respective principles of Federal or State control which have differenced the dominant political parties since the foundation of this Republic.

Since then you have heard the statements of the chairman and attorney of the conservation commission of the State of New York, ·which commission was created during the administration of Gov. Dix to take over the departments of forests, fish, and game, and to conserve them and the other natural resources of the State. It was very interesting to hear an explanation of the ambitious hopes and plans of the conservation commission, which has reported in favor of State ownership and development of water power and the generation therefrom by the State of electricity for transmission and distribution throughout the State by the commission, but your committee are entitled to know and consider that such a policy can not be adopted and carried out until legislation to that end is enacted, and the investigating committee appointed by the New York State Legislature has recently made a voluminous report, after investigations and hearings in Ontario, adversely to the desires and plans of the conservation committee as expressed before you to-day. It is thus apparent that, to use the phraseology of a renowned Democratic President, "A condition, and not a theory, confronts us."

If you will be patient I will now seek to state the facts, as I know and understand them, which I deem essential to a correct and expeditious determination by your committee of the legislation, affecting diversions of water from Niagara River for power purposes, which you shall recommend for passage at this session. Before criticizing the proposed bill submitted by your subcommittee, and before suggesting necessary eliminations and amendments to make it consistent, I beg your indulgence to a brief résumé of the history of the control of the Niagara portage and the Niagara water.

In 1679, La Salle and Father Hennepin first viewed the Falls of Niagara and in that year established settlements at the head of navigation on the lower Niagara at the mouth of the gorge at Lewiston and also at the end of their portage on the upper Niagara at La Salle. Later, the "fortified cabin" of the trader, Jon Caire, was built at Lewiston and block houses for the protection of the portage trail (now called the Military Road) were constructed by the French, who remained in undisputed control of the portage around the Falls of Niagara from the lower lake to the upper lakes for 80 years, employing Seneca Indians to carry the goods on their portage but failing to acquire any territorial rights by cession from the Indians

In 1764 the English, who sought their share of traffic on the upper lakes, established a trading post at Lewiston, constructed a roadway, now called Portage Road, ending at the upper river on lands now owned by the Niagara Falls Power Co., in the city of Niagara Falls, and began the transportation of goods in wagons drawn by oxen or horses. The adoption of an unproved method of transportation by the English enraged the Indians, who had previously monopolized the carrying, and an English wagon train with its military escort and reinforcements was ambushed and annihilated by the French and Indians in what is historically known as the Devils Hole Massacre. Shortly after, Sir William Johnson proceeded to the Niagara frontier on a punitive expedition, the Senecas were threatened by him with extermination, and in reparation for the massacre the Seneca Indians then formally ceded to the English Crown a strip of land 1 mile wide on each side of the Niagara River from Lake Ontario to Lake Erie, and conveyed all the islands in the Niagara River to Sir William Johnson, who that day conveyed them to the Duke of York.

Thus it came about that the "Mile Reserve," so called along the east side of Niagara River and the islands, became vested in the royal colony of New York and passed from the colony to the State of New York, while the strip on the west side of the river became vested in upper Canada, now known as the Province of Ontario; and thus it came about that the State of New York and the Province of Ontario became vested under the then common law of England with the ownership of the land under the waters of the Niagara River, each holding title out to the international boundary line, not as a proprietor but as sovereign, and so in trust for the public. It was in this sense that the Niagara River and the St. Lawrence River were declared to be "public rivers" in Canal Appraisers v. The People ex rel. Tibbetts, decided in 1836 and reported in 17 Wendell Reports at page 623), and this ruling was followed in Kingman v. Sparrow (12 Barbour 201,) decided in 1851; in Matter of the State Reservation (16 Abbott's New Cases 407) decided in 1885; and in Niagara County Irrigation & Water Supply Co. v. College Heights Land Co. (111 App. Div. 770), decided in 1906.

Shortly after the Civil War a canal known as "Day's Canal," for the creation of hydraulic power for grinding grain was constructed from above the upper Niagara rapids to the gorge below the Falls, which has been enlarged from time to time and is now owned by the Hydraulic Power Co., which is controlled by the Schoelkopf family at Niagara Falls. The New York State Reservation at Niagara Falls was created by chapter 336 of the Laws of 1883, entitled "An act to authorize the selection, location, and appropriation of certain lands in the village of Niagara Falls for a State reservation and to preserve the scenery of the Falls of Niagara." By condemnation the present State Park at Niagara was acquired at an expense to the State of $1,433,429.50, and it was made free to a world-wide public in 1884. The example of the State of New York was followed in 1887 by the Province of Ontario which opened, in celebration of the Queen's jubilee, the "Niagara Falls Victoria Park." Scientists thereafter began to become interested in the "harnessing of Niagara," and in 1889, 1891, and 1894 charters of incorporation were enacted by the legislature of the State for the purpose of enabling chartered residents of the village of Niagara Falls, the town of Lewiston, and the city of Lockport to divert waters from Niagara River above the Falls for power development, and work was begun by the Niagara

Falls Power Co. in 1891 under the charter granted to citizens of Niagara Falls.

Work was begun on the canal of the Niagara County Irrigation & Water Supply Co. in 1894 under the charter granted to residents of the town of Lewiston, but no work having been done under the charter granted to citizens of the city of Lockport within the time limit therein specified, and the legislature having refused to extend the time for its canal construction, the financial backers of the Niagara, Lockport & Ontario Power Co., who had given bond for the construction of a power canal to the city of Lockport are locally reported to have agreed as the American distributors of power purchased from the Ontario Power Co. to deliver power at the Lockport city limits at $16 per horsepower in lieu of constructing said canal and to save enforcement of said bond.

The acts creating the three corporations aforesaid were all "passed, three-fifths being present," and when the constitutionality of the act of incorporation of the Niagara County Irrigation & Water Supply Co. was contested by the College Heights Land Co. in the condemnation proceedings instituted by me in 1904, on the ground that under section 20 of article 3 of the State constitution "the assent of two-thirds of the members elected to each house of the legislature shall be requisite to every bill appropriating public moneys or property for local or private purposes," the courts held unanimously (as reported in 111 App. Div. 770) that the State of New York has no property or ownership in the waters of Niagara River within the provision of the constitution in question, though it has dominion over the same and power to regulate the use and diversion thereof and encroachments thereon as navigable waters of the State, and cited Sweet v. City of Syracuse (129 N. Y., 317, at p. 334) and Walter v. State (144 N. Y., 579, at p. 599), in the former of which cases the Court of Appeals of New York says:

It is a principle, recognized in the jurisprudence of every civilized people from the earliest times, that no absolute property can be acquired in flowing water; like air, light, or the heat of the sun, it has none of the attributes commonly ascribed to property, and is not the subject of exclusive dominion or control. * * * Neither sovereign nor subject can acquire anything more than a mere usufructuary right therein, and the State never acquired or could acquire the ownership of the aggregated drops that comprise the mass of flowing water.

Under such precedents, and following the ruling in matter of New York & Long Island Bridge Co. (148 N. Y., 540, at p. 550), the court in the case of the Niagara County Irrigation and Water Supply Co. went further, and held that the act could not be regarded as appropriating any property of the State to the use of the corporation, either in the water or in the bed of the stream, but merely confers power upon the corporation to do what is necessary to carry out its purposes.

All acts incorporating companies with such powers with respect to taking of water from above the Falls of Niagara, except those of the three above mentioned, have been heretofore repealed by an act drawn by me, and the charters of those three companies can not be repealed as the Niagara Falls Power Co. is generating power under one, the Niagara, Lockport & Ontario Power is transmitting and distributing power under another, and the Niagara County Irrigation & Water Supply Co. has complied with the requirements of its charter, acquired riparian lands, spent over $375,000 on its power canal, paid its corporate and real estate taxes, and was only prevented from the completion of its canal by the enactment of the Burton bill.

The CHAIRMAN. You say that these charters have been repealed, except these three?

Mr. SCOVELL. Except these three.

The CHAIRMAN. Mr. Van Keenan did not think that.

Mr. SCOVELL. He did not know.

Mr. COOPER. He said five.

Mr. SCOVELL. I am speaking of the water diversion from Niagara Falls. I had not referred to the Hydraulic Power Co., because that is not a chartered corporation. The Hydraulic Power Co. was not incorporated by an act of the State legislature.

The Hydraulic Power Co. was not chartered by act of legislature, but was the adjoining riparian owner both next above and next below the State Park at Niagara, so in 1896, by act of the State legislature by a two-thirds vote of each house, it had its riparian rights confirmed, and you have all read the brief of Mr. Rome G. Brown and heard the exposition thereof before your committee last winter wherein he showed that the Niagara Falls Power Co. only had the right to divert its 8,600 cubic feet by reason of an agreement with the Hydraulic Power Co., which company as riparian owner claimed the right as against the State under said act to take the remaining 4,400 cubic feet, it being admitted by him that said companies had already agreed on the basis of its division between them, 1,400 cubic feet to the Niagara Falls Power Co. and 3,000 cubic feet to the Hydraulic Power Co., and that such a division was contemplated in the drafting both of the treaty and of the Alexander bill, by which it was proposed to make the treaty effective, but which was defeated before the Rivers and Harbors Committee by my efforts.

Whether the Burton Act resulted from the preservative efforts of the American Civic Association, the monopolistic efforts of the power companies, or the efforts of the coal trust to prevent competition as variously alleged, is immaterial to this argument, but it has prevented further diversion from Niagara River on the American side since its passage on June 29, 1906; by its fourth paragraph the Burton Act requested the President—

to open negotiations with the Government of Great Britain for the purpose of effectually providing by suitable treaty with said Government, for such regulation and control of the waters of Niagara River and its tributaries as will preserve the scenic grandeur of Niagara Falls and of the rapids in said river.

The act was to remain in force for three years, and it was deemed by all parties concerned that a test of its constitutionality was useless, as it would be superseded by a treaty before a final decision could be had. When the President took up the matter, it was decided to make it but a part of a treaty which should control all boundary waters between the United States and Canada, and so it became necessary to extend the Burton bill till after the treaty was proclaimed on May 13, 1910.

By that treaty equal and similar rights are granted to each country and jurisdiction and control of the use and diversion of all boundary waters for domestic, sanitary, navigation, canal, power, and irrigation purposes is given to the International Joint Commission, except in the waters diverted from above the Falls of Niagara for power purposes, as provided in Article V, and in waters diverted from the St.

Marys and Milk Rivers for power and irrigation purposes, as provided
in Article VI. It follows, therefore, that in order to make the proposed bill consistent and correspond to the treaty the words "above
the Falls of Niagara" must be inserted in the third line of the first
page of the proposed bill, in the eighth line of the fifth page, and in
the seventh line of the sixth page; that the words "into the United
States of electrical power generated from water diverted in the
Dominion of Canada from Niagara River above the Falls of Niagara"
must be substituted and inserted after "transmission" in the sixth
line of the fourth page, and that the last clause of section 1 beginning
with the words "the amount" in the ninth line of the first page and
the whole of section 3 must be stricken out.

Mr. KENDALL. What section are you reading from?

Mr. SCOVELL. The sixth line on page 4, that the words, "generated
from water diverted in the Dominion of Canada" must be inserted at
the sixth line of the fourth page. As it reads now the act provides
the importation from Canada of a limitation of 200,000 cubic feet,
regardless of where it may be generated, or from what water.

The character of the Burton Act has necessitated the use of the
words "not exceeding" some definite amount in limiting the diversion
of water or the importation of electricity, but after the treaty was
negotiated, the basis of measuring diversion in both countries was
thereby changed to read, "at the rate of," so I suggest that those
same words, "at the rate of," be substituted for the words, "any one
time the amount," in the ninth line on the second page, by the
insertion thereof in the sixth line on the fifth page of your proposed
bill.

Mr. COOPER. That means at the rate of so many thousand feet per
second.

Mr. SCOVELL. No; "at the rate of" instead of reading, "any one
time the amount of fifteen thousand, six hundred," to read "and a
daily diversion at the rate of fifteen thousand, six hundred." That
conforms to the wording of the treaty.

The CHAIRMAN. This enables them to get more water; if they get
10,000 feet the first hour, then the next hour they could get 30,000
feet?

Mr. SCOVELL. That is quite true. But that would be entirely impracticable in the development and operation, or else they must have
machinery where they develop in units of 10,000 horsepower.

There has been no limitation at any time over that fixed by the
Burton law except that reported in the report of the Chief of Engineers as affecting the Hydraulic Power Co. The value of that item
is in its relation to another matter, in my estimation.

The Chief of Engineers reports that the diversion of water in excess
of the maximum allowance occurred on May 14, 1912. The diversion
on three different occasions has gone beyond, but on two occasions
it was at the time when all the industries were using their power, and
the municipal lights were turned on simultaneously. Those who
negotiated the treaty took this information into consideration, and
Canada in making its limitations upon the persons who used this
power fixed it at that rate, and the United States should be equally
liberal in dealing with its citizens.

Mr. CLINE. What do you mean by equally liberal? Do you mean
the clause should be so loosely drawn that you could exceed the maximum amount and still be within the 8,600 feet?

Mr. SCOVELL. On the 24-hour.

Mr. CLINE. You would average it then?

Mr. SCOVELL. That is what the idea of the treaty is. If you do that you will follow the wording of the treaty, and I am going to suggest——

The CHAIRMAN (interposing). How much would it vary from second to second and hour to hour?

Mr. SCOVELL. It will vary enough perhaps to make a difference of about 4,000 horsepower. It would be accord'ng to the company using it, but it would not exceed 4,000 horsepower.

Mr. CLINE. What is the greatest capacity of your machinery now?

Mr. SCOVELL. You mean the Niagara Falls Power Co.? We can take 8,600 cubic feet, the Schoelkoepf Co. 6,500. The wording of the act makes it possible for the Niagara Falls Power Co. to take a total of 10,000, and for the Schoelkoepf Co. to take a total of 9,500.

Mr. CLINE. Does this condition exist, so that if it became absolutely necessary you can take 10,000 cubic feet?

Mr. SCOVELL. No; it could not. I make the suggestion that those words, "at the rate of," be substituted for the words "any one time the amount" in line 9 on page 2 by the insertion thereof in the sixth line on the tenth page of your proposed bill. That is in regard to the importation of power, using the same expression "at the rate of 200,000 horse-power."

This brings us to the suspension of the limitation to 200,000 horsepower on the importation of electricity. The whole 36,000 cubic feet granted to Canada has been allotted: 500 cubic feet to the International Railway Co., which means the electricity generated therefrom for its corporate purposes; 11,000 cubic feet to the Canadian Niagara Falls Power Co., which can generate about 11 horsepower per cubic foot therefrom; 12,500 cubic feet to the Electrical Development Co., which can generate about 11 horsepower per cubic foot therefrom; and 12,000 cubic feet to the Ontario Power Co., which can generate about 17 horsepower per cubic foot therefrom. Development has steadily progressed and installations for the diversions aggregating about 22,000 cubic feet are now practically complete on the Canadian side.

The CHAIRMAN. The evidence before this committee was that they were only developing 11,000 cubic feet.

Mr. SCOVELL. The difference is between the installations completed and installations in process of being made.

The CHAIRMAN. Within a year.

Mr. SCOVELL. The Ontario Power Co., which was selling less than 7,000 horsepower in Ontario when it obtained its permit to transmit 60,000 horsepower into the United States, is now diverting 8,000 cubic feet, developing 128,000 horsepower, and is selling 70,000 horsepower in Ontario.

Mr. COOPER. Within what time increased 10 times?

Mr. SCOVELL. Five years. When diversion and generation are complete, the 36,000 cubic feet alloted to Canada by the treaty will have produced over 465,000 horse-power, half of which may be brought into the United States if your committee in fixing the limitation at the end of the sixth section of your proposed bill will either use the specific amount, say 232,500 horsepower or the general amount, namely, "one-half the total amount of electricity now or hereafter generated from such diversion."

You can either put in a specific amount, or I would suggest that.

Mr. CLINE. How much has the use of electrical power increased in Canada in the last year by local corporations or local users?

Mr. SCOVELL. I can only speak for the Ontario Power Co., and I should say the past year the amount was increased 62 per cent.

Mr. CURLEY. In one year?

Mr. SCOVELL. In one year; whereas prior to, in the year 1911, we will say, for the purpose of argument, they used 42,000 horse-power, they used in 1912 60,000, which was such an amount in excess of what they used in the previous year that it was equivalent to 62.4 per cent. That gives you an idea of the development and use on the Canadian, American companies getting power there which they can not obtain on the American side.

Now let us consider the limitation on American diversion to 15,600 cubic feet of water per second in the ninth and tenth lines of the second page of the proposed bill. The establishment of this limita-tion——

Mr. CLINE (interposing). Of course, you would not want such a thing as that, as a power trust?

Mr. SCOVELL. That is what your bill provides for; it makes that suggestion, because you limit it to 15,600 cubic feet. The establish-ment of this limitation, taken in connection with the fourth and the eighth sections of the proposed bill, create an absolute power trust or monopoly in the corporation, now actually diverting water on the American side. The Niagara Power Co. had diverted 8,600 cubic feet, and had contracted the sale of all the power generated therefrom before the enactment of the Burton bill, nearly seven years ago. The Hydraulic Power Co. had contracted the sale of the power to be generated from 6,500 cubic feet prior to the enactment of the Burton bill. Most of this power is contracted for use in electro-chemical industries on long-time leases on satisfactory terms, and changes in rates, if required by the public service commission, would not make any additional power available for sale.

Mr. CLINE. What is the objection to an absolute monopoly by those companies that are now generating power if they are fully under the control of the public service commission of the State of New York?

Mr. SCOVELL. Because they are so placed with reference to the water supply of Niagara River that they can not generate under maximum head; I will reach that in a moment.

Because the Niagara Falls Power Co., though the pioneer in the electrical development, was only utilizing 138 feet of head, and pro-ducing therefrom only about 10 horsepower per cubic foot, the Burton bill expressly limited the amount which any one company might take to the 8,600 cubic feet that is taken by the Niagara Falls Power Co., and the Legislature of the State of New York have by joint resolution requested the continuance of this limitation which I would recommend.

Mr. CLINE. What do you think about the section that requires your company to develop its entire——

Mr. SCOVELL (interposing). I am not speaking for any power company.

Mr. CLINE. The Niagara Falls Power Co. You are an expert witness here in this case. What do you say about the proposition to compel those companies to develop the power to its fullest utilization?

Mr. SCOVELL. I will reach that.

Mr. CURLEY. Whom do you represent?

Mr. SCOVELL. I represent myself, individually.

Mr. CURLEY. Whom did you represent the last time you were here?

Mr. SCOVELL. I represented myself.

The nondevelopment of our maximum limitation of 20,000 cubic feet will bring power development to a standstill on the American side.

Mr. COOPER. Twenty thousand?

Mr. SCOVELL. Up to the limits fixed by the treaty. Since the 12th day of November, 1912, a little over two months ago, the Secretary of War has been at liberty to grant an additional 4,400 cubic feet, and it can be done.

Mr. CURLEY. Has he done it?

Mr. SCOVELL. He has not.

Mr. CURLEY. Has application been made for it?

Mr. SCOVELL. I know of no application.

Mr. COOPER. That is an exceedingly important bit of information. Mr. Scovell, has it been authoritatively and finally determined that they are doing that?

Mr. SCOVELL. That they are taking that.

Mr. COOPER. They want to get the exact situation.

Mr. SCOVELL. Here is the report of the Chief of Engineers of the United States Army, dated December 6, House Document No. 936.

Mr. COOPER. He certifies to those facts?

Mr. SCOVELL. He certifies that the Hydraulic Power Co. has now reached its limit of 6,500 cubic feet per second.

Mr. KENDALL. Do you say that Gen. Bixby has certified to the Secretary of War that the fullest amount of diversion, 15,600 cubic feet, has been occurring for six months?

Mr. SCOVELL. He simply says——

Mr. KENDALL (interposing). Equivalent to that?

Mr. SCOVELL. He reports to Congress, and you can get it. You will find it on page 1331, in relation to the importation.

The CHAIRMAN. He has had that power always?

Mr. SCOVELL. After the development has reached that point.

The CHAIRMAN. Where has the development reached that point?

Mr. SCOVELL. There are only two corporations that are now importing up to their limit.

The CHAIRMAN. There is one that is not importing at all, so that they are not importing 160,000, and have not reached the limit?

Mr. SCOVELL. They have not reached the limit.

The CHAIRMAN. So that the Secretary of War could not do that.

Mr. SCOVELL. Not on that proposition.

He takes into consideration how much is taken on the Canadian side. You have got to add what is being used in Canada and what is being used in the United States to determine how much more can be brought into the United States. No application has been made to bring any additional power in, so far as I know. You will find this very matter on pages 1331, 1332, 1333, and 1334 of the report.

Mr. KENDALL. This authority granted to the Secretary of War to allow additional diversion is in one division, but the authority granting increased importation is in another division; they do not seem to be connected at all. They seem to be distinct divisions.

Mr. SCOVELL. The citizens of western New York would like to get this additional water. When I was here last year there were people representing over 100,000 horsepower, but all that was developed on the American side was all sold.

Mr. KENDALL. There is this further thing to be thought of, Mr. Scovell——

Mr. SCOVELL (interposing). There ought to be a computation on that with respect to the three hundred and fifty, but the other one is an entirely different matter.

The increase to 20,000 is available.

The CHAIRMAN. That makes it very important that you do not depend on the Burton law.

Mr. KENDALL. Congress said these provisions herein permitting the diversion and fixing the aggregate horsepower are intended as a limitation on the authority of the Secretary of War and shall in no wise be construed as a direction to said Secretary to issue permits.

Mr. SCOVELL. As I stated, it is in his discretion.

Mr. COOPER. Not mandatory, but permissible.

Mr. KENDALL. It is not directory.

Mr. COOPER. It is permissible.

Mr. SCOVELL. It is permissible.

Undoubtedly Congress has power under the Constitution to limit the diversion so as not to impair the integrity and proper volume of the Niagara River as a defensive boundary, but the above-mentioned report states that the actual and authorized diversions will not appreciably decrease its efficiency as such. These powers of Congress are but confirmed by the treaty. However, Congress has no constitutional power to limit diversion so as not to interfere with the scenic grandeur of Niagara Falls, but even if it had it would be unreasonable to exercise it with respect to the American Falls in the face of the above-mentioned report to the effect that the flow will be decreased only about five-eighths of an inch, being "scarcely appreciable" and affecting only "unimportant changes in the American Falls." It is urged, however, and this proposed bill contemplates that American industries must be denied additional supplies of American-produced power in order that the United States Congress may protect the Canadian end of the Horseshoe Falls by not permitting the use of the balance of 4,400 cubic feet allowed by the treaty to be diverted in the United States, while Canada, in disregard of the reported damage to the beauty of its end of the Horseshoe Falls, continues and plans to continue to take and develop for the aid of its communities up to the full limit of its allotment of 36,000 cubic feet.

That is a fair statement of that position.

The CHAIRMAN. How much power are they under contract to generate in Canada at this time?

Mr. SCOVELL. Gen. Greene's company is under contract to furnish power to the Government up to 100,000 horsepower.

The CHAIRMAN. How much more will they use in Canada?

Mr. SCOVELL. I do not know just how much more?

The CHAIRMAN. Another 100,000?

Mr. SCOVELL. Oh, yes.

The CHAIRMAN. That would make 200,000.

Mr. Scovell. I can say that three years from to-day——

The Chairman (interposing.) I am talking about the present time. That would make 360,000. So the Secretary of War would not have much opportunity to increase importations under the Burton law.

Mr. Scovell. If such is the desire and intention of this committee or of Congress, they should call upon the President to institute negotiations for the joint modification of the amounts now authorized to be diverted by the countries, submitting to the proper officials of the other high contracting party the report of our Army officials, showing the probable impairment to the scenic grandeur of the Canadian end of the Horseshoe Falls. This impairment, however, does not now exist, for the Canadian Park Commission have constructed a parapet and given access on foot and in conveyances out to a line where the water at the west end of the Horsehoe Falls is so deep as not only to greatly increase the wonder and awe at the spectacle, but to make it impossible for either the proposed diversions or the periodic decreases in rainfall in the watershed of the Great Lakes or even a heavy wind from the east on Lake Erie to lessen the scenic grandeur of the cataract at that point, and I beg respectfully to suggest to the park commissioners on the American side that they request a State appropriation to accomplish a similar result at the Amercan end of the Horseshoe Falls.

The Chairman. With 26,600 cubic feet being diverted the fall of water over the Horseshoe Falls on the Canadian side is lowered nine inches, according to Gen. Bixby. With 56,000 diverted is it not fair to assume it would be something like 20 inches?

Mr. Scovell. I think you will find that those estimates when the full amount is taken——

The Chairman (interposing). No; the estimates were based on the diversion at the time they were made.

Mr. Scovell. Those things have been modified by the changes made by the park commissioners on the Canadian side.

The Chairman. It has lessened the width of the falls by 300 feet?

Mr. Scovell. Whatever amount it has been lessened. It is a matter of regret that the members of this committee can not visit Niagara, inspect the power plants on both sides, and see the results attained by the park commissioners in preserving and increasing the natural beauties and wonders on both sides, for then "it would be to laugh" at the fears expressed and the prattle indulged in by those whose visits to Niagara are only imaginary.

But what effect will the taking of the 4,400 feet actually have? Of that amount 400 cubic feet will be taken from the American Falls, and 4,000, or less than 2 per cent more, would be diverted from the flow of over 200,000 cubic feet per second from over the Horseshoe Falls, while Canada with 22,000 cubic feet now diverted from the Horseshoe Falls will not hesitate to take its balance of 14,000 cubic feet.

The Chairman. The contention is that they are just working up some civic pride in Canada, and if this Governement refuses to take 4,400 feet, the Canadian Government will take theirs.

Mr. Scovell. That is a matter for diplomatic negotiations. The effect is not and can not be other than inappreciable. Only the apparent roar is diminished, and that roar is not lost, but changed into the hum of turbines and dynamos, which means industry and commerce and prosperity on the Niagara frontier.

The Legislature of the State of New York is on record in a joint resolution, introduced by Senator George R. Burd, of Buffalo, in opposition to the Alexander bill, adopted unanimously by the State senate on February 20, 1911, and by a vote of 82 to 47 by the assembly on February 23, 1911, a copy of which I have heretofore filed with you. At that time there was no Conservation Commission in the State of New York, which fact of course should receive your consideration. The Commonwealth is entitled to have permits issued and used, so that the whole 20,000 can be made available, and it is entitled that the permits for the additional 4,400 cubic feet be given only where it will be developed under maximum head; that is where the efficiency question comes in. It would be unwise to give a permit directly to the State as its rights might inure; at least no development could be had until after almost interminable litigation to some claimant. But in the plenary power to deal with this matter which Congress has by reason of the wording of the treaty it may well confer the granting of permits either on the Secretary of War, who necessarily has to supervise the diversion and has the facilities therefor, or on the American members of the International Joint Commission, which control of all classes of diversions from all other boundary streams, including even such as may desire to be made from the lower Niagara Rapids. If the State wishes to utilize water from the lower Niagara River or from the St. Lawrence River, it will have to apply to the International Joint Commission. So it would be no hardship for it or any other applicant to be required to apply to the American members of that commission for what is desired to be diverted from above the Falls of Niagara in addition to the 15,600 now diverted. To require the consent of the governor of New York or any commission or any other duly authorized body representing the State and holding such a delegation from Congress of a designating power is but to complicate the method and process of procuring a permit, and so to retard ultimate though necessary development.

I wish in closing to comment on two seemingly minor items. First, I understand the words "for the public benefit," in the fourth line of the second page of the proposed bill, to mean any body corporate empowered with power of eminent domain——.

Mr. COOPER (interposing). Where is that?

Mr. SCOVELL. The fourth line of the second page, "to grant for the public benefit of the State of New York and other States." I want to know what is meant by the words "public benefit of the State of New York"? As I read it legally, it means to any corporation holding the right of eminent domain.

Mr. DIFENDERFER. Legally.

Mr. SCOVELL. Yes. I want to know what is the intention.

The CHAIRMAN. What have you to say?

Mr. SCOVELL. I have nothing to say about it. I would like to know your meaning.

Mr. CLINE. You have an amendment here, Mr. Chairman, upon that score.

Mr. SCOVELL. I inquire if such is your meaning; and, second, the standard of efficiency authorized in the third and fourth lines of the fourth page, to be determined by the Secretary of War, is now based as to companies now diverting 15,600 cubic feet per second on that total fall from the Grass Island-Chippewa Pool to Suspension Bridge.

The CHAIRMAN. You think you ought to go below there?

Mr. SCOVELL. That is the present standard——

Mr. CLINE. Who established that standard?

Mr. KENDALL. I think the War Department found that standard established.

Mr. SCOVELL (continuing). Whereas the standard of efficiency for diversion of the additional 4,400 feet should be based in the future on the total fall from the Grass Island–Chippewa Pool to the lower Niagara River.

The CHAIRMAN. Have you an amendment to suggest?

Mr. SCOVELL. Unless you feel that discretion in the Secretary of War is sufficient.

Mr. KENDALL. I would suggest that there has been no advice to the Secretary of War in any statute which would limit him to the standard he found established.

Mr. SCOVELL. Here is a picture [indicating picture] prepared by the Lake Survey, showing Grass Island Pool and the Upper Gorge to Suspension Bridge. That is the basis of present efficiency, from this pool to here [indicating], and there are the Rapids from Suspension Bridge to the Whirlpool. The result is that the standard of efficiency is such that water taken from the upper to the lower river is capable of being developed under 296 feet of head, which produces anywhere from 26 to 28 horsepower per cubic foot.

The CHAIRMAN. Two hundred and ninety-six as against what at this other point?

Mr. SCOVELL. The maximum there is 208.

Mr. COOPER. And with 296 foot head there would be a great deal more electrical power with the diversion of the same amount of water, would there not?

Mr. SCOVELL. It would be running up to 28, as against between 11 and 15.

Mr. COOPER. Is there any physical or engineering obstacle to the use of that 296-foot head?

Mr. SCOVELL. None. I have heard a prominent engineer connected with one of the Canadian companies say that if he had the right to take 296 feet of water he would take down his plant and take it to the lower river to get a greater efficiency.

Mr. COOPER. For what reason?

Mr. SCOVELL. Because of the difference in efficiency.

Mr. COOPER. And build again down below. That is an exceedingly important thing. If they could get two and one-half or three times the power which they now get, and not divert any more water, and do it easily, and there is no engineering or other practical obstacle, and the Canadian company said if they could get the opportunity to do it they would give up their plant and go there and build a new one, that is a very important thing to be taken into account before we let these lower companies divert so much more water.

The CHAIRMAN. Gen. Greene, I think, made a similar statement. If he did not make it before the committee, he made it to me personally.

Mr. KENDALL. That involves the dismantling of the plant over there.

The CHAIRMAN. He was talking of the Niagara Falls Power Co., and he said it would be a good financial proposition to make a junk pile of that plant and give it this additional head, and the additional power it would get would enable the company to declare a larger dividend on both investments than it can now make on the original investment.

Mr. COOPER. Why could not these companies combine, junk all the plants, and go down there?

Mr. SCOVELL. You can not do that.

Mr. COOPER. We can not make them do it?

Mr. SCOVELL. You can not make them do that.

Mr. COOPER. We can not make them do that.

The CHAIRMAN. Why can not we make them do that?

Mr. KENDALL. You say we have no power to compel them to do that?

Mr. SCOVELL. That is a proposition of law. It concerns their vested rights. I should be very doubtful if you would be able to make them do it.

The CHAIRMAN. It all depends upon our power to establish a standard.

Mr. SCOVELL. If you establish a standard, you might be able to reach such a result. If you wanted those companies to junk their plants and do it, they would not junk their plants unless they had some water to take to the other places, and those companies have not the power under their articles of incorporation as created by the State of New York at the present time to take water.

Mr. COOPER. Do you think the State of New York would grant them power to do it?

Mr. SCOVELL. I do not think the State of New York would be inclined to, if it could get that water for itself.

Mr. COOPER. Do you think the object of legislation to be the greatest good to the greatest number?

Mr. SCOVELL. Yes.

Mr. COOPER. Then let us make a practical application of it right here. You can take the same amount of water and make three times as much power and leave Niagara as beautiful as it is now, and serve the interests of all those people about whom you have been talking and add to the value of industries, add to the taxable property, and to the prosperity of the people, and use less water.

Mr. SCOVELL. I have suggested that it be done as it is done in Canada. Canada has its own canal, from the upper to the lower lake, and not only does it divert water for navigation purposes through the Welland Canal but quite a large amount is taken through that canal and diverted for power purposes, and in going from the upper to the lower lakes they are able to get a maximum efficiency for the development of their water for power purposes. They are spending fifty million for improvement on that 40 miles of canal. The Dominion of Canada is progressive in that respect. If the United States or the State of New York deemed it wise to build a navigable canal from the upper to the lower Niagara which would carry water for navigation purposes and build it of sufficient size to carry in addition 20,000 cubic feet per second, they could say to those companies, "If you move your plants to the lower river, we will let you have the same amount of water you are getting now, provided you will pay to us a reasonable sum which will be some return for the construction of the canal."

Mr. COOPER. That is what the Canadian Government is doing?

Mr. SCOVELL. Practically; yes, sir.

Mr. KENDALL. What is the maximum of horsepower per cubic foot for a fall of 320 feet?

Mr. SCOVELL. You do not get 320 feet at the net head; it is about 298 feet.

Mr. KENDALL. What does that figure?

Mr. SCOVELL. You were told the other day it would be about 11 per foot; you can always figure on 11 per foot. I stated it would run about 28, or about it; perhaps 27.

STATEMENT OF GEORGE C. RILEY, REPRESENTING THE NIAGARA GORGE RAILROAD CO.

The CHAIRMAN. We will now hear Mr. Riley.

Mr. RILEY. Mr. Chairman, much that I had intended to suggest to the committee that bears on the situation has already been stated, and I wish simply to call your attention to what has been said as bearing on our situation, and I want to describe the situation.

Mr. KENDALL. Whom do you represent?

Mr. RILEY. I represent the Niagara Gorge Railroad Co., which owns the land on the American side of the lower river, of the gorge, from a point about a mile below the Falls to a point about 300 feet below the bridges shown on this map [indicating map] and in this photograph [indicating photograph] for over 5 miles to the village of Lewiston.

We acquired that as early as 1894 or 1895, and are the riparian owner which the attorney general has referred to here. We have invested there, in our railroad. which exists only because of the scenic beauty of the gorge and Falls, some $2,000,000. We are entitled, as said by the attorney general of the State of New York, to the riparian rights that go with that ownership. As early as 1898 we contemplated the construction of a canal along there for the generation of power for our railroad and for commercial purposes. We obtained at that time the report of John Birkendon, the eminent electrical engineer, and he proposed, and it is our present plan, to have two units of generation, first, a canal, starting about 300 feet below the bridges and extending to a point on the American shore opposite the whirlpool, which would divert from the rapids at that point, which rapids are our scenic asset, about 10,000 feet of water a second, with a head of 57 feet, generating approximately 40,000 horsepower. The second unit starts below the whirlpool; with a little more water we get a head of about 35 feet and develop approximately the same amount of horsepower.

We are held up in that operation and western New York needs that power, and, as Mr. Sharp stated this afternoon, there has not been any competition and there has not been any great development because of the legislation that has prevented that competition. We want to generate that power; we want to sell it for the commercial advancement of ourselves and the community. The thing that is in our way is the prohibtion of the Burton Act, which applies to the entire river, although the treaty vests in the joint high commission the sole power of granting permits to generate power in that portion of the river. This bill proposes a prohibition the same as in the Burton Act, and I suggest the same amendment suggested by Mr. Richards and the same amendment suggested by Mr. Scoville, that your first section be amended so as to apply only to the river above the Falls. Then we may apply to the joint high commission, and there will be your Federal supervision and we are willing to be controlled absolutely, so far as they may impose conditions, also by the State of New York, because we will be under the jurisdiction of the State of New York when we come to generate and transmit.

The CHAIRMAN. You propose to have the words "above the Falls" inserted where necessary in the bill, and section 3 stricken out?

Mr. RILEY. Yes; because section 3 only provides for a tribunal for the granting of the permit, and I think your enactment would be invalid, because the treaty would be prior to your enactment and would supersede it; and we have always maintained that we are obligated to obtain the consent of the joint high commission. It is not possible to finance any project in the situation that we find ourselves in now. We only say that if this act does not pass and then the Burton Act expires, if in any reenactment of the Burton Act you make that change so that we may apply to the joint high commission, something that the Burton Act has not given us——

The CHAIRMAN (interposing). I will call your attention to this fact. If we reenact the Burton Act, it would have to go through as a hurried measure, and it would have to go through practically by consent, and I do not think Senator Burton would consent to it going through the Senate with that change. I believe he told me he would not.

Mr. RILEY. I can not conceive of any reason which can be urged here in committee for having the Burton Act apply to the entire river, unless it is to give our friends above the falls a monopoly of the power business, and I take it it is not the intention of this committee to perpetuate a monopoly. And what is proposed will not affect the grandeur of the Falls. We will conserve the grandeur of the cataract, or the joint high commission can do that, or, if they do not, I have no doubt the other commissions will attend to that, so that you will have Federal control, and all we ask is the right to exercise our rights without the interference of an enactment like the Burton Act.

STATEMENT OF MILLARD F. BOWEN, ESQ.

The CHAIRMAN. We will now hear Mr. Bowen for 20 minutes.

Mr. BOWEN. Mr. Chairman and gentlemen of the committee, the trend of the hearings last year left the matter in a rather indefinite condition. The International Joint Commission had not at that time gotten to work. Succeeding the hearings I applied to the State Department to have this question that is treated of in that treaty, the use of this additional water, first for sanitation, then for navigation, and last of all for power, ratified by both countries, the United States and Canada and the International Joint Commission. At about the same time, Mr. Simmons put in a special joint resolution, I believe, and asked practically for the same reference to the International Joint Commission, and in furtherance of the requests made jointly to the State Department, the State Department communicated with the Dominion of Canada, and the result was that finally an order of reference was made, so that this whole subject that is treated of in the treaty relating to the pollution of water was referred for report and recommendation to the International Joint Commission. The International Joint Commission have already held several meetings. One was held here in Washington in November, and I presented to them at that time evidence of experts to show that we could take care of this question of pollution as it relates to. the Niagara frontier in order to carry out the pledge of the Government in regard to stopping the pollution of international waters. The treaty, under article 8, makes that the first and paramount question to be considered in any further diversion of water from the river, and therefore it is quite essential that their recommendation be obtained by any company that it to use the balance of this water.

They have a right not only to recommend that 4,400 cubic feet be used for sanitation and navigation, but also an additional amount that would be only limited by the needs of any community as to stopping pollution and in health matters. So that is one of the essential things that has to be considered in this connection. Another very essential thing, it seems to me, is the constant efforts that have been made since the Burton law went into effect to show that that was unconstitutional and should be declared so in the courts. Now, the same thing, it seems to me, will be attached to the bill as now drawn by your committee, because there is no provision in the bill as drawn for any particular work to aid navigation, and in order one time for all to remove that danger of having this bill declared unconstitutional, as has been said time and again about the Burton bill, I have preferred an amendment to the bill to be inserted as section 7 of the bill. That amendment would keep the control of all the waters except the 15,600 feet in Congress. It would not even give the discretion of the Secretary of War to apportion that additional water as the Secretary might see fit. Therefore it would be, it seems to me, a valuable thing for Congress to retain an absolute control over at least one company, so that if the conditions were not carried out that that act giving the grant could be made ineffective and inoperative at any time by your own act.

In this additional section which I have prepared I have made it so conditioned that the Erie & Ontario Sanitary Canal Co. will not only preserve navigation by putting into the river above the Falls such work as the International Waterways Commission has considered or such other works as is found by engineers to be necessary to maintain the lake levels above the Falls. By joining the lake levels with what is already contained in the bill, there can be no possible question about the constitutionality of the bill as a whole, because all of the previous acts of Congress relating to the use of water in any of our navigable rivers have been, except the Burton law, with some express condition in aid of navigation. Every act has contained express conditions in aid of navigation. Therefore that is an added reason why this additional amendment should be added in order to remove for all time this question of the danger of having the whole thing declared unconstitutional in the courts and thus avoid delay. But with this added there can not be any ground for delay. The offer of this company to spend whatever sum is necessary for maintaining lake levels and the beauty of the Falls is also coupled with the offer to allow the canals that we propose to build to be used by all the municipalities on the Niagara frontier and all the corporations and individuals for sewage disposal and the carrying off of the storm water. We have reason to believe that with our greater efficiency we will obtain from every cubic foot of water the greatest amount of power that can be obtained therefrom.

Mr. COOPER. How much fall do you have?

Mr. BOWEN. Three hundred and twelve feet instead of 296 feet. Right there, Mr. Cooper, in order that you may understand how that may be accomplished, the profile of the construction shows the construction of three dams——

Mr. COOPER (interposing). Who is this drawn by?

Mr. BOWEN. By Isham Randolph, of Chicago, and my Buffalo engineers. The flow from Lake Erie to Lockport is just a single drop here of 5 feet, where there would be necessity for a lock, then the fall is continuous to Lockport; there is one fall of 220 feet, and two falls below, so that we get 312 feet in place of 296 feet, the greatest efficiency that can be gotten in Niagara River, by using all three of the falls. By reason of the 312-foot fall we will develop 28.36 horsepower from every cubic foot of water, and we will take 6,000 feet of water, which is less than either the Niagara Falls Power Co. or the other power company is using, and with that 6,000 cubic feet we will be getting such an amount of horsepower that it gives us an income that will enable us to do all this work, and give the free use of it for the purposes mentioned.

Mr. CURLEY. Your maximum development is reached at a point not far distant from the city of Buffalo?

Mr. BOWEN. Lockport is about 26 miles away.

The CHAIRMAN. What will be your comparative charges as compared with the charges now made by the companies operating?

Mr. BOWEN. The city of Buffalo is under contract with the existing distributing companies to pay not to exceed 9 cents per kilowatt-hour. They charge 9 cents to a great many people, others get it for less. Our proposed contract with the city of Buffalo, drawn by the corporation counsel of the city of Buffalo, is for 4 cents per kilowatt-hour. Figuring our maximum and minimum charges, our average is $20 per horsepower. You can see there will be a real benefit in that line to be derived from this particular use of the balance of the water.

A great deal has been said here in regard to the efficiency of all these companies; the Niagara Falls Power Co. could generate with their 136 feet of fall, if they were using it up to 80 per cent of efficiency, if their machinery were modern——

Mr. COOPER (interposing). Which company?

Mr. BOWEN. The Niagara Falls Co. They could, instead of generating 10 horsepower, they could be generating 12.36 horsepower per cubic foot at 80 per cent efficiency, which is now the usual estimate. The other company, instead of getting 17, could be getting, if they were using theirs to 80 per cent efficiency, 19.9, and this company of ours, by reason of their better efficiency, will be getting 28.36 horsepower, so there is 10 horsepower that the Niagara Falls Co. is getting as against 28.36 that this company will be getting.

The CHAIRMAN. Does your company propose to utilize its maximum capacity?

Mr. BOWEN. Oh, yes; every cubic foot for 24 hours per day. The amendment that I have drawn up here makes that one of the conditions. It says, "*Provided further*, That said company shall develop twenty-eight and thirty-six hundredths horsepower from each cubic foot per second of water hereby granted."

The other conditions I have proposed to insert in this amendment are to this effect:

Provided, That said company within two years after the passage of this act and the approval of the International Joint Commission, shall begin the construction of said canal without seeking from State or Nation other aid than that afforded by such cooperation as may properly be effected between Federal and State authorities, and shall with due diligence prosecute the work to completion.

The amendment which I propose is as follows:

SEC. 7. The assent of Congress is hereby given to the Erie and Sanitary Canal Company, a corporation created and organized under the laws of the State of New York, to take six thousand cubic feet of water per second from Lake Erie and Niagara River, in addition to the amount mentioned in section two, for sanitary purposes and canal navigation, to be used lastly for power through a canal to be constructed from Lake Erie to Lake Ontario in the State of New York: *Provided*, That said company, within two years after the passage of this act and the approval of the international joint commission, shall begin the construction of said canal without seeking from State or Nation other aid than that afforded by such cooperation as may properly be effected between Federal and States authorities, and shall with due diligence prosecute the work to completion: *Provided further*, That in consideration of this grant said company shall give to all municipalities on the Niagara frontier and to all public and private corporations and individuals the free use and perpetual right to use said canal for sewage disposal and carrying off storm water, and will build and maintain at its own expense suitable works in Niagara River to maintain the level of Lake Erie and the beauty of Niagara Falls: *Provided further*, That said company may make a proper connection between its canal and Buffalo River and cause the water of Lake Erie to flow backward through Buffalo River into said canal, and may make such changes in Smokes Creek, Ellicott Creek, and other streams in Erie and Niagara Counties as will permit water to enter such streams from Lake Erie and flow through them into said canal and through the same into Lake Ontario; and may build and maintain at the mouths of Smokes Creek and Eighteen Mile Creek such harbors as may be necessary; all of which construction affecting navigation shall be done under the direction of the War Department: *Provided further*, That the provisions of this section shall cease to be operative should it be judicially determined that said company has joined any monopoly in restraint of trade: *And provided further*, That said company shall develop twenty-eight and thirty-six hundredths horsepower from each cubic foot per second of water hereby granted.

We have been promised a conference at Buffalo in the near future, in order to get a decision as to pollution, under the order of reference, by both Governments, and they will proceed as fast as they can to make that approval, and therefore we will have to get to work this year on actual construction.

Mr. COOPER. How long is the canal?

Mr. BOWEN. Forty-seven miles.

Mr. COOPER. Your theory is that would solve the sanitation problem?

Mr. BOWEN. Absolutely; and their approval will do that so Congress does not need to bother about that subject.

Mr. COOPER. Of course, everybody knows Mr. Randolph is a great engineer. I know him by reputation, because I have heard about the Chicago Canal. Has he examined this matter?

Mr. BOWEN. Absolutely, and I have his particular report in regard to it.

The CHAIRMAN. He appeared before the committee last year.

Mr. BOWEN. Since the last meeting of the committee we have obtained the services of one of the greatest lawyers relating to water powers and waterways that there is in this country, George Clinton, of Buffalo, and his brief is in this printed book which I was requested to make up by the international joint commission, and I have copies of it here which I will give to each member of the committee. You will note that this amendment further provides—

"that in consideration of this grant said company shall give to all municipalities on the Niagara frontier and to all public and private corporations and to individuals the free use and perpetual right to use said canal for sewage disposal and carrying off storm water and shall construct and maintain at its own expense suitable works in Niagara River to maintain the level of Lake Erie and the beauty of Niagara Falls."

Those works are being now considered by the engineers of the International Waterways Commission at Buffalo, under George Clinton, Mr. ———, and Gen. Ernst, of the United States Army. That old commission is still in existence for the purpose of determining on these works in Niagara River which have been referred to. You will also notice that the amendment provides further:

"That said company may make a proper connection between its canal and Buffalo River and cause the water of Lake Erie to flow backward through Buffalo River into said canal, and may make such changes in Smokes Creek, Ellicott Creek, and other streams in Erie and Niagara Counties as will permit water to enter such streams from Lake Erie and flow through them into said canal and through the same into Lake Ontario, and may build and maintain at the mouths of Smokes Creek and Eighteen Mile Creek such harbors as may be necessary, all of which construction affecting navigation shall be done under the direction of the War Department.

Whatever we do must be under the approval of the international joint commission, and it must be under the direction of the War Department; it must be under your direction and constant supervision. Therefore I maintain there is no doubt, if you will sufficiently go into this question and examine the possibilities of it, that this grant of additional power from which we will get a limited amount of power to a maximum amount, to this extent should be granted. They are getting 10 horsepower.

Mr. LOVELACE. They are getting 12½.

Mr. BOWEN. Are they, now? Very well; they could get, if they were under this 312-foot head, they could be getting 243,896 horsepower, and the other company that is now getting 124,085 horsepower could be getting under this head 184,340 horsepower.

STATEMENT OF MR. RICHARD B. WATROUS, SECRETARY AMERICAN CIVIC ASSOCIATION.

The CHAIRMAN. Mr. Watrous, do you wish to be heard?

Mr. WATROUS. Only a brief statement, I think, Mr. Chairman. I think it would be a repetition of a good deal that has been said on our side of the case. I simply want to take advantage of this opportunity of calling to your attention, if you need to have it recalled to you, the consideration of the preservation of the Falls for their scenic beauty, and to suggest that you read again and possibly reread the statement of Mr. McFarland at the hearings a year ago, given on page 256 of the printed record of the hearings, in which he states that the beginning of this entire agitation grew out of this desire on the part of both countries, and which was the cause of diplomatic negotiations between them, the desire for the preservation of the Falls from the scenic standpoint.

It would appear to me, Mr. Chairman, that your subcommittee has in drafting this bill recognized that the Burton Act was an instrument that has been efficient, and was a pretty good thing to follow. I believe the hearings of a year ago brought out a very important thing which you have fully recognized, namely, that the companies there have been permitting tremendous waste, and we are insisting that they shall use the water given to them to the greatest possible efficiency, and we do not believe there is any particular occasion for their being granted more, and we stand as we stood a year ago in believing that there should be no increase on the American side, and we believe that there should be no increase in importation. We most certainly stand for the principle that Federal control is the only control. The State of New York demonstrated, before the Burton Act became a law, that it took no particular interest in safeguarding Niagara; it gave water to almost anyone who wanted it, and anyone who came along could get it, and there was no control of the water until the Burton bill was enacted in 1906, and it has been the law of the Nation, and it has proven effective.

Mr. CURLEY. You represent the conservation movement?

Mr. WATROUS. How do you mean, Mr. Curley? I represent the American Civic Association.

Mr. CURLEY. You disagree with what has been said by the representatives of the conservation commission relative to the use of the additional 4,400 feet?

Mr. WATROUS. I certainly disagree with them in their contention that New York State is the proper agency——

Mr. CURLEY (interposing). You believe in preserving the 4,400 feet?

Mr. WATROUS. Yes, sir; and I do so on the statement of the War Department and their representative. In this connection we say this: If you say you go in with the intention of using it to the full amount, and that the authority rests with the Secretary of War to increase those—it says he may—is it at all likely, gentlemen, that when his representatives have been very explicit in saying that there has been that very great damage to the Falls and that there has been damage to the waters of Lake Erie, is it at all reasonable to think that he would take charge of them and give out additional permits for water? I do not think so.

Mr. CURLEY. Has your association ever attempted to confer with the conservation commission relative to the question of preserving the scenic beauty of the Falls?

Mr. WATROUS. I have not, and I do not think the president of the association has.

Mr. CURLEY. Do they not recognize them as an important body there?

Mr. WATROUS. In New York State?

Mr. CURLEY. Yes.

Mr. WATROUS. To be frank, I do not believe we have taken New York into consideration. We have taken the whole United States into consideration. We are separate and distinct from the conservation movement.

The CHAIRMAN. We have had very extensive hearings on this matter, and I would think we want to close these hearings once and for all, to-night if possible.

Mr. CURLEY. Mr. Lovelace ought to have an opportunity to make a statement.

Mr. LOVELACE. I could not correct the inaccuracies of statement that have been made here in an hour.

Thereupon, at 10.45 o'clock p. m., the committee adjourned to meet to-morrow, Friday, January 24, at 10 o'clock a. m.

COMMITTEE ON FOREIGN AFFAIRS,
HOUSE OF REPRESENTATIVES,
Washington, D. C., Friday, January 24, 1913.

The committee met at 10 o'clock a. m., Hon. Henry D. Flood (chairman) presiding.

The CHAIRMAN. Mr. Lovelace, we have not many members here, but what you have to say will be printed in the record and the others can see it. If it is agreeable to you you may proceed now.

STATEMENT OF MR. FREDERICK L. LOVELACE, SECRETARY OF THE NIAGARA FALLS POWER CO.

Mr. LOVELACE. At the outset, gentlemen, I would ask the committee to take into consideration the fact that I am not a trained speaker and accustomed to speaking quickly on my feet, but perhaps I have a little mannerism which may already have been apparent before the committee and possibly have been misconstrued. The emphasis arises only from the extreme interest that I have in the matter and the earnestness that I have in speaking of it is not any animosity toward those who have made statements here.

The CHAIRMAN. Yes, we understand that. Tell us first whom you represent here.

Mr. LOVELACE. I am the secretary of the Niagara Falls Power Co., located at Niagara Falls, N. Y., and I speak in behalf of that company. I am neither a trained speaker, nor am I a constitutional' lawyer. I have listened with profound interest to the addresses that have been made to you yesterday and the day before by the distinguished lawyers who have presented constitutional questions and I personally am unable to determine the merits of the propositions which they have advanced, but I note that in presenting their concrete suggestions, in spite of their arguments they seemed to have admitted the same authority which you apparently have recognized by your subcommittee, at least, in the draft which has been presented here regarding the diversion of water at Niagara. All of the concrete suggestions presented contain provisions by which permits are to be issued by some department of the Federal Government. It seems to me that when you concede that, it goes with it that the Federal Government may attach conditions under which those permits shall be exercised, and that is the whole question, it seems to me.

As I say, I am not a constitutional lawyer, and I do not want to be catechized and asked for the cases, because I do not know the cases, but there are certain fundamental propositions of constitutional law and the constitution of the State of New York which I do understand without having the cases to back them up. I may possibly refer a little later in one phase of this argument to those fundamental propositions. They do not, however, go to the underlying basis on which this bill is drafted. Now, I want to say, gentlemen, in spite of the arguments that may have been advanced by the paid counsel of our company last year, that in practice we have found the Burton law to be admirable as to easy execution and as to being able to place the responsibility for the conditions at Niagara and to control the situation there. The only complaints that we have of the Burton law are the limits which it sets, which are limits inside of the treaty, and I want to say that so far as I am able to judge this submitted provision is one that is admirably drafted, and certainly from the Federal standpoint it will be a practical measure, easy to carry into execution, and certain to carry out its provisions in the most convenient method of easy administration. Personally I have no fault to find with the bill except in three respects, which are not the, basic principles but which are the limits of the bill.

Instead of proceeding as I perhaps suggested to you last night to try to correct the many partly true statements that have been made here, I propose to use my time in going at once to the meat of the proposition and taking this bill and asking this committee to enlarge it and I think that I can present to you, and I am sure that I have in my mind logical reasons, common sense, practical reasons, for each one of the requests that I am going to make. I may not be able to make them clear to you, but I am sure in my mind that they are practical and logical and fair. I will not dwell long on the first point, because it has been presented in other ways, and that is the limit of diversion, within the limits of the treaty. Now, gentlemen, there are two reasons why I think you should make that limit 20,000 cubic feet per second instead of 15,600.

Mr. KENDALL. How did it occur, if you know, that the arbitrary amount of 15,600 cubic feet per second was established? Was it because when the Burton law went into effect the companies were diverting that amount?

Mr. LOVELACE. I can not answer that, yes or no. Yes; I know it accurately. I had determined for the moment to omit that. I know the history of it exactly, and I will give it to you in brief now.

Mr. KENDALL. It is not very vital, of course.

Mr. LOVELACE. Well, it is and it is not, in a way. Now, please trust me, gentlemen, because I mean to be fair, and I am fair. I believe that every member of the committee, even though he puts the questions which, as has been stated here before. seemed like "pretty strong barks," I believe they are sincerely trying to frame a practical and fair measure, in the interests of the people of the United States and those who have put their money in good faith into Niagara power plants. Now, before touching that, let me make this statement. Canada is going to use and is already practically using—it already has plants built to use all of the 32,000 cubic feet per second which they are allowed to divert and they are going to use that power whether you let it come over here or not. There is a glut on the market already.

The CHAIRMAN. I thought there was a power famine up there?

Mr. LOVELACE. The power famine is on the American side and the glut on the Canadian side. We have a part of our power house lying idle to-day and we are purchasing power simply on account of the famine on the American side and the glut on the Canadian side. All of that 32,000 cubic feet of water is practically used in this way. Plants are already built to use every bit of that power, and generators are being installed. There is no reason why you should not give the people of the United States the benefit of the small additional amount between the limits which you have fixed and the limits fixed by the treaty.

Mr. CLINE. How would you distribute the surplus?

Mr. LOVELACE. Well, sir, I would at least give the existing companies an opportunity to compete for it. I would not cut them off entirely, as has been suggested by the concrete suggestions for amendments presented by the conservation commission and by the distinguished lawyer, Mr. J. Boardman Scovell, and he is a distinguished lawyer on this subject, but he has ideas in his mind when it comes to questions outside of law questions. I respect his opinion on legal questions.

Now, just one word as to that 4,400 feet additional. I have here a summary from the report of the Chief of Engineers. I do not ask you to take his offhand statements at the hearing last year, but take his formal document, which is carefully prepared. Now, as to that 4,400 feet additional, this will be the effect upon the Falls: At the crest of the Falls it will be less than one-eighth of an inch; at the Goat Island end of the Horseshoe Falls it will be approximately nine-sixteenths of an inch; at the Canadian end of the Horseshoe Falls it will be less than $1\frac{7}{16}$ inches. That is approximated. At Lake Erie it will be approximately one-fifth of an inch. So that you see it is inappreciable when you consider that the Chief of Engineers has formally reported that due to natural causes on Lake Erie there is 14 feet variation, due to winds, 8 feet one way and 6 feet the other. You will find all that in the report of the Chief of Engineers. That is one of the practical reasons which I advanced why you may well include that 4,400 feet.

The other reason which I desire to urge is this: If you retain in your bill the provision which definitely requires or may require the scrapping of present plants and the building of new plants 7 miles away from where they are now located, it will be impracticable, from the best estimates I can yet obtain, to go down there with 8,600 feet of water. For instance, taking our own case, there is not water enough to do it. The General Electric Co. had a proposition when the Burton law came out, and they claimed that they were bona fide to make developments at the Devils Hole, taking their water above our water, and they stated that they would need all of the treaty amount in order to make that a successful commercial proposition. There are a great many physical conditions, but I am going to come to that. There are a great many legal difficulties, and there are all kinds of financial and commercial difficulties. Now, I am going to answer the interrogation of the Member from the State of Iowa. I had intended not to touch on this point, because I am not sure that touching on it will assist the cause which I am urging before you.

Mr. KENDALL. I was actuated a good deal by curiosity more than anything else.

Mr. LOVELACE. The Burton law, as first drafted by Judge Burton—Senator Burton now—and as it passed the House of Representatives and the Senate of the United States, restricted the diversion of the waters of the Niagara River on the American side to the amount then used by the existing companies, and it was passed after careful consideration, I argued the matter time and time again with Senator Burton, and I think I made his life miserable then, and I think he has made my life miserable ever since. However, it was very carefully considered, and the law passed both branches of Congress. In the Senate, Senator Knox of Massachusetts had inserted an amendment in regard to the requirement of the Pittsburgh Reduction Co., incorporated under the laws of Pennsylvania—now known as the Aluminum Co. of America—which was building its plants on the grounds of the Hydraulic Power Co., and he had an amendment in the Senate covering that situation, so that as it passed the Senate it covered also the diversions which would be made by plants which had their factories in process of construction, which was a very indefinite term and which would have covered many plants on our own land if we had taken advantage of it, but we never undertook to do so. That, of course, necessitated a conference. When the matter came to conference, I had no opportunity——

The CHAIRMAN (interposing). You mean a conference between the House and the Senate?

Mr. LOVELACE. Yes, sir. Judge Burton was one of the conferees from the Senate.

The CHAIRMAN. From the House, you mean?

Mr. LOVELACE (continuing). And that amendment did not please him. He tried to make the bill exact and he did by inserting for the first time this provision limiting the diversion of water in cubic feet per second. Now, he took those figures from Judge Clinton, a very distinguished lawyer from the State of New York, whose name has been respected and revered for generations there, but he arrived at the figures without going to the source that he should have gone to in order to find whether they were exact or not. He had placed in his report as a member of the International Waterways Commission certain figures as to the diversion of water from Niagara River, but these figures were correct to the extent that they were theoretical figures on certain percentages of efficiency which should have been the correct percentages of efficiency.

Those figures Judge Burton adopted and they went into the bill, and they were made up this way: There was 500 cubic feet of water per second for the power users on the Erie Canal at Lockport, 6,500 cubic feet of water per second for the hydraulic company—by the way, Judge Clinton had arranged for them to have 9,500 cubic feet of water per second, which was what he had figured as the theoretical ultimate capacity of their plant, and that has always made their claim for an additional 3,000 feet, which they had insisted on so strongly here, but 6,500 was the figure taken. When it came to our plant, the first tenant that the Niagara Falls Power Co. was able to obtain was the Niagara Falls Paper Co., which afterwards went into what is called the Newspaper Trust and became a branch of the International Paper Co. It was before electricity had really become known in the form of alternating current for use in commercial purposes and for transmission to industries. We sold them 11 acres of land which came close to the river, reserving to ourselves the riparian shore, and gave them the right to develop hydraulic power. Well, I do not know that we gave them the right to develop hydraulic power, but we gave them the right to discharge from their wheelpits and from their small generators into our large tailrace, generating a certain amount of power, and it has been since determined that that amount is 800 cubic feet of water per second. So that 800 cubic feet of this 15,600 feet of water is being used to-day by the Hydraulic Power Co. for hydraulic power and not for electric power. 7,800 cubic feet of water is left for the Niagara Falls Power Co. for the generation of power.

The CHAIRMAN. Did he make any recommendations increasing that to 10,000 feet?

Mr. LOVELACE. No, sir; this was before the Burton law was passed. I am fair to say to you, gentlemen, that in spite of the fact that I revere Judge Clinton's name, I do not think that he was fair in not making a sound investigation before determining that theoretical amount. We afterwards found that it required at Peak Loads more than this 7,800 cubic feet of water that was left to us. There was absolutely no doubt in our minds, there was absolutely no doubt in the mind of Judge Burton, there was no doubt in the mind of everybody, which is borne out by the reports which the Rivers and Harbors Committee made to Congress when they made their reports, that it was the intention of Congress to limit the diversion to what it was then, not increasing the limitation but stopping it right there, not to let another company come in. We determined after the Burton law was passed that those figures were only theoretical; that we ought to divert a thousand feet more. We had never yet been able to operate the entire plant that we had built before the Burton law was passed. Finding that condition to be true, after investigation, we made representations to the treaty commissioners who had been appointed, and I can not give you the exact language, but it was to the effect that if it was true that Congress intended to limit diversions, to the extent that were then in progress at the time of the act, and that if, upon the reports of the Government engineers, they should find out that it did no tinterfere with navigation, that it did not interfere with the integrity of the Niagara River as a boundary stream, and that it did not interfere with scenic beauty, they would rectify the condition.

I know that they did rectify the condition. They took the counsel of the War Department and the engineers did determine these things: That the diversion of 32,000 cubic feet of water per second on the American side of the Niagara River would not interfere with navigation nor with scenic beauty nor with the integrity of the river as a boundary stream—did not appreciably affect the scenic beauty at Niagara. They put in an additional 4,400 cubic feet, for which we did not ask. We did not need all that. Remember this, gentlemen, that we lost another half of our development by the Burton law, which under the law of the State we had the right to make, although the directors told us we had a right to make that additional diversion. We had that one plant completed and we suffered great hardship in being obliged to shut down our machinery.

The CHAIRMAN. Do you mean to say that when the Burton law went into effect you had to abandon part of your plant?

Mr. LOVELACE. We were obliged to. We lost 200,000 horsepower. We abandoned our canal. We purchased 1,200 acres of land on which to locate industries and we though we had purchased substantially 100,000 horsepower.

The CHAIRMAN. What became of the canal?

Mr. LOVELACE. Oh, it is there now.

The CHAIRMAN. That was not lost, then?

Mr. LOVELACE. Not in respect of the initial plant, but it had been constructed for a larger plant.

The CHAIRMAN. You did not lose the land.

Mr. LOVELACE. We have it there, but it is more than we have ever needed up to date, but I am not arguing that point with you.

The CHAIRMAN. But I want to get the facts. You made the statement that under the Burton law you had to abandon plants that cost you millions of dollars.

Mr. LOVELACE. Well, I stated it.

The CHAIRMAN. Is it not a fact that your land is worth more now than it was when you bought it?

Mr. LOVELACE. Well, I hope so. Some of it is and some of it is not.

Mr. GARNER. What kind of industries did you expect to put on this 1,200-acre piece of ground?

Mr. LOVELACE. It was largely a matter of very indefinite prophecy at that time. That was a time when George Westinghouse said it was impossible to carry power to Buffalo. We did not have the industries in mind, but it was to invite all the world to locate there, and they have, very largely, sir. There are industries there that have an investment of $25,000,000 or $30,000,000.

Mr. DIFENDERFER. It is your claim now, is it not, that you have not sufficient head in order to get a full and proper efficiency with the plant that you now have?

Mr. LOVELACE. No; that is not true. That would be a very unfair statement of it, indeed. Our claim is now that we built under the best lights we could get at that time. There had never been a turbine put down to the depth at which we put ours; there never had been a generator in any electric plant in the world with anything like the efficiency that we had. We secured the advice of the most competent engineers of both countries. We did the best we knew how, and we had one of the most efficient plants, not only on the Niagara frontier, but in the world. Now, it is true that we could have located at other places in the world where we could have gotten a much greater head. To carry it to an absurdity, we could have gone to Washington and gotten a drop of 550 feet. Now, I am giving you the history.

Mr. DIFENDERFER. We are here for information.

Mr. LOVELACE. We went there for the reason advanced by Senator Burton and by this association which was represented here last night by Mr. Watrous, the American Civic Association. Now, I have a picture here.

Mr. DIFENDERFER. Wait a moment.

Mr. LOVELACE. I am going to answer your question.

Mr. DIFENDERFER. Let me finish my question.

Mr. LOVELACE. Yes.

Mr. DIFENDERFER. You certainly must have felt justified in selling to the paper company a sufficient amount to run their business out of your allotment, did you not?

Mr. LOVELACE. Yes, sir; that was sold to them in the very first bid that we had for hydraulic power.

Mr. DIFENDERFER. But now you come back and want part of this 4,400 cubic feet per second after disposing of enough to run their business?

Mr. LOVELACE. Oh, that was disposed of long ago.

Mr. DIFENDERFER. It does not make any difference whether it was disposed of long ago. You had your plant built.

Mr. LOVELACE. That is exactly what it was built for. Most of the gentlemen thought that plants would all be like the paper company, and George Westinghouse said that those were the only kinds of industries that could be built there, because they could use the power on the spot. That is what the paper company is doing.

Mr. DIFENDERFER. Then, do you not think that the Government itself might as well have given it to the paper company?

Mr. LOVELACE. I do think to-day that that was the proper method; that we should have taken advantage of it. The Burton law contains a provision that no one company shall apply for a permit in excess of 8,600 cubic feet of water per second. Now, instead of making the International Paper Co. a part of ourselves we should have asked the International Paper Co. to go to the Secretary of War and make application for 8,600 cubic feet. We could have done the same thing, but it would have been selfish.

Mr. DIFENDERFER. But you made a profit out of it?

Mr. LOVELACE. Out of which? We were glad to get the International Paper Co. as a tenant. This thing had to be financed, and it could not finance itself. Local men tried to finance it not only in this country, but in Europe; but it was only men of undaunted courage and faith that did get hold of it and put it into effect. I believe that if anybody else but these particular men got hold of it it would not have been a success. Of course, the world would have come to it in time, but not as soon as they did. Now, this is why we went up the stream [referring to maps and pictures]. Do you see all those streams coming down here? That is the Falls there. That is the footbridge down here. Here is the Hydraulic Power Co. You see those mills right there in front of the Falls. Now, gentlemen, this same agitation as is now made was in the air at the time this development began.

The beginnings of the Hydraulic Power Co. started back in the fifties, and they had put up the flour mills and all kinds of mills in front of the Falls and defaced the Falls, but the men who finally took our enterprise in hand were men of broader views and they determined for the very purpose of preserving the scenic beauty of the Falls to go a mile and a half up the river and there they got the lands and obtained a river frontage and constructed their plant. Now, gentlemen, they might have gone away down in the other direction and not stopped at Niagara Falls and not got such a head, but this head is the greatest that has ever been used by any company before on a turbine wheel for power purposes, and that is why we are there now. Now, I have got some arguments on this and I want to progress. That is my first request. My second request is in respect of the limitation of transmission of power from Canada. The arguments on that subject need not be repeated, but I would ask you to remove your limits on that. Trust Canada. Why not? She has contracted with the United States to limit her diversion of water to a certain amount, and she is certainly going to make that diversion. Now, it seems to me that the comity of nations requires that we should trust her to carry out her part of the treaty, and we will carry out our part. If you are going to limit it at all, you can limit it to one-half of the limit now used over there, which is entirely, too low.   The actual figures are 500,000 horsepower, which can be produced by 32,000 cubic feet of water, possibly more if they get greater efficiency.   But they are going to produce their 500,000 from this 32,000 feet.   Now, I am going to bring out this point: Seven miles from there, there is a fourth development, not from the Niagara River but from the Welland Canal.   I understand that its maximum load there to-day is 40,000 horsepower.   I was told last night by Mr. Scovell—I am not sure that it was Mr. Scovell, but it might have been the counsel for the Ontario Power Co., Mr. Bowen—that they have contracts made by which they will sell, at peaks, at least 60,000 horsepower.

Now, that power is just as available for transmission into the United States as the other.   I do not think it will be, but it is just as available.

They have the whole head of the river there.   The water is really taken from Lake Erie and discharged into Lake Ontario.

Mr. DIFENDERFER. Do you not think it would be well for this Government to encourage the transmission of power into this country for this reason: That we would be encouraging enterprise on this side rather than on the other side?

Mr. LOVELACE. There is absolutely no doubt in my mind on that, and the only sensible way and the only polite way is to trust Canada herself to put into effect this sacred obligation on her part.

Mr. DIFENDERFER. Would there not be a possibility of collusion to prevent transmission—a gentlemen's agreement?

Mr. LOVELACE. Now, I want to answer that.   There have been various references to "interlocking trusts" and "interlocking boards," and I want to say that there is no place in the world where there is more active competition in water power than at Niagara Falls. President Taft, when he was Secretary of War, in his opinion, or rather in his order directing that permits should be issued for the transmission of power into the United States, the question having been raised by the Seneca Association, said that he had looked into the matter and had not found the slightest evidence of collusion, and that if he found any, he would take care of it.

Mr. DIFENDERFER. How about the MacKenzie-Mann people? Has there been any effort to restrain those people from bringing power into this country?

Mr. LOVELACE. No, sir; they have a permit for 37,500——

Mr. DIFENDERFER (interposing). I believe the testimony here is 40,000?

Mr. LOVELACE. No; it is 37,500.

Mr. DIFENDERFER. And they bring it to the center of the river?

Mr. LOVELACE. Now, wait a minute.   They have never constructed a plant for transmitting any part of it into the United States.   They own the Electric Light Co. in Toronto and the railways radiating out from Toronto, and they did come to the Secretary of War under the Burton Act and got a permit.

Mr. DIFENDERFER. Did they buy a gas plant at Niagara Falls?

Mr. LOVELACE. Yes, sir; and if you ask me if they have any intention of coming into the United States I will say that they have.   I will give you the facts if you will give me the time.   They have themselves transmitted no power under the Burton law.   We have a great market at Niagara Falls and at Buffalo; all of Buffalo is dependent on our company, not because there is no open competition, but because the other gentlemen are not willing—take the Niagara, Lockport & Ontario Power Co.—they could not do it now, because they have sold out, but before that they were unwilling to supply them. So Buffalo is dependent on us entirely for her power, and we have a very large market there and we have a very large market at Niagara Falls.

Under our permit for the transmission of power from Canada and for the production of power on the American side, we are unable to supply all of the demands that are made on us, and we have either got to take power from somebody at Niagara Falls, which needs it badly, or take it from Buffalo, which is dependent on us for its public utilities. In that state of affairs, not being able to get our power from Canada, where we would have ample, we have gone to the Toronto Power Co. and contracted with them to purchase 25,000 horsepower, or at least our subcompany has done it, and they are taking that power and distributing it in Buffalo, and that contract can be revoked any day. That is the fact as regards the Ontario Power Co. and the Toronto Power Co.

Mr. CLINE. Do you not think it is better to make definite the amount of power that is to be brought over, for the reason that if it is left as you say it would involve the Government to a very large extent in controversy with the people getting the power, as to whether they were getting more than they ought to have?

Mr. LOVELACE. I say "yes" to that, but I qualify it. I believe that if you are going to put any limit on it at all, that the limit should be definite, but I do not think there should be any limit. If there is to be a limit I believe that it should be 250,000 horsepower, which is nearer one-half than 200,000, and it is less than one-half if you count the power used at Kew Falls, which is near St. Catherine.

Now, gentlemen, this brings me up to what is really on my mind, the third point, which is the point in respect of efficiency, as you have called it. Now, gentlemen, nobody can quarrel with you on the basis of that requirement; on the logic of it as an academic proposition it is absolutely correct. But I want to say that, placed in this definite manner which would absolutely require, within five years, I should say, the "scrapping" of our plant and very likely the "scrapping" of the plant of the Hydraulic Co., although it is practically the efficiency between the two levels, the level above the Falls and the level immediately below the Falls, I say that that provision is fraught with great danger. It may be—I will not say that it is, but it may be—a commercial, a physical, and a legal impossibility to do that, and I will advance some of the reasons why it may be. It is a matter of course; it is not a matter of exact estimate, because you can not make an exact estimate. For instance, take our company— and even new companies would be in substantially the same condition as we are—take our company, the Niagara Falls Power Co. That distinguished lawyer, Mr. J. Boardman Scovell, who I say is a distinguished lawyer in that particular branch of the law, told me privately last night that our company did not have the power to go down there and build a plant where we would have to divert water to comply with this provision——

Mr. GARNER (interposing). What do you mean by "power"?

Mr. LOVELACE. It is not in our State charter. I am not a constitutional lawyer, but I have some of the fundamentals of constitutional law as applied in the State of New York that I am sure of.   But it is not a matter of cases whether it is right or not.

The CHAIRMAN. Why not answer his question?

Mr. GARNER. He said he did not have it in his charter.

Mr. LOVELACE. We can get the permit from the Secretary of War, but it is another question to have the power.

Mr. GARNER. Haven't you a general incorporation act of the State of New York for the purpose of furnishing power to the public?

Mr. LOVELACE. Yes, sir.

Mr. GARNER. Could not you incorporate under that law and ask for a new permit?

Mr. LOVELACE. That would be a new permit, but I am talking about the present power.

The CHAIRMAN. And he was, too.

Mr. LOVELACE. But let me show you some of the difficulties that are apparent to me.   As I say, I am not a constitutional lawyer, but it is a fundamental constitutional law upon which you will all agree with me, I think, that in the State of New York there are certain rights—I will not name the rights that have been stated before you— but there are certain rights that belong to riparian owners.   They may not have the right to divert water for power purposes, but they have at least the right to have the water flow by their shores, and no company can divert water and go around the lower riparian owner and return it below without impairing the latter's rights.   I am almost certain that we have not the power to condemn their rights because a large number of them are using it already for public purposes, for railway purposes, and could we condemn a public use, if we had the power, for our own use?   That is possibly the legal obstacle in our way.   We would also, of course, have to condemn a right of way over the source of intake and the source of discharge in addition to these riparian rights.   So there may be legal objections and there may be commercial objections which may be insurmountable, and the physical objection is the ice question.

Now, that has not been brought up here; but, gentlemen, I am sure that a canal 7 miles long in which we do not divert more than 8,600 cubic feet of water per second, and carried not at a very great pitch, would very likely so fill itself up with ice in winter as not to be a practical proposition, a practical operating proposition.   Now, the Hydraulic Power Co. found itself in that position many years ago, and until they deepened and widened their canal beyond all the powers they had from the State of New York every winter they were locked up in ice.   The ice proposition is a very serious question in that climate, and the great public utilities depending on us for their power can not stand a restriction.   The city of Syracuse to-day, in spite of all the money the Niagara, Lockport & Ontario Power Co. has spent to get its power down to Syracuse, is full of complaints of citizens about the service in that city.   To-day in the city of Buffalo we have eight independent lines depending on our plant, which can be switched together in any way, and we are just barely enabled to give them a pretty fair service.

Now we come to what I believe to be the real solution of it.   I believe that such an absolute, definite requirement is fraught with grave danger; but, as I said before, I can not quarrel with you on the logic of the requirement, and there is no doubt that by the provision which you have already put into the law, and which you will put into any law that you pass, limiting the amount of water that may be used for power purposes, you are going to compel us, who have already found the market, to do that very thing, if it is practicable, if it is feasible, if it is possible.

Now, these three requests I am urging to you. I believe, irrespective of my interest in the subject——

Mr. GARNER (interposing). You are a lawyer?

Mr. LOVELACE. Well, I was admitted to practice law, but I found it more to my advantage to settle down as an officer of this corporation and draft its contracts; but I am not——

Mr. GARNER (interposing). Then you do not care to express an opinion as to the constitutionality of this provision or as to the power of your State legislature to force you to do the same thing?

Mr. LOVELACE. No; I do not care to go into a discussion of the cases. But I have already said to this committee that, having listened with great interest to the learned arguments that have been made to you, I am still of the opinion that your subcommittee has prepared a measure which is absolutely practicable as regards its administrative features.

The Burton law has been in operation for years without the slightest friction between the Secretary of War and the companies and has been found to be a practical measure for the control of the waters of the Niagara River. The only matter of complaint that I have at all is the matter of the two limits which you have set and this exact, definite provision for efficiency. Now, as regards that question of efficiency. I do not know that I have it here, but I talked with the engineers who made the report upon which the table of efficiency is based, and those gentlemen said to me last night that they did not mean that table to be exact; that it was a mistake to insert it in that report; that it was merely a comparison by which the head of the department could see the relations of the various companies at Niagara; and that the 100 per cent was not intended as a standard of efficiency.

Mr. CLINE. In all the discussion before this committee by constitutional lawyers and other lawyers the question of the power of the Federal Government or the State government to require this efficiency has not been raised by anyone.

Mr. KENDALL. I understood Judge O'Gorman to state——

Mr. GARNER (interposing). He said the Federal Government had no power. He was only discussing the Federal Government; he did not say anything about the State power.

Mr. LOVELACE. I want to repeat that I am not a constitutional lawyer with cases to cite, but I believe I have already said that if this committee of Congress has the right to provide for the issuing of permits for the diversion of water from the Niagara River—and every gentleman who has spoken before you except, perhaps, Senator O'Gorman, certainly Gen. Carmody, did admit that right—if you have that right, then it seems to me that you can regulate the conditions under which the permits shall be given and exercised.

Mr. KENDALL. What is your objection to the substitute here—the proposed substitute? You read that, I suppose?

Mr. LOVELACE. The substitute of the Conservation Commission?

Mr. KENDALL. No, sir; of the subcommittee.

Mr. LOVELACE. I have already stated it.

Mr. KENDALL. I know, but does it substantially meet with your approval?

Mr. LOVELACE. Yes, sir; I believe it is an absolutely workable bill.

Mr. KENDALL. If your three suggestions are adopted?

Mr. LOVELACE. Yes, sir. Now, just a minute. These questions keep coming up in my mind. I would not object at all to your inserting the amendment asked for by the Conservation Commission, which is absolutely fair, if it would not encumber your bill, but I want to say that, such a lawyer as I am, I am sure that the Public Service Commission of the State of New York has the power to regulate the rates of our generating company, and they can very easily acquire the power the regulate the rates of the other companies. The Hydraulic Power Co. since the institution of the public service commission has separated itself into two separate bodies. It has one body which is producing hydraulic power and it sells to its other self that mechanical power thus produced, and its other self turns that into electrical power and distributes it. That is their condition. I take it from what Congressman Smith said that their hydraulic part, although not an electrical corporation, has refused to comply with the regulations of the public service commission and the reason why they do that is this: The public service commission law of the State of New York contains a provision that all its requirements and provisions shall apply to electrical corporations. We are purely an electrical corporation, but only one-half of the Hydraulic Co. is an electrical corporation, the other half being a hydraulic corporation. As a matter of fact, we have turned ourselves inside out, voluntarily and gladly, for the benefit of the Public Service Commission of the State of New York.

Let me say this in respect of Judge Hammond's argument before you a year ago: Judge Hammond has since that time tried the case——

The CHAIRMAN (interposing). Is that the corporation counsel of the city of Buffalo?

Mr. LOVELACE. Yes, sir. He made complaint to the public-service commission that the rates in Buffalo were unfair, and that case has been tried at great length, and there is no doubt in my mind that it will be settled before the 1st of February, when the term of the chairman of that commission expires.

The CHAIRMAN. That is merely speculation?

Mr. LOVELACE. Well, it certainly will be decided before the 1st of February, and you will find, gentlemen, that the public-service commission has duly asserted its power absolutely to regulate rates in the city of Buffalo, and you will find that Judge Hammond has not been altogether unsuccessful in that litigation.

Mr. HARRISON. You have a live Canadian company there and the Niagara Falls Power Co.?

Mr. LOVELACE. Yes, sir.

Mr. HARRISON. Which charges the higher rates, the Ontario Power Co. or the Niagara Falls Power Co.?

Mr. LOVELACE. The glut of the market in Canada and the extreme famine on this side has reduced the power rate in Canada.

Mr. HARRISON. Notwithstanding the fact that the Canadian company pays rentals to the Canadian Government?

Mr. LOVELACE. They pay very much less than we do.

Mr. HARRISON. You have more of a monopoly on this side?

Mr. LOVELACE. Oh, no; there are two competing generating companies on this side, and in addition to that two of the other companies competing on the other side bring their power into the United States, and I am asking for an enlargement of that right in order that there may be greater competition. I would be very glad to give Mr. Bowen what he wants provided you do not distrub the Niagara River.

Mr. KENDALL. Have you any objection to Mr. Bowen's proposition?

Mr. LOVELACE. Not the slightest.

Mr. CURLEY. What is the real value tax per thousand in Canada?

Mr. LOVELACE. It is very small. You understand this is practically a country district where the plants are located.

Mr. CURLEY. Is it $8 a thousand?

Mr. LOVELACE. All the taxes put together will not amount to that, but the real thing about it is that the assessments are low.

Mr. CURLEY. What is the rate in Buffalo?

Mr. LOVELACE. The aggregate of the rates is about $25 or $26.

Mr. CURLEY. Then the tax rate is about three times as great as on the Canadian side?

Mr. LOVELACE. Oh, yes. We paid in taxes on our American plant last year about $3 per horsepower and a dollar per horsepower for improvements.

Mr. CURLEY. What did you pay the Canadian Government?

Mr. LOVELESS. It runs up to 80 cents per horsepower. It is a sliding scale, beginning at a dollar for 50,000 horsepower and then 50 cents——

Mr. DIFENDERFER (interposing). That goes into the park improvement commission fund, does it not?

Mr. LOVELACE. Yes, sir; it is called by them "park rental."

Mr. CURLEY. So that, as a matter of fact, it is twice as expensive on this side as on the other side?

Mr. LOVELACE. It is very much more expensive. I thank you very much, and I hope you do not think that because I have raised my voice I have anything but an earnest interest in the subject.

Mr. KENDALL. You have a general counsel, however?

Mr. LOVELACE. I do not know that we have. I am the attorney for the company. I am, you might call it, the local attorney. I am called the attorney as well as the secretary. Now, I am not going to hide anything. Our board of directors is one of the most distinguished boards in the United States and it contains three lawyers; two of them, at least—and I do not want to slight the third—are considered among the most eminent lawyers of our State, if not of the country, and they have never considered themselves as attorneys, never charged a dollar for their services. One of them is the father of the company, one of the men most responsible for what the world has learned of power development.

Mr. KENDALL. This bill may require your company to transfer its plant.

Mr. LOVELACE. In its present form.

Mr. KENDALL. Now, there may be legal difficulties in the way of doing that; that is, that your New York charter may not be compre hensive enough to permit it?

Mr. LOVELACE. That may be one of the smaller difficulties.

Mr. KENDALL. I want to know what your legal department thought about that proposition, whether you could jump your plant, start below, and get increased head.

Mr. LOVELACE. There is no doubt that under the constitutional law of the State of New York we have not the power of eminent domain sufficient to condemn other public uses. For instance, there is this Gorge Railroad which was before you last night. We would be obliged to condemn their rights and also the rights of the Hydraulic Power Co., their riparian rights, in order to get by them.

Mr. CURLEY. I believe Mr. Scovell or somebody else raised the contention last night that this committee had no power to compel you to take power from below the Falls and that the only body that had the power was the public utilities commission or the public service commission.

Mr. LOVELACE. Oh, no; that is the joint high commission.

The CHAIRMAN. The treaty gives the jurisdiction over that to the joint high commission.

Mr. LOVELACE. I really think that is right. Of course, you have the treaty before you.

The CHAIRMAN. Now, gentlemen, that ends the hearings on the bill.

77396—13——8

DIVERSION OF WATER FROM THE NIAGARA RIVER

HEARINGS

BEFORE THE

COMMITTEE ON FOREIGN AFFAIRS

HOUSE OF REPRESENTATIVES

JANUARY 24,
FEBRUARY 15 AND 17, 1913

ON

BILL PROPOSED BY THE SUBCOMMITTEE
ON NIAGARA FALLS LEGISLATION,
DATED, JANUARY 15, 1913

STATEMENTS OF

THE SECRETARY OF WAR

AND

MR. FREDERICK L. LOVELACE (Revised)

WASHINGTON
GOVERNMENT PRINTING OFFICE
1913

COMMITTEE ON FOREIGN AFFAIRS.

House of Representatives.

[Committee room, gallery floor, west corridor. Telephone 230. Meets on call.]

HENRY D. FLOOD, Virginia, *Chairman*.

JOHN N. GARNER, Texas.
GEORGE S. LEGARE, South Carolina.
WILLIAM G. SHARP, Ohio.
CYRUS CLINE, Indiana.
JEFFERSON M. LEVY, New York.
JAMES M. CURLEY, Massachusetts.
J. CHAS. LINTHICUM, Maryland.
ROBERT E. DIFENDERFER, Pennsylvania.
WILLIAM S. GOODWIN, Arkansas.
CHARLES M. STEDMAN, North Carolina.

EDWARD W. TOWNSEND, New Jersey.
BYRON P. HARRISON, Mississippi.
WILLIAM B. McKINLEY, Illinois.
HENRY A. COOPER, Wisconsin.
IRA W. WOOD, New Jersey.
RICHARD BARTHOLDT, Missouri.
GEORGE W. FAIRCHILD, New York.
N. E. KENDALL, Iowa.
J. HAMPTON MOORE, Pennsylvania.

B. F. ODEN, *Clerk*.

II

DIVERSION OF WATER FROM THE NIAGARA RIVER.

House of Representatives,
Committee on Foreign Affairs,
Saturday, February 15, 1913.

The committee met at 10.30 o'clock a. m., Hon. Henry D. Flood (chairman) presiding.

The Chairman. This meeting was called to hear the Secretary of War in reference to the Niagara Falls bill which we have already reported. We are sorry we did not have the Secretary with us before the bill was reported, but we will be glad to hear him and consider any changes he may suggest to the bill.

STATEMENT OF HON. HENRY L. STIMSON, SECRETARY OF WAR.

Mr. Stimson. I have brought Col. Kernan with me, who was on this committee that I spoke to you about.

The Chairman. We are glad to see you, Col. Kernan. Mr. Stimson, you may proceed.

Secretary Stimson. Mr. Chairman, my function in coming here to-day is reduced, since the report of your bill, to the very pleasant one of expressing my hearty sense of appreciation of the position which the committee took there in regard to the control by the Federal Government of that property. When I wrote to you the other day expressing the suggestion that possibly there might be some facts which had developed in the experience of the War Department in the administration of the old Burton law which you might want to have, I wrote before your report had been made and before I had seen the bill. But since this came out it has reduced very materially what I had to say, and I will not take very long.

The experience which the department has had has particularly emphasized, to my mind, the importance of treating this great waterway which runs through the Lakes as a single system; and has emphasized very strongly the effect which diversions of water at any one part of the system may have upon any other part of the system. For instance, I have just had to decide the question of the effect of diversion at Chicago, Ill.—the effect of additional diversion there upon the entire system of the lakes and rivers below that—and the evidence which that hearing brought out as to the effect which might be produced as far down as Montreal by the taking of water from Lake Michigan was very striking and very strong and emphasized two things—first, that what might seem to be a very slight matter in one part of this great waterway system might very seriously affect a more distant part; and, secondly, it brought out the fact that the only branch of our Government which was qualified to treat that whole system impartially and as a whole was the entire Federal Govern-

115

ment. At the hearings, for instance, of the Chicago case before me, there were six or seven States in opposition. If the position taken by the State of Illinois was correct, the positions taken by the States of Wisconsin, Michigan, Ohio, and New York were absolutely wrong, and it brought out very clearly the fact that State control could not be trusted to deal fully and absolutely impartially with the situation where the interests of the different communities were so different and diversified.

Mr. GARNER. May I interrupt you there?

Secretary STIMSON. You may, sir, at any time you wish.

Mr. GARNER. I do not know that it has ever been contended by anyone that the Federal Government should not control as to the amount of water to be taken from a lake or other navigable stream, but the question here is that after you determine the amount of water to be taken and the effect it will have on navigation, then who is to control the water after it is taken?

Secretary STIMSON. I was going to take that feature up, if you will allow me, right there.

Mr. SHARP. Isn't the position you have just announced here—hasn't that been the position taken by the United States Corps of Engineers in reference to rivers and harbors—that all of the improvements must be by the Central Government; that the Central Government shall not allow the State or local interests to undertake to make improvements?

Secretary STIMSON. Let me say, Mr. Sharp, that the evidence before me showed that the United States Government had spent between ninety and a hundred million dollars on the improvement of harbors on the different lakes, all of which would be affected by any diversion of water at Chicago. It also showed that a change in the draft of the vessels which used that waterway, by even so slight a degree as an inch in draft, would have a total effect on the year's tonnage in transportation capacity of very tremendous amounts, very surprising amounts, so that it would be emphasized to the mind of anyone who studied it that any injury to this great waterway would mean injuries amounting to millions of dollars.

Mr. KENDALL. Have you recently had a hearing in the Chicago case?

Secretary STIMSON. The one I was speaking of was a hearing about one year ago.

Mr. KENDALL. That hearing was upon the application of Illinois for the diversion of more water from Lake Michigan into the sanitary canal, and it was resisted by interests in other States?

Secretary STIMSON. Yes, sir; by interests from other States.

Mr. KENDALL. So that the interests of Illinois came into direct conflict with the interests of Wisconsin, Ohio, and New York?

Secretary STIMSON. Precisely. Now, the proposition, of course, here in regard to the Niagara River is a somewhat different one, but it is one over which, as your report points out, the United States Government has taken jurisdiction in a treaty with Canada, so that there is the additional ground that not only do the diversions or the changes in levels affect different communities of our own country, but they affect the interests of a foreign country with which the Central Government has assumed treaty relations. Of course, that 's brought out so clearly by this report that it is unnecessary to revert to it, except that I want to call your attention to the fact that that treaty affects in certain ways the entire waterway, not only above the Falls but below them.

As I read the treaty, there are several sections, notably section 8, wherein the United States Government has assumed certain obligations toward Canada in respect to all boundary waters, and having done that, the Federal Government necessarily must put itself and keep itself in a position where it can make good those obligations. And that would apply, so far as the treaty is concerned, to the entire length of the Niagara River. Now, Mr. Garner was asking me a moment ago as to the further questions. Of course the first question is the amount of the diversion. The experience of the War Department has shown this—that the question of measuring the amounts taken out and the amounts of their production into electricity is a thing which requires the utmost scientific care, and it is not yet thoroughly settled as to what is the best scientific method. What I mean is, that it is not a question of merely reading a gauge; it is not a question of looking at it with your eye and telling methodically what has gone, but it is a very complex problem, and therefore I should say that the second step was perfectly clear, that the amount of diversion is of such a character that it makes it absolutely necessary that the same power which has to measure and decide what will affect the Lakes should have the right of inspection, thorough and careful, and absolute control down as far as the machinery by which that power is turned into electricity.

Mr. FAIRCHILD. And no further, Mr. Secretary?

Secretary STIMSON. I will take you one step at a time. Of course it is a border-line question of how far it should go.

The CHAIRMAN. That involves the question of which authority should designate the parties to whom the use of the water should go.

Secretary STIMSON. My own view is that that necessarily follows as an incident. It is so tied up with the efficiency of reproduction into electricity that it is difficult to divorce it. That brings me into the next question, which is the efficiency of transformation. That is brought out very carefully in your bill and your report, Mr. Cline, and as to that it seemed to me that our experience very strongly corroborated the position you take there. The first question that comes up, the first practical question, is whether you are going to enlarge the amount of water which the Burton law allowed, up to the amount which the treaty allowed. Now, in my mind a decision of that question turns upon and is tied up with the question of the efficiency of production.

Mr. SHARP. You mean on the American side?

Secretary STIMSON. I am speaking of diversions now, not importations. I am speaking of the American side. In other words, speaking in general language, this seems to be the situation: We have got at Niagara the biggest power-producing natural phenomenon in the country. It is perfectly clear and manifest that the object of all lawmaking should be to give the public in every way the most effective results. That is the position which I understand is taken in the report of the committee.

Mr. CLINE. Yes.

Secretary STIMSON. Now, that is the practical question which underlies, it seems to me, the whole thing here. In the first place, we are up against the question of constantly increasing demand for power, and at the same time the question of preserving the beauty of the Falls comes into conflict with that all the time. The report of my engineers, which I have just sent out, indicated that if the power which we take now were used in the most effective manner it would produce very nearly double the amount of horsepower now produced there.

It is estimated by the Corps of Engineers that the water now authorized to be diverted for power purposes produces at present about 229,000 horsepower—no; that it can produce under the existing fall about 229,000 horsepower. It is also estimated that the same quantity of water, if carried through a canal extending from a point above Niagara Falls to Lewiston, would generate at the latter point about 412,000 horsepower, an amount which would, among other things, postpone for a time pressure to take more water from the Falls. That represents the extreme of the problem. In between that there are the constant intermediary positions that you have struck in your investigations as between the different companies, some obtaining better results than others. Now, it seems to me that that question of efficiency is so tied up with the question of diversion that the Government has got to determine the amount of water to be diverted and its effect upon navigation, and it has also got to determine the way in which that is to be transformed into electricity; otherwise you will have a conflict of authority and a conflict of interests which will result in its not being used to its most effective capacity.

Mr. COOPER. There is a point right there. I understood you to say that the amount possible to be generated by the plants as they are now is about 229,000 horsepower.

Secretary STIMSON. That is the statement I have here. It is estimated that the total amount of power which can be generated by existing water-power plants on the American side at Niagara Falls and with the quantity of water now authorized to be diverted for power purposes on that side is about 229,000 horsepower.

Mr. COOPER. And with the other plant, what is the estimate?

Secretary STIMSON. They estimated about 412,000 horsepower if the same quantity of water was carried through a canal from a point above Niagara Falls to Lewiston.

Mr. COOPER. Now, what horsepower do they actually produce? That is an important item, and I think it ought to be put in right there. I want to have the three figures right together in the record.

The CHAIRMAN. They produce less than that now.

Secretary STIMSON. On January 1, 1913, the approximate power developed by the Niagara Falls Power Co. was 88,000 horsepower and by the Hydraulic Power Co. 105,000 horsepower, making a total of 193,000, as against 229,000 horsepower that could be developed from the amount of water now authorized to be diverted.

The CHAIRMAN. Then there is 500 cubic feet of water reserved for the canal?

Secretary STIMSON. Yes.

Mr. LINTHICUM. I would like to ask whether or not there has been any computation as to what would be the removal cost in order to get this increased horsepower?

Secretary STIMSON. There has not been a very accurate estimate, although I can give you some figures that I have here. One of the suggestions I was going to make, Mr. Chairman, if you care to have suggestions in regard to possible amendments to the bill, would be this: That this subject of possible maximum production is so important, and the data on it is so imperfect now, that I would suggest a survey be made and an estimate made through a board of engineers of the cost of making the change that they suggest of carrying the water through a canal down to Lewiston, where it would have a fall of something like 300 feet.

Mr. GARNER. Haven't you that power under this bill now?

Secretary STIMSON. I may have the power, but I haven't the money.

Mr. GARNER. I want to ask you a general question there. There are three lines of thought developed in this committee and, so far as I know, by different Members of the House. One of them, as you doubtless have noticed, was by Senator O'Gorman, that the limit of the authority of Congress should be to determine from the standpoint of navigation how much water should be taken out of this stream, and then it should be left to other legislative bodies to determine who should take it. There is another line of thought suggested by you this morning, that we should not only determine the amount of water to be taken from a navigation standpoint, but you should be given further power to determine who should take it, and the character of the plants to be used, which means efficiency. There is another and quite a large element among the membership of the House which believes that having that authority the Government should still go further and make conditions as to the cost to the consumer. Now, could you give us your idea as to the power of Congress to follow this up and determine the cost to the consumer?

Secretary STIMSON. I want to preface this by saying that this is a border-line question, and I speak with great modesty there.

Mr. GARNER. You are speaking now as a Cabinet officer rather than a citizen of New York, as I understand it.

Mr. SHARP. It makes quite a difference, doesn't it, Mr. Secretary?

Secretary STIMSON. I have found it so.

Mr. FAIRCHILD. You do not assume that the Secretary would not be absolutely loyal to the State of New York, do you?

Mr. GARNER. I assume that he is absolutely true to his administration first.

Secretary STIMSON. My own view of that last question, the question of the price paid by the consumer, is that it is, particularly in a State like New York, where there is an active public-service commission, a matter for the regulation primarily of the local authorities, and to speak in short language, I should say that the efficiency of the performance of the Federal function of regulating the navigation of the Lakes required that the Federal authorities should supervise the process of transformation into electricity down to the point where it went out for distribution—that is, where the electricity went out for distribution. That is to say, the Federal officers shall be given authority to say, first, how much water shall be diverted, by whom it shall be diverted, and how those diverters shall transform it into electricity, all with a view to its most economical and efficient use in the interest of minimizing such diversion of water. Thereafter the distribution of that electric current so produced, the prices paid for it by the local consumers, and the regulation of the service to them—that is, for example, who should have preference, municipal users, private users, or manufacturers. I should say that was a matter primarily for the State to regulate and control.

The CHAIRMAN. That is the bill.

Secretary STIMSON. As I read it that is the substantial position taken by your bill.

Mr. HARRISON. You believe that the Secretary of War should designate the parties who should utilize the power and not the State authorities?

Secretary STIMSON. The parties who should utilize the water.

Mr. HARRISON. Who should divert it?

Secretary STIMSON. Yes. The question of utilizing the water and utilizing the electricity afterwards made from the water are two quite different things.

Mr. LINTHICUM. In answer to my question a few moments ago, I understood the Secretary to say that he had some figures upon the cost of removal of these plants.

Secretary STIMSON. I would be very glad to give you what I have, but I think it is a summary of evidence taken before this committee.

Mr. LINTHICUM. I think it would be well to get it into the hearing at this point anyhow.

Mr. KENDALL. That means for the reconstruction of the plants?

Mr. LINTHICUM. Yes: the approximate figures for reconstruction.

Secretary STIMSON. I have here in memorandum form from the engineers one estimate for $60 per horsepower and the other from $95 to $100 per horsepower to make this transfer.

Mr. LINTHICUM. That is the entire horsepower you would obtain, not for the excess?

Secretary STIMSON. No: that is for the 412,000 horsepower.

Mr. COOPER. What would that cost in dollars?

Secretary STIMSON. The statement I have here I would like to make subject to correction. The statement has been made that the initial cost of installation at Lewiston would be about $60 per horsepower, which would make the cost of such an installation, including canal for 412,000 horsepower, amount to $24,720,000. That is for the plant entirely. That is the memorandum submitted by the engineers; but Gen. Greene has stated that the actual cost of installing a power plant at Niagara Falls is about $95 to $100 per horsepower, and that latter price would make the cost of such an installation, including canal for 412,000 horsepower, amount to $41,200,000. There is such a wide divergence there that I would like to have further information on it before determining the cost.

Mr. SHARP. Mr. Green says there that that is what would be the cost of changing their existing plants to new plants?

Secretary STIMSON. No: the words are, "Actual cost of installing a power plant at Niagara Falls."

Mr. FAIRCHILD. That would entirely eliminate the present investments there.

The CHAIRMAN. I notice the estimates you have made are based entirely upon the horsepower produced.

Secretary STIMSON. That was merely the way of expressing the cost of the undertaking by calculating the cost per horsepower which it finally produces.

Mr. GARNER. You utilize in there the water the Government permits to be taken, the horsepower that would produce, and then divide that by the total cost of the canal to get the price per horsepower.

Mr. KENDALL. The difference between the cost of constructing a canal for 20,000 cubic feet under the treaty, and 15,600 cubic feet provided by the Burton law would be negligible, wouldn't it?

Secretary STIMSON. There would not be much difference.

Mr. KENDALL. That was the chairman's idea, I think.

Mr. GARNER. I do not know whether you care to give an opinion as a lawyer, but you did not say in your reply to my question whether you thought the Federal Government had the power to regulate the cost to the consumer.

Secretary STIMSON. That is on such a debated ground, and it is on a ground in which there are so few decisions to guide us so far that I hardly like to say.

Mr. COOPER. And it is something that is not involved there.

Mr. GARNER. It may become involved, because there is a large sentiment in the House of Representatives at this time to regulate the price to the consumer where the Federal Government undertakes control. The debate in the House on various subjects has shown that very conclusively, that there is a line of thought in the House that where the Federal Government undertakes to control power generated under its jurisdiction, that it will also have something to say about the price to the consumer.

Secretary STIMSON. Mr. Garner, that is a question to which I have given a great deal of thought and care, and I only want to call this to your attention. The situation here is a very different one from the situation where the water power is produced as an incident or a by-product to a navigation work, created either by the Federal Government itself, built with its money and by its engineers in a lock and dam of its own, or where such a dam is built according to plans of the Federal Government for the purpose of promoting navigation, even if the Federal Government choose to use some private agent for the purpose of further improving navigability. The situation you have in either of those dam cases is really a water power which is created by a work in the interest of navigation. It is really a by-product of navigation, and I should say it is more closely allied to navigation than the situation you have here at Niagara. In the case of water power created by such dams I believe that the electricity— as has been held by the Supreme Court in the Kaukauna case (172 U. S., 58)—being electricity produced as a by-product of such a navigable work by the United States is wholly within its disposition and can be sold by the United States to consumers. Notwithstanding even there, as well as in this case, my own view as a matter of policy would be to leave the question of price to the consumer to the State, so long as the States are adequately exercising their function.

Mr. GARNER. We have agreed on that; but there is one other case in the United States that is very similar to this, and that is along the Rio Grande River.

Secretary STIMSON. I have read that very carefully. 174 United States, and there the United States Supreme Court held that a corporation would not be allowed to divert water upon the Rio Grande River, even for such high purposes as municipal purposes, if it interfered with navigation lower down the river.

Mr. CLINE. I would like to ask a question, if I might be permitted. I would like to ask if it is not a fact that the Federal Government never has sought to intervene to fix the rates of a product produced by a local corporation doing business strictly within the State that incorporated it?

Secretary STIMSON. I think not, with this possible exception—of course where the United States is a proprietor and owns the land on which the water power is produced, there you have a totally different question. The United States there is acting not in a governmental capacity, it is acting in a proprietary capacity. It owns the whole thing and it can put what conditions on it it chooses. It is not a question there of limitation of Federal power, but a question of the rights of an owner.

Mr. TOWNSEND. As, for instance, if they would create electricity by using the Falls for some other purpose.

Secretary STIMSON. Yes.

Mr. CLINE. In the case under consideration in the Senate now the Federal Government does not attempt to go any further than to say what shall be done with the power it produces.

Secretary STIMSON. Precisely. In that case now pending in the Senate the power produced there is power produced by navigation work—work built for the purpose, so far as the Government is concerned, of making navigable the Enfield Rapids in the Connecticut River, so that ships can go around part of the river now nonnavigable. There the proposition is that the corporation in question has agreed to pay over to the United States part of its profits, provided it is allowed to build the dam in question for the development of its water power. It is a wholly different question, and, as you say, Mr. Cline, there is no attempt to regulate the price to the consumer, and the whole arrangement is made in such a way that even the rates paid to the Government are merely a certain percentage of the profits, and if the public-service commission chooses to do so—the Connecticut Public Service Commission—it can regulate the rate there so that the Government will not get anything.

Mr. GARNER. There is a practical feature of this situation, and that is that very likely there will be no legislation upon this subject at this session of Congress, judging from the condition of affairs in the House and Senate.

Secretary STIMSON. Might I suggest right there, if this bill is not going through it is a very vital matter that a joint resolution be adopted to continue the present Burton Act.

Mr. GARNER. That is what I was going to ask you. Have you examined the law in connection with the treaty to see how effective your department could control this situation, without any law whatever, under the common law and under the treaty?

Secretary STIMSON. I know it is the opinion of the Chief of Engineers that we could not control it effectively, and I wrote a letter to the Congress when the act expired before, in the summer of 1911, pointing out that fact and inclosing a letter from the Chief of Engineers to that effect, and I should like to refer you to that, inasmuch as the situation exists now.

Mr. SHARP. I would like to anticipate what you may be coming to. You may not have anything of that kind in mind, but we have been hearing from time to time arguments on diversion above the falls of a sanitary canal and a power canal to be operated through the city of Buffalo, and so on, and now we have the statement that erosion caused by the waters going over the Falls is so great that unless preventive measures are taken soon by the Government it will make a V-shape there and destroy the beauty of the Falls. It has been stated to me and other members of the committee that that could be very much prevented, and I wondered if you could give us any information about that.

Secretary STIMSON. I have not given any careful thought to it, Mr. Sharp, so that I would rather not state. I have seen the statement made that it could be prevented to a large extent by a wier built across there.

Mr. SHARP. One thing I am interested in particularly is to prevent that erosion, if it can be done. I do not care anything about the other projects, but if we can by any means, at reasonable expense, stop that erosion I think we ought to do it.

The CHAIRMAN. I would suggest to the gentlemen of the committee that if the Secretary is going to finish his statement we will have to allow him to proceed.

Secretary STIMSON. My time is very limited, as I have to meet the President at 11.45 o'clock.

Mr. SMITH of New York. I would like to ask you, Mr. Secretary, if you are willing to say how far the Federal Government should go in controlling the situation—whether it should control the distribution of power or whether the State of New York should control that?

The CHAIRMAN. That has been all gone over, Mr. Smith.

Mr. HARRISON. I want to speak about section 3 of the bill, where it says:

In granting permits for the diversion of water from the Niagara River above the Falls of Niagara, as authorized by this act, the Secretary of War shall have due regard for investments already made in the construction of power plants under the grants of authority issued by the State of New York and the Secretary of War.

I want to ask you what is your opinion of what is meant by "due regard for investments already made"?

Secretary STIMSON. Well, I was going to ask you that.

Mr. HARRISON. I might say that I am opposed to that section in the bill, and that is why I asked you.

The CHAIRMAN. That is asking a judge of a court to construe a law before it is presented to the court.

Mr. CLINE. I want to call to the attention of the Secretary that that is the very statement as used in the treaty.

Secretary STIMSON. But in the treaty it is a statement of the intention of the two contracting parties.

Mr. CLINE. Yes; I understand that.

Secretary STIMSON. In this it is a direction to a ministerial officer. When you call upon a ministerial officer to have due regard for investments already made, you do not fix any standards by which he is to measure that due regard.

Mr. HARRISON. Do you think it ought to be in there?

Secretary STIMSON. Unless you mean it as a general statement of advice I do not see that it means much else.

The CHAIRMAN. That is about all it does mean. It was meant to convey the idea to the Secretary of War that Congress thought existing investments ought to have a preference.

Secretary STIMSON. If you meant it as a suggestion to the Secretary of War that he is not to run amuck, that is about all I can see that it means.

The CHAIRMAN. That is about all.

Mr. GARNER. He would necessarily keep that question in view in construing the treaty, without any direction in this bill?

Secretary STIMSON. Yes.

The CHAIRMAN. If we want to hear the Secretary on this subject we will have to let him proceed.

Secretary STIMSON. I wanted especially to call your attention to several things in regard to importation of current. while I am right on this matter. In the first place, as to this amount of diversion. raising it up to the amount of the treaty. I wanted simply to add to what I have already said that it seems to me the position taken by the bill was a wise one in the interest of withholding any further diversion until the United States is in a position to see that it is most effectively used: that is, that the greatest efficiency possible is derived from it. I think the difficulty is that if that extra diversion were granted now it would not be as effectively used as it would be after a careful study was made of the whole situation in the way I have suggested.

Mr. SMITH of New York. You do not oppose it on the ground that it would injure the Falls?

Secretary STIMSON. The statement of the engineers is that the Falls have been injured already. and that any further diversion would continue to injure them.

Mr. CURLEY. Do I understand you to say that this applies to the amount allowed to be diverted under the treaty. the amount of importation?

Secretary STIMSON. I am talking now about further diversion. I think that is the thing you should consider, and further you now in your present bill propose to restrict your provisions as to diversions to water above the Falls of Niagara. I think it may be a very serious problem if that same regulation does not apply all the way down.

The CHAIRMAN. You know the control of the water below the Falls is vested in the joint high commission. and that is the reason we put that provision in.

Secretary STIMSON. As I understand it, the United States agreed that certain diversions would not be done without a report of the joint high commission. I thought legislation on that point, at least, whether necessary or not, would not be inadvisable. It just struck me in reading it that it might be less in the air.

The CHAIRMAN. The treaty vests it apparently exclusively in the joint high commission, and we thought we would be legislating against the provision of the treaty to vest power over this water in another tribunal.

Secretary STIMSON. I may be wrong in that, but I thought the language in the treaty was not sufficiently in detail and that further supplementary legislation was necessary.

Mr. SMITH of New York. Wouldn't it be wise to leave it in the control of the joint high commission as it is in the treaty?

Secretary STIMSON. You have got to, under the treaty.

The CHAIRMAN. We will look into it again, but that was our view at the time that the law was drafted.

(See letter of the Secretary of War dated Feb. 20, 1913, on this subject printed at p. 152.)

Secretary STIMSON. In the second place, I notice in the bill you have provided for 30 days' notice to the party holding a permit for diversion, and to Congress, before revoking such permit. That is in the second section, but you make no provision as to what would happen in case Congress was not in session. The effectiveness of the notice might be entirely offset by that.

The CHAIRMAN. The notices to the parties which are to be transmitted to Congress?

Secretary STIMSON. The bill says that he shall revoke any permits granted after giving 30 days' notice to the party and to Congress of his intention.

Mr. KENDALL. Suppose Congress adjourned on the 1st of May, and this notice was given on the 5th of May, then the permit would run until Congress met again in December.

Mr. CLINE. That is simply a matter of changing the conjunction "and" to "or." Make it read, "to the party holding the same or to Congress."

Secretary STIMSON. Now, I thought I would also call your attention to this point, that the five-year provision for the revocation and reconstruction of plants is so long that it would necessarily carry the matter over to another administration, and that always makes for ineffectiveness.

The CHAIRMAN. We were told that they could not reconstruct these plants in less than five years.

Secretary STIMSON. That may be so, but I should provide for some intermediate step to start the thing in operation. You might give them five years before it is completed, but if all you can do is to give them notice that five years from now you are to have them reconstructed, my experience is that at the end of five years they will not be reconstructed, and they will be counting on a new Secretary to let them out.

Mr. KENDALL. Can you come back here again, Mr. Secretary?

Secretary STIMSON. Yes.

Mr. KENDALL. I think it would be the sense of the committee that we ought to have these hearings when there is no restriction as to time. This has been a very valuable hearing this morning.

Secretary STIMSON. I still have 20 minutes.

Mr. KENDALL. But we haven't but 5.

Mr. COOPER. I would like to have Col. Kernan come back also.

The CHAIRMAN. What time can you come back Monday morning, Mr. Secretary?

Secretary STIMSON. Monday morning at the same time will suit me.

The CHAIRMAN. At 10.30 Monday morning. Col. Kernan, will you be here also?

Col. KERNAN. Yes, sir.

The CHAIRMAN. Very well, we will adjourn, then, until 10.30 Monday morning next.

HOUSE OF REPRESENTATIVES,
COMMITTEE ON FOREIGN AFFAIRS.
Monday, February 17, 1913.

STATEMENTS OF HON. HENRY L. STIMSON, SECRETARY OF WAR, AND LIEUT. COL. FRANCIS J. KERNAN, UNITED STATES ARMY.

Secretary STIMSON. Mr. Chairman, I do not think I have very much more to say, but I wanted to say something about the question of the importation of power. On Saturday I confined what I had to say to the question of the diversion of the water. The question of the importation of current from Canada is, of course, wholly a different question, both as to the constitutional power to deal with it on the part of the Federal Government and as to the economic questions involved. Of course, the power of the Government to deal with the importation of any current is absolute and complete. There is no question of doubt about it. The Government can impose any conditions in any way it chooses and has sole jurisdiction.

My study of the question has indicated there are two questions of policy involved. The first is whether there should be any limitation in the amount of current imported, and the second whether there should be any supervision over what is allowed to be imported. Those are two different questions.

As to the first, after a good deal of hesitation and a good deal of study I have come to the conclusion—and it was upon the unanimous report of the committee of engineers whom I had investigate it—that there are no substantial reasons subserved by putting any limitation on the importation of current.

The CHAIRMAN. You understand, Mr. Secretary, the limitation we imposed was all we thought could possibly be brought in under the laws and regulations of Canada. If they divert 36.000 cubic feet of the water and make all the power they can from it, they can only export half of it to this country, and 250,000 horsepower we thought would certainly cover that half, and consequently there is practically no limitation.

Mr. SMITH. They could bring over more than that until Canada wanted it.

The CHAIRMAN. But at the same time we are informed that Canada will want it very soon.

Mr. SMITH. Yes; that is true.

Secretary STIMSON. The investigation which has been made by the engineers indicates that Canada, if we do not take it, will use the entire amount that the treaty permits in a very brief time, so that whatever effect any restrictions on importations would have would not protect the Falls for more than a very brief period, and it would result in giving to Canada, very possibly, a large number of industries which otherwise would be established on this side of the Falls.

The CHAIRMAN. The committee agrees with you, and we put that limitation of 250,000 horsepower——

Mr. DIFENDEFER (interposing). As the maximum.

The CHAIRMAN (continuing). As the maximum that could possibly be brought in, and there is practically no limitation, but it satisfies some conservationists better than taking off the limitation entirely.

Mr. SHARP. May I ask you, Mr. Secretary, whether you are familiar with the way in which these power rights are granted by the Canadian Government? I ask that because during the hearing this fact was brought out, I think by some Canadian gentlemen here, when he was asked what restriction would be placed by the Canadian Government upon the use of their own power, he said in all probability such a limitation would be incorporated in the grant that as soon as their own people wanted to use that power, or perhaps not as soon, but within a certain period of years, then they would have the right to take the power back that they did grant for importation purposes here when it would be required by the needs of their own manufacturers.

Secretary STIMSON. I have heard that statement made, and of course it does involve a certain amount of peril from the fact that reliance may be placed upon the importation of current by concerns here who would be embarrassed when it was withdrawn; but, on the other hand, I do not see that it is a very good argument to refuse to allow a man to get for one year a benefit just because he can not have it for five years.

Mr. SHARP. Certainly; that is no argument.

The CHAIRMAN. And the risk is the risk of the investor.

Secretary STIMSON. Yes; he takes that risk with his eyes open, and so far as I can see the benefit outweighs the danger.

When I come to the second question, the question of the supervision of importations, I think there is a very real need of supervision, the object being to see that such current as is imported goes to the most useful channels for benefiting the public. In other words, I can give you a concrete example of what has come within my own experience. The old Burton law provided that after the importation, I think, of 160,000 horsepower was permitted, in the discretion of the Secretary of War a certain amount more could be imported. Apparently no application for that was made until about a year ago, when an application was made for the importation of power at Detroit by a concern there. That caused me to look up the entire subject matter, and I found there was apparently a possibility of importing more current, and there might be demand for it in places where the wastage of transportation of the current would not be quite as great as at Detroit, and where the uses might be more public uses, and various other things of that sort. At any rate, the investigation resulted in my directing the Chief of Engineers to advertise throughout the country in the neighborhood of the Falls, as far as Detroit on one side and as far east on the other side as Syracuse to find out what demand there would be for that power before we granted this single, casual application in Detroit, and that resulted in a very careful report made to me by Col. Sanford upon the result of those advertisements. I have the report here and can file it with the committee if you desire to see it, and also file my own order directing the investigation.

In other words, it seems to me if we are going to import a limited commodity, such as Canadian electricity certainly is, we ought to see at least that public users get the first whack at it.

Mr. GARNER. Will you permit an interruption there?

Secretary STIMSON. May I just finish this statement?

Mr. GARNER. Yes.

Secretary STIMSON. I was simply going to suggest that you add to your bill where you say that permits for importations shall be granted by the Secretary of War some such provision as this:

> In granting such permits the Secretary of War is to give preference, so far as possible, first, to applications of municipalities or to applicants contemplating the distribution of power to municipalities; second, to those contemplating distribution for the use of public utilities; and, third, to those contemplating distribution to small consumers.

In other words, I think there is a distinct duty upon the Government where there is a limited amount of cheap power available to get, if possible, into the hands of public users rather than private users.

Mr. COOPER. Is not that the only way to prevent an absolute monopolization of the electric power of the United States?

Secretary STIMSON. It is one of the ways.

Mr. COOPER. It is the way.

Mr. GARNER. Now, Mr. Secretary, I want to follow that up and see whether or not it is going to be effective. You grant a permit to some concern or municipality or corporation, after you conclude at the time they are going to use it for the greatest good to the greatest number, if you want to put it in that language. A little later on somebody else buys out that corporation or somebody else gets in possession of the municipality and directs it in a different channel from what it was at the time you admitted the current or gave the permit. Now, is there any way you can change that? In other words, how far are you going in the direction of directing what shall be done with the power after it comes into this country? That is the question I am interested in.

Secretary STIMSON. I think the result of any investigation, Mr. Garner, will show in such a case, where the amount of power is so limited, there are always a great many people who want it; some of them will be public users, some of them will be cities, some of them will be public utilities, and others will be private concerns or private manufacturers. My suggestion is, where there is a great demand—much greater than the supply—there should be a standard set, under which the Secretary should use his discretion in giving it to the public users rather than to the private users first.

Mr. GARNER. First; but after you have done that——

Secretary STIMSON (interposing). Oh, if there are not enough public users who want it, then by all means give it to the others.

Mr. GARNER. What I am trying to ascertain is what power you would have to revoke such a permit or transfer it to somebody else who would use it for a public purpose?

Secretary STIMSON. You would have at least all the powers this bill proposes to give in the case of diversions of water.

Mr. KENDALL. That is true. That could be reserved in the permit.

Secretary STIMSON. It is much easier to control the use of these importations, because our authority is greater.

Mr. GARNER. The reason I ask that is. as you will doubtless recall if you have had occasion to look at the hearings, the people who now own these power plants at Niagara Falls claim certain rights existing there that can not be taken from them by act of Congress or otherwise.

The CHAIRMAN. Not the people on the other side of the river.

Mr. GARNER. No; I am speaking of those on this side of the river. Of course that is a legal question.

Secretary STIMSON. Mr. Garner. so far as the importation of commodities into this country is concerned. like the importation of human beings into this country, the power of Congress is absolute and unrestrained.

Mr. HARRISON. Why would you not make those conditions apply to the power generated on the American side?

Secretary STIMSON. I should if it were an open question.

Mr. HARRISON. But you could not in view of section 3 with respect to " due regard for investments already made in the construction of power plants."

Secretary STIMSON. I will be very glad to answer that question in full. if you desire it. The question of diversion, as I understand, presents quite a different question, because this committee and this bill do not propose to authorize any increase in the amount of diversion, and the amount which is now being diverted is following the distribution that was made some six years ago, when the Burton Act was first passed and when Congress authorized it to be diverted primarily among the then users of the water.

Now, I understand the situation to be as to that simply this: When the question of using Niagara power was first begun, a good many years ago. there was a great deal of money spent and a great deal of money lost by the original applicants for the power. I am told—and, of course, I am speaking from hearsay entirely—that the original companies which went in there spent a great deal of money in developing the method of transporting electricity, and that it was through their efforts more than through any other experiments that have been conducted that the development and control of electricity was made as practicable as it is now. They made their investment; they put their plants there; and they established themselves there and have invested a great deal of money to that end. out of which to a certain extent the public have gotten the benefit. Now, as to a man who is in a position of that sort, I believe he should be treated with due regard to the sacrifices he has made and the investments of capital he has made. and that he should be allowed a fair return for that sacrifice and such investments. I do not believe he should be allowed a monopolistic return; I do not believe he should be allowed an undue return; but I do believe he should be treated with a fair regard for the sacrifices he has made and the money he has invested.

The CHAIRMAN. The committee. or a majority of them, had that same idea in mind in framing the bill.

Secretary STIMSON. Yes: I was just going to say, in other words, I think the cases of people who have gotten established there can be treated and regulated by the regulative power of the Federal and

State Governments, however you may determine to distribute that power, so that they shall continue to get, so long as it is fair, a fair return on their investment, and yet shall not be allowed to use their priority of possession to get any more. In other words, so long as the State public service commission is able to regulate and does regulate the prices at which electricity from Niagara is sold to consumers, so that these licensees of water power do not get an unfair return upon their investment, the matter can well rest where it does now. But if the time should ever come when, in spite of the public service commission, they obtained an undue or monopolistic return on their investment, Congress should take up the question again with a view to Federal regulation or charge for the privilege.

Mr. GARNER. And that could be done without having section 3 in this bill.

Secretary STIMSON. I do not recall which section that is.

Mr. GARNER. Section 3 provides that the Secretary of War shall have due regard to present investments. It is in your discretion now.

Secretary STIMSON. If I were in a position where I had the discretion to do that, that would be the rule I should follow.

Mr. GARNER. You would have that discretion under this bill without section 3.

Secretary STIMSON. I think so.

Mr. KLINE. Then section 3 does not do the bill any violence at all?

Secretary STIMSON. I do not think it does any harm.

Mr. GARNER. And it does not do it any material good.

Secretary STIMSON. It does this much good, I think, Mr. Garner: It gives the Secretary of War, who has these views, the sanction and backing of an expression of the views of Congress.

The CHAIRMAN. And that is all that was intended by that section.

Mr. HARRISON. It may materially affect the passage of the bill on the floor of the House.

Mr. GARNER. May I ask you a question different from the question of the duties of the Secretary of War or the rights of the State of New York? The committee has proposed a limitation of 15,600 cubic feet. What is the judgment of yourself and your engineers as to the effect on the scenic beauty of the Falls if the other 5,400 feet were permitted to be taken?

Secretary STIMSON. The report of the engineers has been made a number of times to the effect that the beauty of the Falls has already been diminished by the diversions which have been already allowed.

Mr. GARNER. What would be the effect, if any, of the additional diversion?

Secretary STIMSON. That would still further diminish it.

The CHAIRMAN. Let me ask you right there in reference to your statement, Mr. Harrison, that section 3 would weaken the bill on the floor of the House?

Secretary STIMSON. I did not say that.

The CHAIRMAN. No; Mr. Harrison made that remark.

Mr. HARRISON. It is merely my opinion that it would materially affect its passage on the floor of the House.

The CHAIRMAN. Of course, there are a good many things in the bill that would weaken it with some people on the floor of the House. I had a letter from Mr. McFarland which I wish to file and have printed in this hearing, in which he states that the allowance by this committee of the importation of 250,000 horsepower from Canada would absolutely defeat the bill in Congress. That letter I will file, to be printed in this hearing.

Mr. SHARP. On what ground?

The CHAIRMAN. On the ground that the conservationists of the country will not allow any more power to come in from Canada.

Secretary STIMSON. To be perfectly frank, I do not agree with that position. I think I am as much alive to the beauty of Niagara as anybody, but the result of our investigation is to show that that amount of power will be used in the very near future, anyhow, by Canada, even if we do not use it.

Mr. GARNER. That statement is simply in accord with the chief advocate of that particularly erratic theory of conservation in telling Congress it can or can not do as it may see proper.

Mr. KENDALL. Mr. Chairman, I think I know what Mr. McFarland's view is, and while it may be an erroneous view I sympathize very strongly with him in his——

Secretary STIMSON (interposing). So do I.

Mr. KENDALL (continuing). In his general purpose to conserve the Falls. His notion is that every horsepower which we authorize to be imported into the United States simply means the diversion of enough water from the Falls to create that horsepower, entailing the diminishment of the scenic beauty of the Falls, and that if we limit the importation from Canada that power will not be used in Canada, hence the water will not be diverted. I think, however, he may be wrong.

Secretary STIMSON. That was the view of the Burton bill in forbidding importations. The Burton bill imposed a much more stringent restriction than your present bill.

Mr. KENDALL. Yes.

Secretary STIMSON. I happen to have before me an investigation showing what the effect of the Burton bill has been, and it shows that that restriction did not operate to prevent the diversion of water on the Canadian side, but that, on the contrary, it has increased enormously, the only difference being it goes to Canada instead of coming here.

Mr. KENDALL. Naturally it will increase. Mr. McFarland's position may be erroneous, but I doubt if it ought to characterized as erratic.

Secretary STIMSON. I did not say that.

Mr. GARNER. I did not say his opinion was erratic, but I said his message to the committee telling them what Congress would do is in line with the statements of some other distinguished citizens in declaring that this, that, or the other could or could not be done.

Secretary STIMSON. I want to make my position perfectly clear. I have the highest sympathy with Mr. McFarland's efforts to protect the beauty of the Falls.

Mr. GARNER. So have I, Mr. Secretary.

Mr. KENDALL. I did not attribute that suggestion to you, Mr. Secretary.

The CHAIRMAN. All of us have sympathy with Mr. McFarland's desire to prevent any diversion that would affect the scenic beauty of the Falls, but we simply do not agree with him as to the result of excluding power from Canada.

Mr. BARTHOLDT. Mr. Chairman, referring to section 3, suppose this section remains in the bill—this is more a suggestion of an executive nature—and the House votes it down, what will be the effect of that upon the judgment of the Secretary of War? After Congress explicitly votes down such a proposition could he give preferential treatment to such cases?

The CHAIRMAN. I should think so.

Mr. GARNER. He would consider the naked law and not the reasons given for its passage.

Mr. SMITH. Mr. Chairman, I want to call attention to section 4, where it says that " all persons, companies, or corporate bodies granted permits under the provisions of this act for the diversion of water from Niagara River above the Falls of Niagara for power purposes shall, if necessary, reconstruct the plant they are now operating," etc. Would not that be regarded as practically a direction to the Secretary of War to give permits to these companies? Is not the assumption in the bill that these companies are to have the permits?

The CHAIRMAN. I should not think that construction would be put upon it. If he does give the permits to them, then that section would apply.

Mr. GARNER. Mr. Secretary, where would you have your amendment inserted in the proposed bill?

Secretary STIMSON. On page 5, line 6, after the word " delivered," would be as good a place as any.

Mr. KENDALL. That relates to the importation of power?

Secretary STIMSON. Yes.

Mr. GARNER. And directs the Secretary as to preferential permits.

Mr. KENDALL. Mr. Chairman, I should want to think about that. I doubt the propriety of inserting that amendment.

The CHAIRMAN. We will consider that in executive session.

Mr. KENDALL. Because it will complicate the bill and only furnish some other ground on which the measure can be attacked on the floor.

Secretary STIMSON. Of course that is a question for you gentlemen to determine. I simply wanted to tell you the experience that we had had in the development of it and one of the points that was most sharply brought to my mind was the propriety of some such treatment by the Secretary of War. As a matter of fact, it is left open to his discretion to do it now.

Mr. KENDALL. You will observe this unqualified authority in the third line of the bill, on page 5:

And he may designate the persons, companies, municipalities, or bodies corporate by whom the same may be transmitted and to whom the same may be delivered.

Secretary STIMSON. No doubt he has the power to do it. My suggestion was merely in the way of guiding——

Mr. GARNER (interposing). Merely an expression of Congress as to what policy he should pursue?

Secretary STIMSON. As to what policy the Secretary, who might not have it in mind, should pursue. He could do it now, because I have done it now.

Mr. CLINE. I would like to ask a question which I think is quite pertinent in this connection. To include that amendment in this bill would give the bill the character of attempting to administer this same subject matter in two different methods; that is, the power that is imported is to be distributed under the direction of the Secretary of War, but as to the power that is generated upon this side, it only goes so far as to say that it shall be given to certain companies without respect to their relationship of the commerce of the country or the manufacturing interests of the country. Do you not anticipate, Mr. Secretary, that that would give rise to very serious complications?

Secretary STIMSON. I do not undertake to advise the committee at all on what would be the effect on Congress; that is for you gentlemen to say. I simply call your attention to the fact that two situations are entirely different. In one case we are dealing with new importations, and in the other case we are dealing with an old situation, former investments and already existing investments.

Mr. GARNER. And I understood you to say, Mr. Secretary, that if it was clear you had the power you would not mind if the same conditions were imposed with reference to the diversion on our side of the Falls.

Secretary STIMSON. As to future diversions.

Mr. SHARP. Does not the fact that the authority of the State of New York somewhat differentiate the two?

Secretary STIMSON. Of course, the State of New York has no authority as to importations.

Mr. SHARP. Not at all; but I mean with reference to the diversion of water and its use here. They would certainly have certain rights even under this bill.

Mr. COOPER. What was the exact proposition you advanced as to your amendment?

Secretary STIMSON. My exact proposition was in regard to importations of electricity—that the bill should provide that the Secretary of War in granting permits to use that current and import that current should prefer public users to private users.

Mr. COOPER. Mr. Secretary, this power being generated at the Falls, first entering this country, would go through the State of New York and would have to cross the territory of the State of New York before it could get into any other State?

Secretary STIMSON. Not necessarily. I said I had an application to import it at Detroit, Mich.

Mr. COOPER. I mean up Pennsylvania way. Is there a way to get it into Pennsylvania without going through the State of New York?

Secretary STIMSON. Not if it came across at Niagara or at the east end of Lake Erie; but they are already carrying that current on the Canadian side as far west almost as Detroit.

Mr. COOPER. I understand that; but how can it get through the State of New York, or can it be brought through the State of New York without the consent of that State, under the theory of this bill?

Secretary STIMSON. Of course not; by the exercise of eminent domain it could not.

Mr. COOPER. Suppose that manufacturers in Pennsylvania 100 or 150 miles away should want some of that power——

Mr. SHARP (interposing). Mr. Cooper, it will go by wireless before that time.

Mr. COOPER. It goes 150 or 200 miles in the State of New York now; but suppose that New York should pass a law preventing it from going into the State of Pennsylvania?

Secretary STIMSON. There is a decision of the Supreme Court, Mr. Cooper, on a situation that is almost on all fours with your question, where the State of Oklahoma passed an act forbidding the exportation of natural gas or oil—I have forgotten which it was—developed in that State, and the Supreme Court held that such an act was unconstitutional. (Oklahoma v. Kansas Co., 221 U. S., 229.)

Mr. COOPER. But this is not an exported product of that State.

Secretary STIMSON. It was not held to be unconstitutional on that ground, but on the ground of its being an interference with interstate commerce.

Mr. COOPER. But this is the crossing of a State line.

Secretary STIMSON. That is interstate commerce.

Mr. COOPER. It is in one sense of the word, but you have to use a part of the territory permanently for the wires.

Secretary STIMSON. I said, Mr. Cooper, the State could undoubtedly pass laws which would make it impossible for them to condemn a right of way, but if those Pennsylvania manufacturers obtained a right of way by purchase, I doubt very much whether the State of New York could prevent them from using it.

Mr. COOPER. You understand there is quite a distinction between commerce, for instance, a box of dry goods going across a State line, and a permanent easement of poles and wires in the territory of a State.

Mr. TOWNSEND. They would have to get a charter from the State before they could do that, and if the State wanted to forbid them from doing it, they would probably refuse to grant them a charter.

Mr. COOPER. Exactly. Then you have the manufacturers in the State of New York having the very great advantage of the enormous power of Niagara Falls for the purpose of manufacturers in Pennsylvania right close by, much closer than Syracuse, deprived of it.

Secretary STIMSON. I have not heard of any such steps being taken yet, and it seems to me——

Mr. COOPER (interposing). Is it possible to prevent such steps being taken, is the question; not wait until the evil is accomplished and then inquire about it?

The CHAIRMAN. The States and cities west of New York would use all of this power?

Secretary STIMSON. I should doubt very much whether the State of New York could directly forbid the exportation of electricity out of its borders.

Mr. COOPER. But that is not the question. Could the State of New York prevent the establishment to the extent of prohibiting poles and wires being erected in its territory for a company which is to take this power into another territory?

Mr. TOWNSEND. That would be a question for the State public service commission, would it not, Mr. Secretary?

Secretary STIMSON. No; the right of condemnation is not necessary to such a situation as that. A great many transportation companies are able to get their transportation lines established by private purchase, and if it was wanted very much in Pennsylvania I have no doubt it could be obtained.

Mr. SMITH. Arrangements have already been made to carry it into that State, so the question will not arise practically.

Mr. COOPER. During the time of the Confederacy all the States were trying to take advantage of each other, and that is the reason the Union was established and the power given to the Congress, but this transmission of power through a wire which requires an easement in property is quite a different thing from carrying goods across a State line.

Secretary STIMSON. Mr. Cooper, I think I agree with you perfectly that there should be no restriction put on the use of this current where it is imported by any State or any municipality that fulfills the conditions, but I do not understand what the point is you suggest now.

Mr. COOPER. The charter of a company in New York might be restricted so that it would not have interstate possibilities.

Secretary STIMSON. But foreign corporations can do business in New York, you know.

Mr. COOPER. Yes; but a foreign corporation might not have any access to Niagara Falls, whereas New York corporations have it now.

Secretary STIMSON. You are talking about importations?

Mr. COOPER. I was talking about the electricity generated at the falls by the companies already in existence or any other companies.

Mr. KENDALL. Let us consider line 9, in section 2, of the bill, which contemplates the authority of the Secretary of War:

Provided, That as a condition precedent to the issuance of any permit the applicant therefor shall stipulate and agree to comply with all regulations respecting rates, tolls, service, and otherwise that may be established by any State in which the power created under such permit is generated, transmitted, used, delivered.

It seems inconceivable that the State of New York would establish a regulation of that sort.

Mr. COOPER. They did it during the times of the Confederacy.

Mr. GARNER. We have got to assume in this day and time that each State is going to pass laws for the best interests of the whole people.

Mr. COOPER. Is that so? Your own State of Texas sought to prevent the traveling men from my State from coming in there under a statute which was declared unconstitutional. You thought it interfered with the industry of Texas to have our people coming down there, and your statute was thrown out by the courts. What has become of your humanitarian views in Texas?

Mr. GARNER. Whenever we pass one of those inhumanitarian statutes the courts will always do that.

The CHAIRMAN. We will consider those questions in executive session. We had better let the Secretary proceed with his statement.

Secretary STIMSON. I was very careful in my statement on Saturday—at least, I intended to be—to point out simply the extent to which I thought it was necessary for the Federal Government to go in protecting the use of the water taken from the river in the interest of the functions of that Federal Government. Now, I did not mean to say you might not find it for other reasons advisable to go further; but I did say I thought it was necessary to exercise the Federal control down as far, at least, as the converting plants, which turn water power into electricity. My own impression was when you asked me the further question—when it came to the distribution of that power in that neighborhood—certainly the matter could be left safely to the State authorities, in view of the fact that New York had an active and vigorous public-service commission. But there may be other questions as to interstate transportation of it which you may care to take up; but I was speaking of navigation naturally, and of the views of my department, so far as it was concerned with that side of it. I understand that is what you were alluding to, Mr. Cooper, in your questions.

Mr. Cooper. I had in mind the possibility that some day New York might not have an active public-service commission.

Secretary Stimson. My view of that has been right along, as I think you know very well, that the main object in the regulation of water powers is to see that the public gets the benefit of what is a great natural resource. Now, that benefit can be gotten in one of two ways: It can be gotten either from the furnishing of cheap power to the public or it can be gotten by using the sale or lease of that power to diminish taxation. It depends very much on the local situation which one of those methods should be used. The Federal Government ought to stand ready to use its power to see that that general aim is accomplished in one of those ways.

Mr. Garner. Mr. Secretary, suppose New York did not have any public-service commission whatever and had no law on the statute books with reference to the regulation of these power companies, do you contend that after you have ascertained the amount of water to be taken and the efficiency of the plant you could follow it up under the Federal law as to all the whys and wherefores and see what it was used for in the State of New York?

Secretary Stimson. Mr. Garner, you are opening up a question——

Mr. Garner (interposing). You said a moment ago, in view of the fact that New York had those things, that that was as far as you would go, intimating you would go further as to a Federal law if New York did not have an efficient public-service commission. Now, I want to know as a lawyer and as a representative of the Federal Government how far you believe we can go.

Secretary Stimson. Is that up here?

Mr. Garner. Yes; a good many think we ought to go further, and there are a great many who have not the same view of the public-service commission of New York you have. They do not believe it is efficient. There are some people in New York who do not believe that.

Secretary Stimson. Mr. Garner, I do not think anything is to be gained by a discussion of an academic subject here. I will say frankly that in view of the situation I believe it would be inexpedient to go further in the case now before us. As I think I told you the other day in a case where the water power is the direct product of a Federal navigable work, where the Federal Government, for instance, has built a dam and acquired the riparian rights that go with that dam, I have not the slightest doubt of its authority to sell that power at such prices as it chooses and regulate those prices to any consumer in any part of the country. That, I believe, has already been settled by the Supreme Court.

The question you now asked me has not been stated, and I do not think there is anything gained by you and me discussing it here as lawyers. By this I do not mean at all to assert that further power in the Federal Government does not exist. I simply mean that I doubt the advisability of debating it now before this committee when under the circumstances now before us the need of the exercise of such power does not seem to me to exist.

Mr. GARNER. I did not know but what I might get your opinion, in order to quote it in case of discussion on the floor of the House. Of course, if you do not care to give an opinion I will not press you for one.

Secretary STIMSON. Mr. Chairman, that is all I desire to say unless there are any questions you desire to ask.

Mr. SHARP. Mr. Chairman, I want to ask Mr. Bartholdt what his idea was as to raising that question about section 3 and selecting that particular section, referring as it does to the rights of those who have already made investments there, and referring to the probability of its being questioned or defeated, perhaps, on the floor? I want to know your thought, Mr. Bartholdt.

Mr. BARTHOLDT. My thought was that if Congress, for instance, votes down a certain proposition there may be a question in the mind of the executive officer who has to administer the law as to whether he could administer it in violation of an express judgment of Congress.

Mr. SHARP. Section 3, if you will notice, deals exclusively with the rights of those who already have investments there.

Mr. BARTHOLDT. As I understand it, it gives the Secretary of War the right to accord preferential treatment to the companies who are now enjoying those privileges, but if Congress should vote that down there may be a question in the mind of the Secretary as to whether in defiance of Congress he could execute such a section if it was not the law.

Mr. SHARP. Then it is your theory that a provision being in the bill that the Secretary of War should have due regard for fixed investments, and that provision being defeated by the Congress, it would be deducible by the Secretary of War that Congress did not intend him to have due regard for fixed investments?

Mr. BARTHOLDT. That is exactly what I had in mind.

Mr. COOPER. Mr. Secretary, is it true or not that Col. Sanford recommended the extension of the Burton Act?

Secretary STIMSON. I do not recall whether he did or not, but the Chief of Engineers has recommended several times, and so have I.

Mr. COOPER. Gen. Bixby?

Secretary STIMSON. Yes.

Mr. GARNER. That is only in case Congress does not pass a general bill covering the subject.

Secretary STIMSON. Yes; I say with the utmost earnestness, in case this bill does not pass, I sincerely hope the Burton Act will be extended.

The CHAIRMAN. Col. Kernan, do you want to present your views to the committee this morning?

Col. KERNAN. No, sir; not unless the committee wants to ask me something.

Mr. COOPER. Colonel, were you on the board that recently visited the Falls?

Col. KERNAN. Yes, sir.

Mr. COOPER. For what purpose did you go?

Col. KERNAN. Under an order from the Secretary to make a report to him on the general subject.

Mr. COOPER. Have you submitted a report?

Col. KERNAN. We have.

Mr. COOPER. What, in substance, did you find, and have you made any recommendations?

Col. KERNAN. Yes, sir; we have made a number of recommendations. They were made, however, to the Secretary of War.

Secretary STIMSON. There was a division in the board, Mr. Cooper, on certain questions, and I have given the unanimous report here where it was unanimous, and where I have not quoted the board I have used their information and my own views.

Mr. GARNER. And those views will be in the record?

Secretary STIMSON. My views are already in the record.

Mr. HARRISON. Are the minority views also in the record?

Secretary STIMSON. No; the views cover a great variety of topics. Some of them are in the record and some of them are not.

The CHAIRMAN. As I understand it, you only put in the record their views upon questions about which the board was unanimous.

Secretary STIMSON. Yes. Of course, the board gave me facts, on which I do not think there was any division, and then they submitted to me recommendations, on which they did divide, and as to those I have only given to the committee here the recommendations that were unanimous, and the rest of it has been my own view.

Mr. COOPER. You have given the facts substantially?

Secretary STIMSON. Yes.

Mr. COOPER. That, I think, covers the ground. The facts, of course, are what we want.

Mr. HARRISON. If the committee should desire to have all the views with respect to Niagara Falls, whether unanimous or not, would the Secretary of War object to giving them?

Secretary STIMSON. Not at all; only I was trying to act as the coordinator as far as I could. I had all of these gentlemen in my office and discussed the whole matter with them and tried to reconcile and harmonize their views so far as I could, and to save your time I have produced them in this way.

(The report of the board of engineers and the order of the Secretary of War referred to here follow:)

MEMORANDUM IN RE APPLICATION OF THE FEDERAL LIGHT & POWER CO. TO IMPORT WATER POWER FROM NIAGARA FALLS.

WAR DEPARTMENT,
Washington, August 24, 1913.

Requests for permits for the importation of water power available from the Canadian side of the Niagara Falls under the authority of the Burton Act, entitled "An act for the control and regulation of the waters of Niagara River, for the preservation of Niagara Falls, and for other purposes" (approved June 29, 1906, 34 Stat. L., 626), are applications for commercial privileges of great value and corresponding importance to the municipal and commercial interests which are within a proper radius to avail themselves of them. The grant of such a privilege by the Federal Government, particularly when the extent of its enjoyment is so limited, as is this power from Niagara, should be controlled by general standards and not depend on the chances of isolated applications. The only way to secure the largest usefulness from the Niagara importation and at the same time most effectively protect the public interests is to subject the grant of such privileges to public bidding under terms just to the Government, to the investing public, and to the consumers.

This necessity is emphasized by the fact that the present applicant seeks to import electric power at such a long distance from the place of its creation as to involve a loss of wastage in transmission of from 20 to 40 per cent, according to the statements at the hearing. Care should evidently be taken before granting such a permit to ascertain whether this is the wisest economy or whether the power may not be more needed at places where there will be less waste in its development.

I am therefore compelled to deny the application of the Federal Light & Power Co. in its present form, and to direct the Chief of Engineers to invite public bids from various cities interested in Niagara power importation, in accordance with the notice marked "Schedule A" and the form of application marked "Schedule B," made a part of this memorandum. The bids are to be received at the place and places designated by the Chief of Engineers not later than November 1, 1912.

H. L. STIMSON, *Secretary of War.*

SCHEDULE A.

OFFICE OF THE SECRETARY OF WAR,
Washington, D. C., October 7, 1912.

NOTICE.

Acting under authority of the act of Congress approved June 29, 1906, entitled "An act for the control and regulation of the waters of Niagara River, for the preservation of Niagara Falls, and for other purposes," the Secretary of War hereby announces that applications for permits for the transmission across the international boundary from Canada into the United States of electrical power generated in Canada from the waters of the Niagara River, will be received from municipalities, from individuals, and from companies duly incorporated under the laws of the States in which they operate, up to 2 p. m., October 31, 1912, and the applications then received will thereupon be publicly opened, and will be considered upon a competitive basis with a view to alloting a maximum of 80,000 horsepower, or any portion thereof, and to issuing revocable permits for the importation of the several allotments, which permits, in accordance with the provisions of the act referred to, will be issued only to companies legally authorized therefor, and to such companies as will insure to the ultimate consumers, in the judgment of the Secretary of War, the maximum amount of benefit from the imported power. The permits will be issued subject to the conditions of the aforesaid act of Congress (a copy of which is appended) and under provisions of that portion of the act reading:

"*Provided further*, That the said Secretary, subject to the provisions of section 5 of this act, may issue revocable permits for the transmission of additional electrical power so generated in Canada, but in no event shall the amount included in such permits, together with the said one hundred and sixty thousand horsepower and the amount generated and used in Canada, exceed three hundred and fifty thousand horsepower."

The original amount of 160,000 horsepower named in section 2 of the act has already been provided for by permits or reservation.

The conditions under which applications will be received are as follows:

1. All applications must be submitted in triplicate and must be accompanied (*a*) with satisfactory evidence that the amount of power for which application is made can and will be provided to the applicant, if successful, at the international boundary from one or more of the power stations generating electrical energy from the waters of the Niagara River on the Canadian side; (*b*) with a clear and concise statement of the use for which the power is intended and

the class of customers to be served; and (c) with a complete schedule of maximum rates to be charged bona fide consumers.

2. Applications must state the maximum, or peak load, in horsepower for which the application is made and the minimum amount of such peak load for which permit will be accepted and utilized, also the amount or percentage of power lost in the course of transmission from Niagara.

3. Applications must be accompanied by certified copies of the articles of incorporation of the company making the application, together with a list of the officers and stockholders of the company, a statement of the paid-in capital, and satisfactory evidence that the financial resources of the company are sufficient to enable it to undertake and carry on the enterprise successfully.

4. In considering the comparative merits of the applications and the allocation of power to be made thereon, preference will be shown, first, to applications contemplating the distribution of power to municipalities, and, second, to those contemplating distribution to individuals or companies who propose to distribute energy to individuals, or small consumers, and for the use of public utilities.

5. Each permit when granted will provide that the holder of such permit shall be equipped, within two years from the date thereof, for the distribution of at least 50 per cent of the full amount of power allowed by the permit, and shall then actually be receiving and distributing at least 30 per cent of the full amount to bona fide customers; that the books and records of the company shall be kept so as to show clearly the cost of transmitting and distributing power and the earnings gross and net; and such books and records and the plant shall be open to the Secretary of War and all persons authorized by him, who will be given opportunity to determine that the provisions of the permit are complied with, and that the schedule of rates accompanying the application, or the schedule of rates lawfully regulated by any State or municipal authority, is not exceeded by the charge to bona fide consumers; that sufficient and satisfactory means will be provided by the successful applicant for the continuous measurement of power at or near the point of importation, and that the cost of all such measurements and inspections must be borne by the holder of the permit. Referring to that portion of section 2 of the act of Congress approved June 29, 1906, which provides with reference to permits for the transmission of additional electrical power, that " in no event shall the amount included in such permits, together with the said one hundred and sixty thousand horsepower and the amount generated and used in Canada, exceed three hundred and fifty thousand horsepower," applicants are informed that each permit granted for the transmission of additional electrical power will also include a condition that the amount authorized for transmission into the United States will be subject to such reduction as may be directed by the Secretary of War when the amount of electrical power generated in Canada by diversion of water from the Niagara River or its tributaries or from the Welland Canal, exceeds 350,000 horsepower.

6. Distributing companies or agents will not be considered as bona fide consumers.

7. Any violation of the terms of a permit or of the restrictions imposed by the act of Congress under which it is issued will be considered just and sufficient reason for its revocation.

8. The Secretary of War will, at his discretion, reject any or all of the applications that are received, and will likewise withhold the allotment of any or all of the additional power which he is authorized to distribute, if, in his opinion, the terms of the application do not sufficiently protect the interests of the public.

Blank applications may be had from the office of the Secretary of War, Washington, D. C.

***

[Public, No. 367.]

AN ACT For the control and regulation of the waters of Niagara River, for the preservation of Niagara Falls, and for other purposes.

Be it enacted by the Senate and House of Representatives of the United States of America in Congress assembled. That the diversion of water from Niagara River or its tributaries, in the State of New York, is hereby prohibited.

except with the consent of the Secretary of War as hereinafter authorized in section two of this Act: *Provided*, That this prohibition shall not be interpreted as forbidding the diversion of the waters of the Great Lakes or of Niagara River for sanitary or domestic purposes, or for navigation, the amount of which may be fixed from time to time by the Congress of the United States or by the Secretary of War of the United States under its direction.

SEC. 2. That the Secretary of War is hereby authorized to grant permits for the diversion of water in the United States from said Niagara River or its tributaries for the creation of power to individuals, companies, or corporations which are now actually producing power from the waters of said river or its tributaries in the State of New York or from the Erie Canal, also permits for the transmission of power from the Dominion of Canada into the United States to companies legally authorized therefor, both for diversion and transmission, as hereinafter stated, but permits for diversion shall be issued only to the individuals, companies, or corporations as aforesaid, and only to the amount now actually in use or contracted to be used in factories the buildings for which are now in process of construction, not exceeding to any one individual, company, or corporation as aforesaid a maximum amount of eight thousand six hundred cubic feet per second, and not exceeding to all individuals, companies, or corporations as aforesaid an aggregate amount of fifteen thousand six hundred cubic feet per second; but no revocable permits shall be issued by the said Secretary under the provisions hereafter set forth for the diversion of additional amounts of water from the said river or its tributaries until the approximate amount for which permits may be issued as above, to wit, fifteen thousand six hundred cubic feet per second shall for a period of not less than six months have been diverted from the waters of said river or its tributaries in the State of New York: *Provided*, That the said Secretary, subject to the provisions of section five of this Act, under the limitations relating to time above set forth is hereby authorized to grant revocable permits from time to time to such individuals, companies, or corporations, or their assigns for the diversion of additional amounts of water from the said river or its tributaries to such amount, if any, as, in connection with the amount diverted on the Canadian side, shall not injure or interfere with the navigable capacity of said river, or its integrity and proper volume as a boundary stream, or the scenic grandeur of Niagara Falls, and that the quantity of electrical power which may by permits be allowed to be transmitted from the Dominion of Canada into the United States shall be one hundred and sixty thousand horsepower: *Provided further*, That the said Secretary, subject to the provisions of section five of this Act, may issue revocable permits for the transmission of additional electrical power so generated in Canada, but in no event shall the amount included in such permits, together with the said one hundred and sixty thousand horsepower and the amount generated and used in Canada, exceed three hundred and fifty thousand horsepower: *Provided always*, That the provisions herein permitting diversions and fixing the aggregate horsepower herein permitted to be transmitted into the United States as aforesaid are intended as a limitation on the authority of the Secretary of War, and shall in nowise be construed as a direction to said Secretary to issue permits, and the Secretary of War shall make regulations preventing or limiting the diversion of water and the admission of electrical power as herein stated, and the permits for the transmission of electrical power issued by the Secretary of War may specify the persons, companies, or corporations by whom the same shall be transmitted, and the persons, companies, or corporations to whom the same shall be delivered.

SEC. 3. That any person, company, or corporation diverting water from the said Niagara River or its tributaries, or transmitting electrical power into the United States from Canada, except as herein stated, or violating any of the provisions of this act, shall be deemed guilty of a misdemeanor, and on conviction thereof shall be punished by a fine not exceeding $2,500 nor less than $500, or by imprisonment (in the case of a natural person) not exceeding one year, or by both such punishments, in the discretion of the court. And, further, the removal of any structures or parts of structures erected in violation of this act, or any construction incidental to or used for such diversion of water or transmission of power as is herein prohibited, as well as any diversion of water or transmission of power in violation hereof, may be enforced or enjoined at the suit of the United States by any circuit court having jurisdiction in any district in which the same may be located, and proper proceedings to this end may be instituted under the direction of the Attorney General of the United States.

SEC. 4. That the President of the United States is respectfully requested to open negotiations with the Government of Great Britain for the purpose of effectually providing, by suitable treaty with said Government, for such regulation and control of the waters of Niagara River and its tributaries as will preserve the scenic grandeur of Niagara Falls and of the rapids in said river.

SEC. 5. That the provisions of this act shall remain in force for three years from and after date of its passage, at the expiration of which time all permits granted hereunder by the Secretary of War shall terminate unless sooner revoked, and the Secretary of War is hereby authorized to revoke any or all permits granted by him by authority of this act. and nothing herein contained shall be held to confirm, establish, or confer any rights heretofore claimed or exercised in the diversion of water or the transmission of power.

SEC. 6. That for accomplishing the purposes detailed in this act the sum of $50,000, or so much thereof as may be necessary, is hereby appropriated from any money in the Treasury not otherwise appropriated.

SEC. 7. That the right to alter, amend. or repeal this act is hereby expressly reserved.

Approved. June 29, 1906.

[Public resolution No. 56.]

[H. J. Res. 262.]

JOINT RESOLUTION Extending the operation of the act for the control and regulation of the waters of Niagara River, for the preservation of Niagara Falls, and for other purposes.

Whereas the provisions of the act entitled "An act for the control and regulation of the waters of Niagara River. for the preservation of Niagara Falls, and for other purposes," approved June twenty-ninth, nineteen hundred and six, will expire by limitation on June twenty-ninth. nineteen hundred and nine; and

Whereas a date for the termination of the operation of said act was provided therein, but with a view to the more permanent settlement of the questions involved by a treaty with Great Britain and by further legislation appropriate to the situation, and such treaty not having been negotiated, it is desirable that the provisions of said act should be continued until such permanent settlement can be made: Therefore be it

Resolved by the Senate and House of Representatives of the United States of America in Congress assembled, That the provisions of the aforesaid act be, and they are hereby, extended for two years from June twenty-ninth. nineteen hundred and nine, being the date of the expiration of the operation of said act. save in so far as any portion thereof may be found inapplicable or already complied with.

Approved, March 3, 1909.

[Public resolution No. 9.]

[S. J. Res. 3.]

JOINT RESOLUTION Extending the operation of the act for the control and regulation of the waters of Niagara River, for the preservation of Niagara Falls, and for other purposes.

Resolved by the Senate and House of Representatives of the United States of America in Congress assembled, That the provisions of an act entitled "An act for the control of the waters of Niagara River, for the preservation of Niagara Falls, and for other purposes," be, and they are hereby, extended and reenacted from June twenty-ninth, nineteen hundred and eleven, being the date of the expiration of the operation of said act. to March first, nineteen hundred and twelve.

Approved, August 22, 1911.

[Public resolution No. 24.]

[H. J. Res. 232.]

JOINT RESOLUTION Extending the operation of the act for the control and regulation of the waters of Niagara River, for the preservation of Niagara Falls, and for other purposes.

Whereas the provisions of the act entitled "An act for the control and regulation of the waters of Niagara River, for the preservation of Niagara Falls, and for other purposes," approved June twenty-ninth, nineteen hundred and six, and extended to June twenty-ninth, nineteen hundred and eleven, by joint resolution (public resolution numbered fifty-six), and further extended to March first nineteen hundred and twelve, by joint resolution (public resolution numbered nine), approved August twenty-second, nineteen hundred and eleven, expires March first, nineteen hundred and twelve: Be it therefore

Resolved by the Senate and House of Representatives of the United States of America in Congress assembled, That the provisions of the aforesaid act be, and they are hereby, reenacted and extended from March first, nineteen hundred and twelve, being the date of the expiration of said act, to March fourth, nineteen hundred and thirteen.

Approved, April 5, 1912.

SCHEDULE B.

[Office of the Secretary of War, Washington, D. C.]

APPLICATION FOR PERMIT.

————, *1912.*

To the honorable the SECRETARY OF WAR,
Washington, D. C.

SIR: In accordance with your notice of October 7, 1912, inviting applications for permits to receive at the international boundary and to transmit from the Dominion of Canada into the United States electrical energy generated on the Canadian side of the Niagara River from the waters thereof, and subject to all the conditions and requirements of said notice, a copy of which is hereto attached and, so far as it relates to this application, is made a part of it, the undersigned, ————, does hereby file application for a permit to receive a maximum of ———— electrical horsepower, measured at or near the international boundary, from ———— company, and to transmit the same from the Dominion of Canada into the United States for the purpose of distributing and supplying to consumers the electrical energy so imported.

Under an allotment of the power, for which the Secretary of War is authorized to grant permits, the undersigned applicant agrees to accept and utilize, under the conditions and requirements of this application and the attached regulations, a permit for a minimum peak load of ———— electrical horsepower or any allotment between the maximum and minimum amounts herein named.

In accordance with the requirements of the attached notice from the Secretary of War, there are inclosed herewith and made a part of this application the following papers and documents (see condition 1 of notice): (*a*) ————, (*b*) ————, (*c*) ————. (See condition 3 of notice.) ————. ————.

We (or I) make this application with a full knowledge of the conditions and requirements to be met by the successful applicant, and of the competitive basis upon which the awards are to be made, and, if granted a permit for the importation of power to an amount between the limits named herein, will at once pledge ourselves (or myself) with such reasonable sureties as the Secretary of War may demand, to acquire and equip transmission lines, distributing stations, etc., to an extent and within the time specified in paragraph 5 of the attached notice, and otherwise to meet fully and faithfully the requirements of the permit.

(Signature) ———— ————.
(Address) ———— ————.

[Signed in triplicate.]

WAR DEPARTMENT,
UNITED STATES LAKE SURVEY OFFICE,
Detroit, Mich., January 6, 1913.

From: Lieut. Col. J. C. Sanford, Corps of Engineers.
To: The Chief of Engineers, United States Army.
Subject: Transmitting applications for permission to import Niagara power, with report and recommendations.

1. In compliance with instructions in seventh indorsement on memorandum of the Secretary of War dated August 24. 1912 (E. D. 80899/128), advertisements announcing the receival of applications for permission to import Niagara power were duly published in the daily and weekly journals authorized by the Secretary of War. Also notices and blank applications were mailed to the mayors and city councils of all towns and cities that were thought to be directly interested and to all individuals and companies that were known or believed to be concerned in the matter. In accordance with the advertisement and notice (Schedule A) applications were received at this office up to 2 p. m. October 31. 1912. and were then publicly opened.

2. The following companies filed applications for permits in accordance with the terms of the notice. with request for allotment of power within the amounts stated:

	Maximum.	Minimum.
	Horsepower.	*Horsepower.*
Niagara Falls Power Co.	60,000	(1)
Niagara, Lockport & Ontario Power Co.	40,000	10,000
The Federal Light & Power Co.	50,000	25,000

¹ Any lesser amount.

3. There was also received a letter of application submitted by the city clerk of Detroit, Mich., for the common council, requesting permission for the city of Detroit to import Niagara Falls power.

4. The latter application, being wholly indefinite and not in required form, is not recommended for consideration.

5. With a view of comparing the formal applications on a competitive basis to determine which applicant will grant the greatest benefit to the ultimate consumers there are four chief points for consideration, namely, which companies propose to distribute the greatest proportion of power to municipalities and to small consumers, which will make the earliest use of the power, which will grant the lowest rates to the ultimate consumers, and which will obtain and distribute power with the least economic waste. These points are discussed seriatim.

USE OF POWER AND CLASS OF CUSTOMERS.

6. The applicants all propose to make general distribution of the power for which permits are requested. this power to be used in each case for municipal lighting, for operation of public utilities. and for power and lighting by the small consumers. The proportion of power for these various uses is not stated, and there appears to be no distinction in the kind of use or class of customers to be served by the applicants upon which preference may be based, as contemplated in paragraph 4 of the notice.

EARLY UTILIZATION OF PERMITS.

7. There is no question but that Niagara Falls power will soon be utilized to the fullest extent allowed by governmental restrictions. If advantage of the power generated in Canada can not be had on the American side, manufacturers will be attracted to Canada by this cheap power. and the industries of this country will suffer accordingly. The effect of present restrictions on the importation of power is becoming noticeable. Except for the permit of the transmission companies receiving power from the Electrical Development Co. of Ontario (Ltd.), the permits for diversion of water and for the importation of power for use in the United States are now fully utilized. and manufacturers at present contracting for additional Niagara power must locate and are

locating in Canada. It therefore seems advisable to permit immediately the importation of Niagara power to the fullest extent permissible under the law, and, other things being equal, to grant permission for its importation to the company or companies which will make the earliest use of such power. The Niagara Falls Power Co. and the Niagara, Lockport & Ontario Power Co., of the above-named applicants, are both equipped for importing and distributing power largely in excess of the amounts allowed by their present permits, and as their customers are reported to be urgently demanding more power there is no doubt that permits for importation of additional power, if granted, will be quickly utilized by these companies. For this reason the applications of the Niagara Falls Power Co. and the Niagara, Lockport & Ontario Power Co. are recommended for first consideration.

SCHEDULES OF RATES.

8. In compliance with conditions upon which applications were to be received and considered, the three applicants have submitted schedules of maximum rates to be charged the ultimate consumers for electrical energy that may be imported and distributed under the proposed permits.

The Niagara Falls Power Co. and the Niagara, Lockport & Ontario Power Co. propose to import and distribute additional power on transmission lines already in use. This power will be transmitted in parallel with that now being imported, and will be distributed in larger quantities to present consumers and to additional consumers of the same class. There can be no practicable way of separating this from power imported under former permits. These companies therefore submit the schedule of rates for which they are now distributing power through local companies to ultimate consumers. The Federal Light & Power Co., which proposes to import such power at the international boundary at Detroit, Mich., and to distribute such power to consumers in that city, quotes rates of the Detroit Edison Co. as a basis for its charges.

It will be noted that the schedules are complex and, in the form submitted, are practically incomparable. The manner of measuring and charging for light and power by local distributing companies is variously on the basis of average kilowatt-hour use, maximum demand, connected load, or some combination or modification of these, and the distributing companies to be served by the applicants quote rates in these various forms. An attempt has been made to analyze the scheduled rates, but it is found that there are in vogue various arbitrary methods of applying charges for power and lighting, and without full details exact comparison is impossible. For instance, where residence lighting is charged on the basis of connected load some distributing companies include "convenience" lights in basement, attic, porch, bathroom, etc., while other companies do not include these. Some companies furnish initial lamps and all renewals, while in some communities the consumer must furnish either or both. Where the charge is graded according to hours of service per day the kilowatt-hour use between meter readings is divided by the length of time and by the connected load, of which quantities the latter may be an arbitrary factor or may be determined by test, according to the practice of the company. Other arbitrary methods of making charges are also in practice. For example, the Detroit Edison Co., whose schedule is the basis of that submitted by the Federal Light & Power Co., charges for residence lighting 12.6 cents net per kilowatt-hour during each month for the total use of energy up to 2 kilowatt-hours for each living room, excepting the kitchen, and for each bedroom above three, and 3.6 cents net per kilowatt-hour for use above this.

The power rates scheduled by the various distributing companies are about as complicated as the lighting rates, and without full details regarding arbitrary charges and methods of applying rates, together with statistics of distribution, it is manifestly impossible to make any definite comparison of the rate schedules submitted by the applicants for Niagara power.

It has been ascertained that during the year 1911 the average consumption of electrical energy in Detroit for residence lighting was 331 kilowatt-hours per meter, for which the average charge was 6.04 cents per kilowatt-hour. There was no additional charge for initial lamps or renewals. It would appear from this that present rates for residence lighting are less in Detroit than for the other cities and towns named in the applications.

Similar data concerning distribution and rates for electric power in Detroit are not available. It is claimed that the charges for intermittent power to small consumers—that is, to consumers using a small amount of power for a few hous each day—are less in Detroit than in many communities using Niagara power. I have been unable to verify this. The Federal Light & Power Co. proposes to distribute light and power in Detroit at rates 15 to 20 per cent below those of the Edison Co., and there appears no reason for doubting the sincerity and good faith of this proposal. Assuming that the present established rates for light and power to small consumers in Detroit are as low as those granted by the two applicants now operating in New York State— and I believe this to be true—the application of the Federal Light & Power Co. may be accepted is the one offering the cheapest rates to the individual or small consumers, and should receive consideration accordingly.

ECONOMIC WASTE.

9. In comparing the merits of the applications with respect to the loss in transmission of power, it seems proper to consider also the efficiencies of the generating plants from which it is proposed to receive the power, as these efficiencies enter into the question of conservation of resources. Of the three applicants the Niagara, Lockport & Ontario Power Co. and the Federal Light & Power Co. propose to receive electrical energy generated at the plant of the Ontario Power Co. The loss in the development of power for these two transmission companies will therefore be the same. The Niagara Falls Power Co. proposes to receive energy developed by the Canadian Niagara Power Co. This latter company is generating power on a head of 140 feet with an efficiency of 71 per cent, according to the report of Lieut. Col. C. S. Riche, Corps of Engineers, dated September 30, 1911 (p. 16, H. Doc. 246, 62d Cong., 2d sess). The same report states that the Ontario Power Co. was then generating with a head of 193 feet and with 74 per cent efficiency. This operating head will eventually be reduced to 180 feet. It may be assumed that the mechanical efficiency will remain the same on the reduced head. Comparing the developments of the Ontario Power Co. and the Canadian Niagara Power Co. it is found that the latter will develop 30 per cent less power for the same quantity of water diverted under conditions existing in 1911, and 25 per cent less power when the head of the Ontario Power Co. has been reduced to 180 feet.

In compliance with the conditions of the notice—Schedule A—the applicants have stated the estimated losses in transmission of power from the generating stations to the ultimate consumers as follows:

Niagara Falls Power Co., from the generating plant of the Canadian Niagara Power Co. to Buffalo, 8 per cent, and from the same station to Niagara Falls, N. Y., 2½ per cent. The amount of power transmitted to these two cities is widely fluctuating, but will average about equal in amounts, so that the average transmission losses may be taken as the mean of the losses to Buffalo and to Niagara Falls, or 5¼ per cent.

The Niagara, Lockport & Ontario Power Co.'s average loss on all power transmitted into the United States as actually measured is stated to have been as follows: 1907, 11.5 per cent; 1908, 9.5 per cent; 1909, 8.3 per cent; 1910, 8.2 per cent; 1911, 4.8 per cent; and 1912 (9 months) 7.3 per cent. In explanation of the varying results the company has stated informally that the low percentage in loss shown for the year 1911 is probably erroneous, due to meter errors. The gradual reduction in loss from 1907 to date, as shown by these figures, is stated to be due to the improvement of measuring equipment at the receiving ends, and is not due to actual reduction of the losses. Based on the figures given, it may be assumed that the actual loss on all transmission by this company is approximately 8 per cent.

The Federal Light & Power Co. in its application makes the simple statement that the loss transmission from Niagara Falls to Detroit will be 7 per cent. As this figure appeared to be unreasonably low, the officers of the company have been requested to verify it. In informal reply it was stated that the question of transmission losses from Niagara Falls to Detroit had previously been submitted to the Hydro-Electric Commission of Canada, and that the commission had estimated the probable average loss to be from 7 to 10 per cent. The lower figure was inserted in the company's application. The Federal Light & Power Co. was further requested to furnish a statement from the Hydro-Electric Commission of Canada covering this question, with details of transmission such as size of cables, etc., so that the theoretical losses could be checked. This the company promised to do if possible, but it is now understood that the said commission refuses to furnish the data. Without further information it may be assumed that the statement of the company is correct, and that the transmission losses from Niagara Falls to the ultimate consumers at Detroit will not exceed 10 per cent.

From the information at hand it appears that the percentage losses in transmission by the applicants are the least for the Niagara Falls Power Co., second for the Niagara, Lockport & Ontario Power Co., and largest for the Federal Light & Power Co. However, when generating efficiency is also considered, the Niagara Falls Power Co. delivers the least amount of power per unit of diversion from the Niagara River, instead of the greatest, as indicated by the transmission losses. The order of preference, then, on the basis of efficiency, is as follows: First, Niagara, Lockport & Ontario Power Co.; second, Federal Light & Power Co.; and third, Niagara Falls Power Co.

GENERAL CONSIDERATIONS.

10. Each application presents certain advantages over one or both of those submitted by the competing applicants. The value of these various advantages are not such as will admit of careful mathematical comparison. The points for consideration can not be weighed or measured, and therefore the proper allocation of power for "the greatest good to the greatest number" must be a matter of opinion, and the allotment must be more or less arbitrary. As noted in paragraph 7 above it is my opinion that the Niagara Falls Power Co. and the Niagara, Lockport & Ontario Power Co. should receive first consideration on account of their ability to make immediate delivery of the power; and for the present these companies should be allowed to import all of the power that the law will allow. On the other hand, the Federal Light & Power Co. proposes to enter competition with an established monopoly, whereas additional permits to the other applicants will increase and strengthen distributing companies which now practically enjoy monopolies in the territory in which they operate. In my opinion this consideration should insure to the Detroit Co. the right to a portion of the power to be allotted as soon as it is in position to use such power.

As between the Niagara Falls Power Co. and the Niagara, Lockport & Ontario Power Co., the former distributes power with less loss in transmission, but there is much greater waste in the generation of the power which it receives. Its rates appear to be somewhat less, but distribution is made to fewer consumers in larger amounts and thus benefits a less number of people directly than the power ditributed by the latter company. A division of the power between these companies whereby the economic waste of each from the potential power of the water to the electrical energy delivered to the consumer is equal in absolute amount seems to be equitable.

Consideration of the various points hereinbefore discussed has led to the recommendations made in the concluding paragraph of this report.

AMOUNT OF POWER TO BE ALLOTTED.

11. By the provisions of the act of Congress approved June 29, 1906, under which permits for the importation of Niagara power are issued, the quantity of electrical power which may be allowed to be transmitted from the Dominion of Canada into the United States is limited to 160,000 horsepower, except that the Secretary of War is empowered to issue revocable permits for the transmission of additional electrical power generated in Canada, "but in no event shall the amount included in such (revocable) permits, together with the said one hundred and sixty thousand horsepower and the amount generated and used in Canada, exceed three hundred and fifty thousand horsepower."

12. The permits already issued for the importation of power from Canada are as follows:

	Horsepower.
Niagara Falls Power Co	52,500
Niagara, Lockport & Ontario Power Co	60,000
Niagara Falls Electrical Transmission Co. et al	46,000

The additional 1,500 horsepower of the 160,000 horsepower allowed in the first instance by the act of Congress was reserved in 1907 for the International Railway Co., pending the settlement of a controversy between that company and the Dominion Government regarding the rights granted by the company's charter. It is understood that the question is still unsettled. It would seem that further reservation of the 1,500 horsepower is not warranted, and it is recommended that it be now considered available for allocation. The total amount of power that may still be allotted by permits for importation is determined by subtracting from 350,000 horsepower the 158,500 horsepower already allotted and deducting from the remainder the amount of power generated and used in Canada. The amounts named in the law are limiting, and hence maximum amounts; but the law does not specify how they shall be measured. In commercial practice, maximum power may be determined as the mean load during definite periods of time or as peak loads of certain specified duration, such as momentary, one minute, two minutes, hourly, etc., occurring within certain units of time. As the law is not specific in this matter, it is necessary to arrive at some reasonable interpretation. In formulating the permits for importation which were issued in 1907 the Secretary of War has named the maximum amounts in each for which the respective permits are issued, with exceptions for excessive loads not exceeding 1 hour in duration at any one time nor for more than 2 hours during any 24 hours. This is virtually limiting the importation on the basis of hourly peaks, with not more than the equivalent of two such peaks allowed in one day. This method has proven sound and reasonable in practice, in so far as making the limitations for the companies agree with the apparent intent of the law.

13. There is naturally a tendency for the peak loads of the several companies to coincide or overlap, and when all companies are operating to their limits it will undoubtedly occur that the aggregate importation for very short periods of time will exceed the total amount specified in the law. However, under present limitations the extra diversions of water due to this excess load will practically be provided for by the storage capacity of the upper river so long as the average daily importation does not exceed the specified amount; and so the flow of water over the Falls will at no time be decreased appreciably below the amount corresponding to the aggregate specified limit of importation. The records of inspections do not show that the importation under any permit has averaged more in any one day than the specified limit of such permit. At the same time the concession of hourly peaks has permitted the companies to compensate themselves for periods of the day when the demand is light by excess loads during hours of maximum demand.

14. The principal objection to the present method of limiting importation is the difficulty attending proper supervision. Graphic meter records for each circuit must be scaled, the readings corrected for meter error and transmission loss, and the summation line plotted graphically before it can be ascertained positively that the restrictions of the permit have been complied with. This same difficulty in determining the amount of importation affords the operators easy and plausible excuse in case of a violation of permit. However, the Burton Act is due to expire on March 4 next, and as any material change in method of measuring the limit of importation would probably involve changes in installation that could not be accomplished before the expiration of the law, it is recommended that no change in existing permits be considered during the present term of the Burton Act.

15. The applications for revocable permits herewith from the Niagara Falls Power Co. and the Niagara, Lockport & Ontario Power Co. contemplate transmitting additional power in parallel with that transmitted under their previous permits. It will be impossible to measure this power separately, and a new permit to either of these two applicants will be, in effect, an increase of tis old permit. To prescribe different methods of limiting the importation would involve very complicated methods of supervision, and it is doubtful if effective supervision would be practicable without depriving the companies of the privilege of working close to their limits. It is therefore recommended that the revocable permits, if issued, shall be in the same general form as the permits issued by the Secretary of War in 1907, and that the understanding be that the manner of measuring the limitations will be modified later providing congressional action is such that present or similar limitations are to become permanent.

16. Under the terms of the Burton Act the amount of power which may still be imported under further permits is determined to be 191,500 horsepower, less the amount of power generated and used in Canada. An interpretation of the meaning of the law as to the manner of determining the amount of power used in Canada was requested from the department on October 24, 1912. No interpretation has yet been received in reply to this request, but on December 7, 1912, the Secretary of War directed that applications for permits be forwarded with a report considering the facts in the light of the two possible methods of

determining the amount of power used and generated in Canada, to wit, (a) peak-load measurement or (b) average daily amount.

Each company generating power in Canada from waters of the Niagara River has been requested to submit estimates of its operations during the year 1913, these estimates being requested in various forms to be used in determining the amount of power generated and used in Canada according to various interpretations of the law. These estimates have been submitted by the several companies in terms of maximum momentary peak, maximum load which will not be exceeded more than 1 hour at any one time nor more than 2 hours in 24 (in terms of previous permits), average load for the year, and maximum daily average. These estimated amounts are shown in the following table:

Estimated output in horsepower to Canadian consumers during 1913 from stations generating power in Canada.

	Maximum momentary peak.	Maximum loads in terms of permit.	Average load throughout the year.	Maximum daily average.
Canadian Niagara Power Co.	1,600	1,600	1,200	1,450
Ontario Power Co.	81,000	79,000	60,000	74,260
Electrical Development Co.	70,000	62,000	30,000	36,290
International Ry. Co.	2,000	1,600	628	1,117
Dominion Power & Transmission Co.	33,000	(1)	17,000	19,260
Total	187,600	....	108,828	132,378

1 The records of the Dominion Power & Transmission Co. do not afford means of estimating the amount of output from its power station which would not be exceeded more than 1 hour at any one time nor more than 2 hours in 24.

17. It will be noted that the aggregate of the various momentary peaks is 187,600 horsepower, which is close to the amount provided in the Burton Act to cover the power generated and used in Canada and the power to be imported under revocable permits. Under this interpretation there would be very little power to allot. It is believed, however, that the conditions of operation and a fair interpretation of the Burton Act would not require such restrictions. The maximum momentary peaks in the various plants are not coincident, and in the aggregate do not represent the probable total output at any one time (although they might happen to do so at intervals).

The maximum loads, in terms of previous permits, are estimated for each of the power plants except in the case of the Dominion Power & Transmission Co. This company diverts water from the upper level of the Welland Canal, in the vicinity of Allanburg, Ontario, from whence the diversion flows through a channel into a fairly large storage basin on top of the escarpment near De Cew Falls. From this storage basin the water passes through penstocks to the power station as it is used for generating power. The output of power from the Dominion Power & Transmission Co. varies greatly, the greater amount of power being used for only a short portion of each day. It will be noted that the maximum momentary peak is 33,000 horsepower, while the average load throughout the year is 17,000 horsepower. The conditions attending the operations of this plant are different from other Canadian stations which draw water from the river as it is used. Its diversion from the Welland Canal, and hence from Lake Erie, is nearly uniform throughout the day. The fluctuation in output in the power station is provided for by the storage reservoir. It would therefore seem proper to adopt the output from the De Cew Falls power station as estimated for the maximum daily use, namely, 19,260 horsepower in connection with the maximum loads in terms of previous permits for the other Niagara power stations if this manner of interpreting the law is to be adopted. This gives a total aggregate output of all stations for Canadian use of 163,460 horsepower, leaving 28,040 horsepower which may be imported into the United States under permits still to be issued.

The combined average output estimated for the year 1913 for Canadian use from all power stations diverting water from the Niagara River or its tributaries is 108,828 horsepower, and if this average output is accepted as the interpretation of the law in determining the amount of power generated and used in Canada there remains a total of 82,872 horsepower which may be imported into the United States in addition to that being imported under previous permits. It is seen from the table above that the maximum daily average output for Canadian use exceeds largely the average for the year, and this excess in output above the yearly average is practically coincident for the several stations. For instance, the output during winter months is considerably larger in each station than that during the summer season. It would seem therefore that it would not be proper to adopt the yearly average as the basis for determining the amount of power to be allotted for importation, since the method would allow importation in excess of the amount defined in the law for long periods of time, and this can not be accepted as a reasonable interpretation. Accordingly it is recommended that the yearly averages be not considered in this computation.

The aggregate of the estimated maximum daily average outputs for Canadian use during 1913 of each Canadian power station diverting water from the Niagara River is 132,378 horsepower. If the maximum daily average for each station is to be used as the amount generated and used in Canada by the respective companies, there remains a total of 59,122 horsepower to be allotted under new permits.

18. It was recommended by Lieut. Col. Patrick in letter to the department dated October 24, 1912, that the aggregate of the estimated maximum daily averages of each Canadian power station for Canadian use during the year 1913 be accepted as the amount generated and used in Canada in the meaning of the Burton Act in defining the amount of power which may be imported into the United States under permits issued by the Secretary of War. I concur in this recommendation and believe that this is a fair and reasonable interpretation of the law. It is true that this manner of determining the amount of power generated and used in Canada does not accord with the limitations of permits for importation into the United States that have already been issued, but I can see no practical difficulties in the coordinating of the two methods for the present, and it is hoped that the method of limiting importation will be changed in the near future.

The records of importation of power under previous permits have shown that the use of allowable excess over the stipulated amounts has been due to the overlapping of the lighting load in the fall and winter months with the ordinary daytime load. These peaks occur outside of daylight hours, and the daylight loads average approximately the same as the average load during the 24 hours; and it is the daylight load that visibly affects the grandeur of the Falls. The use of maximum daily averages as the basis of determining the amount of power generated and used in Canada will allow greater importation of power into the United States than the like use of hourly peaks; but in my opinion this is as it should be, so long as the spirit and intent of the law are fulfilled; and I believe that the former method does this.

Furthermore, as has been noted previously in this report, there has been difficulty in performing proper supervision of the companies importing power under the present form of permits; and it can be foreseen that inasmuch as the revocable permits must be modified from time to time in order to keep the amount of power generated and used in Canada and imported into the United States under 350,000 horsepower, the issue of these new permits will necessitate supervision of the entire operations of all Canadian companies, and much greater difficulties can be predicted for such supervision if the present method is followed throughout. In fact, it is doubtful if it will be practicable to determine at any or all times the amount of power generated and used in Canada and imported into the United States on the basis of output which does not exceed a certain amount more than one hour at any time nor more than two hours in twenty-four. The records of these companies are not uniform, and a summation of their outputs in such terms would be difficult if not impossible.

RECOMMENDATIONS.

19. For the reasons stated in paragraph 7 above, it is recommended that, whatever interpretation may be made as to the amount of power that may be allotted for importation under revocable permits, the total amount of power so determined be allotted at once to the two companies who are prepared to start

utilizing such power immediately, namely, the Canadian Niagara Power Co. and the Ontario Power Co. As stated in paragraph 10 above, the merits of the applications of these two companies can not be compared definitely, and whereas any apportionment of power to the said companies must necessarily be more or less arbitrary, it is suggested that this apportionment be made so that the economic loss from the potential energy of the water to the power delivered to the ultimate consumer shall be of equal amounts when using the maximum limits of the respective permits. On this basis, and for a total of 59,000 horsepower, which is the amount to be allotted if the aggregate of maximum daily averages for each plant is used to define the amount of power generated and used in Canada, the allotment of power would be 24,000 horsepower to the Niagara Falls Power Co. and 35,000 horsepower to the Niagara, Lockport & Ontario Power Co.

If the maximum amounts of Canadian power from each plant which will not be exceeded more than 1 hour at any one time nor more than 2 hours in 24 be used in determining the amount of power generated and used in Canada, there remains, in round numbers, 28,000 horsepower to be allotted for importation into the United States. A division on the same basis as above will give to the Canadian Niagara Power Co. 11,000 horsepower and to the Niagara, Lockport & Ontario Power Co. 17,000 horsepower.

It is recommended that permits be issued to the Niagara Falls Power Co. and to the Niagara, Lockport & Ontario Power Co. at once, and for the amounts named above, according to the decision in regard to the interpretation of the Burton Act, and that these permits be formulated similarly to the permits now held by the same companies.

20. For reasons stated in paragraphs 8 and 10 above, it is believed that the Federal Light & Power Co., of Detroit, should have its application considered liberally. There is little doubt but that the rates named by this company are generally lower for the small consumer than the rates of the competing applicants; and also this company proposes to enter competition with an established monopoly, whereas additional permits to the other applicants will generally serve to increase and strengthen subsidiary companies which now practically enjoy monopolies in the territories in which they operate. But for the fact that the Federal Light & Power Co. is not now in a position to utilize power which might be allotted to it, I would recommend that the entire amount of additional power for allocation, or as much of it as could be used, be allotted to it immediately. However, I do recommend that a provisional permit be issued to this company, allotting to it the full amount of power that may be available for distribution under revocable permits, or as much of it as this company may be able to use, to become effective two years from date of such provisional permit, and that the limitation of such permit be increased from time to time, as the needs of this company may require, until the total amount available for allotment under the provision for revocable permits shall be permitted to be imported by the Federal Light & Power Co.

All permits that may be issued to these applicants should include provisions for revocation or modification, so that the aggregate amounts of such permits be not greater than the amount permissible to import under the law; and, in the case of the permits recommended to be issued to the Niagara Falls Power Co. and the Niagara, Lockport & Ontario Power Co., conditions should be named whereby the Secretary of War reserves the right to withdraw any portion or all of the amounts so allotted for reallotment to any other company at any time. (This reservation being for the purpose of reallotting the power to the Federal Light & Power Co. as recommended above.)

21. Inclosed herewith are the applications and other papers in connection therewith, all in duplicate, as follows:

(a) Application of Federal Light & Power Co., with attached exhibits and accompanying brief.

(b) Application of the Niagara Falls Power Co. and attached schedules.

(c) Application of Niagara, Lockport & Ontario Power Co., with 12 inclosures accompanying; also copy of charter and certificate of increase in capital.

(d) Application of Detroit City Council.

J. C. SANFORD.

(The letter of Mr. McFarland, referred to by the chairman, is as follows:)

AMERICAN CIVIC ASSOCIATION,
Harrisburg, Pa., February 3, 1913.

Hon. HENRY D. FLOOD,
  Chairman Committee on Foreign Affairs,
    House of Representatives, Washington, D. C.

DEAR SIR: I am in receipt of yours of January 31 referring to my letter in regard to action in the Committee on Foreign Affairs on the preservation of Niagara Falls.

I beg now to call your attention to the fact that you can not properly secure the passage in the Congress of any legislation which proposes to materially extend the diversion of water at Niagara Falls directly or indirectly. I know of what I speak, and the reporting to the House with a favorable recommendation of any bill which proposes an extension of diversion beyond the terms of the Burton bill will be certain to bring down an avalanche of justified protest and as certain to bring about eventual defeat.

I am advised that your committee has favorably considered a proposition to increase the admission of power from Canada to the total extent of 250,000 horsepower. This is 90,000 horsepower beyond the Burton bill limitations. It means the eventual abstraction of approximately 7,000 cubic feet per second beyond that now possible under the law.

Such a proviso is not only inconsistent but unfair. If there is additional water to be stolen from the cataract at Niagara it ought to be taken on the American side and not the Canadian side. The effect on the grandeur of the Falls is the same in any case, despite any specious statements which may be made to you, as you can ascertain by inquiring of the engineers of the Lake Survey.

Your committee can not, I believe, in consistency and with propriety depart from your wise determination to limit the diversion on the American side to the fair amount set by the Burton bill in 1906 at 15,600 cubic feet per second, neither can you properly or with fairness exceed materially the admission from Canada established in the Burton bill of 160,000 horsepower. These limitations were calculated to give full power and effect to all proceeding investments at the time the United States took possession of Niagara Falls in 1906. The urgency for the admission of more power from Canada is, I believe, almost entirely in behalf of the Ontario Power Co., which in defiance of the expressed will of the American people has doubled its power-producing works since the limitation was established.

Any statement that the power will be sold in Canada if not sold in the United States is absolutely untrue. Canada can demand, and will demand, up to 50 per cent of the capacity of the power authorized on that side and all transmitted to the United States is in direct additional depletion of the Falls.

In other words, Mr. Flood, the United States will be 59 per cent more guilty if the Congress admits 90,000 horsepower additional from Canada than she will be if Congress permitted the diversion of the 4,400 cubic feet per second directly on the American side.

Yours, truly,   J. HORACE MCFARLAND, *President.*

SUPPLEMENTAL STATEMENT OF THE SECRETARY OF WAR.

WAR DEPARTMENT,
Washington, February 20, 1913.

MY DEAR MR. FLOOD: Since my appearance before your committee in regard to the Niagara River bills I have carefully considered the provisions of the treaty with Canada as to the restrictions upon the diversion of water below the Falls. Article 3 of the treaty provides that no diversion of such waters shall be made " except by authority of the United States or the Dominion of Canada within their respective jurisdictions and with the approval, as hereinafter provided, of a joint high commission, to be known as the International Joint Commission." It is evident, therefore, that the treaty looks for the protection of such waters to governmental action of each of the countries and, in addition, requires the approval of the joint high commission. The bill as now drawn is silent as to the attitude of this Government in regard to the diversion of water below the Falls. I think there should be some affirmative declaration by the Government of the United States, and I therefore suggest that there be an express provision in your bill prohibiting the diversion of water below the Falls on the American side without express authority from the Secretary of War. In other words, in any new bill, as in the Burton Act, diversion below the Falls should be assimilated to diversion above the Falls, so far as authority from the United States is required, which still leaves, of course, in full operation the provision of the treaty requiring the approval of the joint high commission, even after permission for diversion should be granted by the Secretary of War. May I ask to have this letter incorporated in the minutes of the hearing?

Allow me to take this occasion to thank you and your committee for the courtesy extended to me in giving me a full opportunity to present my views.

Very respectfully,

HENRY L. STIMSON,
Secretary of War.

Hon. HENRY D. FLOOD,
Chairman of the Committee on Foreign Affairs,
House of Representatives.

REVISED STATEMENT OF MR. F. L. LOVELACE.

COMMITTEE ON FOREIGN AFFAIRS,
HOUSE OF REPRESENTATIVES,
Washington, D. C., Friday, January 24, 1913.

The committee met at 10 o'clock a. m., Hon. Henry D. Flood (chairman) presiding.

The CHAIRMAN. Mr. Lovelace, we have not many members here, but what you have to say will be printed in the record and the others can see it. If it is agreeable to you, you may proceed now.

STATEMENT OF MR. FREDERICK L. LOVELACE, SECRETARY OF THE NIAGARA FALLS POWER CO.

[Revised by Mr. Lovelace.]

Mr. LOVELACE. At the outset, gentlemen, I would ask the committee to take into consideration the fact that I am not a trained speaker, accustomed to thinking quickly on my feet. I have a little mannerism which may already have been apparent before the committee and possibly have been misconstrued. The emphasis arises only from the extreme interest that I have in the matter, and the earnestness that I show in speaking is not evidence of any animosity toward those who have made statements here.

The CHAIRMAN. Yes; we understand that. Tell us first whom you represent here.

Mr. LOVELACE. I am the secretary of the Niagara Falls Power Co., located at Niagara Falls, N. Y., and I speak in behalf of that company. I have listened with profound interest to the addresses made to you yesterday and the day before by the distinguished lawyers who have discussed constitutional limitations, and I personally am unable to determine the merits of the propositions which they have advanced, but I note that in presenting their concrete suggestions, in spite of their arguments they seem to have admitted the same authority as your subcommittee in the draft bill presented here regarding the diversion of water at Niagara. All of the concrete suggestions presented contain provisions by which permits are to be issued by some department of the Federal Government. It seems to me when you concede that it goes with it that the Federal Government may attach conditions under which such permits shall be exercised, and that is the whole question.

I am not a constitutional lawyer, and I do not want to be catechized and asked for the cases, because I do not know the cases, but there are certain fundamental propositions of constitutional law and of the constitution of the State of New York which I do understand. I may possibly refer a little later in one phase of this argument to those fundamental propositions. Now, I want to say, gentlemen, in spite of the arguments for State control that may have been advanced by counsel for our company last year, in practice we have found the Burton law to be admirable as to easy execution and as to being able to place the responsibility for the conditions at Niagara and to control the situation there. The only complaints we have of the Burton law are the narrow limits which it sets, limits narrower than those of the treaty. I want to say that so far as I am able to judge this submitted measure is admirably drafted, and certainly from the Federal jurisdiction standpoint it will be a practical measure, easy to carry into execution, and certain to carry out its provisions in the most convenient method of easy administration. Personally I have no fault to find with the bill except in three respects, which are not its basic principles.

Instead of proceeding, as suggested last night, to try to correct the many untrue and partly true statements that have been made here, I propose to use my time in going at once to the meat of the proposition, asking the committee to enlarge and amend the measure now being considered. I am sure that I have in my mind and shall present to you logical reasons—common sense, practical reasons—for each one of the requests that I am going to make. I may not be able to make them clear to you, but I am sure in my mind that they are practical and logical and fair. I will not dwell long on the first point, because it has been presented in other ways, and that is the limitation of diversion to the limits prescribed by the treaty. Now, gentlemen, there are two reasons why you should make that limit 20,000 cubic feet per second instead of 15,600.

Mr. KENDALL. How did it occur, if you know, that the arbitrary amount of 15,600 cubic feet per second was established? Was it because when the Burton law went into effect the companies were diverting that amount?

Mr. LOVELACE. I can not answer that yes or no. I know the history of it exactly, and I will give it to you in brief.

Mr. KENDALL. It is not very vital, of course.

Mr. LOVELACE. Well, it is and it is not, in a way. Now, please trust me, gentlemen, because I mean to be fair. I believe that every member of the committee, even though he puts questions which, as has been stated here before, seem like " pretty strong barks," is sincerely trying to frame a practical and fair measure, in the interests of the people of the United States as well as of those who have put their money in good faith into Niagara power development and distribution. Now, before touching that, let me make this statement: Canada is going to use and is already practically using—it already has plants built to use all of the 36,000 cubic feet per second which under the treaty they are allowed to divert and they are going to use that power whether you let it come over here or not. Power is now a glut on the Canadian market.

The CHAIRMAN. I thought there was a power famine up there.

Mr. LOVELACE. The power famine is on the American side and the glut on the Canadian side. We have a part of our Canadian power house lying idle to-day and we are purchasing power simply on account of the famine on the American side. All of that 36,000 cubic feet of water is practically appropriated for use. Plants are already built to use every bit of that water, and generators are being rapidly installed to turn it all into electric energy. There is no reason why you should not give the people of the United States the benefit of the small additional amount between the limits which you have fixed in the measure before you and the limits fixed by the treaty.

Mr. CLINE. How would you distribute the surplus?

Mr. LOVELACE. Well, sir, I would at least give the existing companies an opportunity to compete for it. I would not cut them off entirely, as has been suggested by the concrete suggestions for amendments presented by the Conservation Commission and by the distinguished lawyer, Mr. J. Boardman Scovell, and he is a distinguished lawyer on this subject, but he has ideas in his mind when it comes to questions outside of law questions. I respect his opinion on legal questions.

Now, just one word as to that 4,400 feet additional. I have here a summary from the report of the Chief of Engineers. I do not ask you to take his offhand statements at the hearing last year, but take his formal documents, which were carefully prepared. Now, as to 4,400 feet additional diversion, this will be the effect upon the Falls: At the crest of the Falls it will be less than one-eighth of an inch; at the Goat Island end of the Horseshoe Falls it will be approximately nine-sixteenths of an inch; at the Canadian end of the Horseshoe Falls it will be less than $1\frac{7}{8}$ inches. That is approximated. At Lake Erie it will be approximately one-fifth of an inch. So that you see it will be inappreciable when you consider that the Chief of Engineers has formally reported that, due to natural causes, Lake Erie has a 14-foot variation, due to winds, 8 feet one way and 6 feet the other. You will find all that in the report of the Chief of Engineers. That is one of the practical reasons advanced why you may well include that 4,400 feet.

The other reason for including it which I desire to urge is this: If you retain in your bill the provision which definitely requires or may require the scrapping of present plants and the building of new plants 7 miles away from where they are now located, it will be impracticable, from the best estimates I can yet obtain, to operate the required long-surface canal with 8,600 feet of water. Every winter it would fill with ice, and public utilities as well as industrial uses dependent on the power be paralyzed. The General Electric Co. had a proposition when the Burton law came out, and they claimed to be about to make bona fide developments at the Devils Hole, taking their water above our water, and they stated that they would need all of the 20,000 cubic feet, the treaty amount, in order to make that a successful commercial proposition with such a long (7 miles) surface canal. There are a great many physical difficulties, but I am coming to that. There are a great many legal difficulties and there are all kinds of financial and commercial difficulties in scrapping the pioneer hydroelectric plant of the world and instituting in its place a plant .7 miles away, supplied by a long, slow-moving canal from a point above the Falls.

Now, I am going to answer the interrogation of the Member from the State of Iowa. I had intended not to touch on this point, because I am not sure that touching on it will assist the cause which I am urging before you.

Mr. KENDALL. I was actuated a good deal by curiosity more than anything else.

Mr. LOVELACE. The Burton law, as first drafted by Judge Burton—Senator Burton now—and as it first passed the House of Representatives and the Senate of the United States, restricted the diversion of the waters of the Niagara River on the American side to the amount then used by the existing companies, and until a treaty could be negotiated permitted no new diversions. It was passed after careful consideration. I argued the matter time and time again with Senator Burton. I think I made his life miserable then, and I know he has made mine miserable ever since. However, it was very carefully considered, and the law passed both branches of Congress. In the Senate, Senator Knox, of Pennsylvania, had inserted an amendment in regard to the requirements of the Pittsburgh Reduction Co., incorporated under the laws of Pennsylvania—now known as the Aluminum Co. of America—which was building its plants on the lands of the Hydraulic Power Co., the amendment in the Senate covering that situation, so that as it passed the Senate it also provided for diversions which would be made by plants which had their factories in process of construction. This was a very indefinite term and would have covered many plants on our own land if we had taken advantage of it, but we never undertook to do so. That, of course, necessitated a conference.

The CHAIRMAN. You mean a conference between the House and the Senate?

Mr. LOVELACE. Yes, sir. Judge Burton was one of the conferees from the Senate.

The CHAIRMAN. From the House, you mean?

Mr. LOVELACE (continuing). And that amendment did not please him. He tried to make the bill exact, and he did so by inserting for the first time this provision limiting the diversion of water in terms of cubic feet per second. Now, he took those figures from the Hon. George Clinton, a distinguished lawyer from the State of New York, the bearer of a name respected and revered for generations; but he arrived at the figures without going to the source that he should have gone to in order to find whether they were exact or not.

He had placed in his report as a member of the International Water-ways Commission certain figures as to the diversion of water from Niagara River, but these figures were correct only to the extent that they were theoretical figures on certain percentages of efficiency.

Those figures Judge Burton adopted and they went into the bill. They were made up this way: Five hundred cubic feet of water per second for the power users on the Erie Canal at Lockport, 6,500 cubic feet of water per second for the Hydraulic Co.—by the way, Judge Clinton had assigned them 9,500 cubic feet of water per second, which was what he had figured as the theoretical ultimate capacity of their plant, but 6,500 was the figure taken and allowed by Judge Burton. When it came to our plant, the first tenant that the Niagara Falls Power Co. was able to obtain was the Niagara Falls Paper Co., which afterwards became a branch of the International Paper Co. It was before electricity had really become known in the form of alternating current for use in commercial purposes and for trans-mission to industries. We sold them 11 acres of land near the river, reserving to ourselves the riparian rights, and gave them the right to discharge the tail waters from their development into our large tailrace tunnel, generating a certain amount of mechanical power, and it has been since determined that their diversion from the river is 800 cubic feet of water per second. So that 800 cubic feet of the 15,600 feet of water is being used to-day by the International Paper Co. for hydraulic power and not for electric power. Seven thousand eight hundred cubic feet of water was assigned to us, and is now the amount permitted by the Secretary of War to be used by the Niagara Falls Power Co. for the generation of electrical power.

The CHAIRMAN. Did he make any recommendations increasing that to 10,000 feet?

Mr. LOVELACE. No, sir; this was before the Burton law was passed. I am frank to say to you, gentlemen, that in spite of the fact that I revere Judge Clinton's name, I do not think he was fair in not making a sound investigation before determining that theoretical amount. We afterwards found that it required more than this 7,800 cubic feet of water that was left to us to operate the plant which we had already built and had been operating before the enact-ment of the Burton law, with about 10,500 cubic feet of water. There was absolutely no doubt in our minds, there was absolutely no doubt in the mind of Judge Burton, there was no doubt in the mind of any-body, which is borne out by the reports which the Rivers and Harbors Committee made to Congress, that it was the intention of Congress to limit the diversion to what it was then, not increasing the limita-tion but stopping it temporarily at the amount then being diverted by existing companies and permitting no new diversions to be begun until a treaty should be made covering the entire matter on both sides of the river. We found soon after the Burton law was passed that those figures were only theoretical; that we had previously at peak loads been diverting about 2,000 feet more. We found we were not able to operate the entire plant that we had built before the Burton law was passed. Finding that condition to be true, after in-vestigation, we made representations to the treaty commissioners who had been appointed, who replied that if it was true that Con-gress intended to limit diversions, to the extent that were then in progress at the time of the act, and that if, upon the reports of the

Government engineers, they should find out that it did not interfere with navigation, that it did not interfere with the integrity of the Niagara River as a boundary stream, and that it did not interfere with scenic beauty, they would rectify the condition.

I know that they did rectify the condition. They took counsel of the War Department and the engineers did determine these things: That the diversion of 20,000 cubic feet of water per second on the American side of the Niagara River, together with 36,000 on the Canadian side, would not interfere with navigation nor with scenic beauty nor with the integrity of the river as a boundary stream—would not appreciably affect the scenic beauty at Niagara. Remember this, gentlemen, that we also lost half of our development by the Burton law, which under the law of the State of New York we had the right to make. We had one plant completed and we suffered great hardship in being obliged to shut down a part of our machinery, as well as being deprived of our right to complete our original plans for 200,000 horsepower.

The CHAIRMAN. Do you mean to say that when the Burton law went into effect you had to abandon part of your plant?

Mr. LOVELACE. We were obliged immediately to shut down a considerable part of our completed plant. Besides that we lost one-half of our authorized 200,000 horsepower for which we had constructed a canal and made other substantial constructions, and had purchased 1,200 acres of land on which to locate industries.

The CHAIRMAN. What became of the canal?

Mr. LOVELACE. It is in use supplying water to our existing plant.

The CHAIRMAN. That was not lost, then?

Mr. LOVELACE. Not in respect of the initial plant, but it had been constructed for that plant and also to supply water to a second development of a like amount of power.

The CHAIRMAN. You did not lose the land.

Mr. LOVELACE. We have it there, but it is more than we have ever needed up to date; but I am not urging that fact for the purpose of the present argument.

The CHAIRMAN. But I want to get the facts. You made the statement that under the Burton law you had to abandon plants that cost you millions of dollars.

Mr. LOVELACE. Yes; and it is true.

The CHAIRMAN. Is it not a fact that your land is worth more now than it was when you bought it?

Mr. LOVELACE. Well, I hope so. Some of it is and some of it is not.

Mr. GARNER. What kind of industries did you expect to put on this 1,200-acre piece of ground?

Mr. LOVELACE. It was largely a matter of very indefinite prophecy at that time. That was a time when George Westinghouse said it was impossible to carry electric power to Buffalo. We did not have the industries in mind, but it was to invite all the world to locate there. and they have, very largely, sir. There are industries there that have an investment of $25,000,000 or $30,000,000, requiring all the power we can produce with the water now allowed us, and their success and growth urgently demanding more.

Mr. DIFENDERFER. It is your claim now, is it not, that you have not sufficient head in order to get a full and proper efficiency with the plant that you now have?

Mr. Lovelace. No; that is not true. That would be a very unfair statement of it. The efficiency of the machinery in our plant to-day is unsurpassed by that in any similar plant in the world. Our claim is that we built under the best lights we could get at that time. There had never been a turbine put down to the depth at which we put ours; there never had been a generator in any electric plant in the world with anything like the output of power and efficiency. We secured the advice of the most competent engineers of both continents. We did the best we knew how, and we have to-day one of the most efficient plants, not only on the Niagara frontier but in the world. Now, it is true that we could have located at other places in the world where we could have gotten a much greater head. To carry the argument to an absurdity, we could have come to Washington and gotten a drop of 550 feet.

Mr. Difenderfer. We are here for information.

Mr. Lovelace. We went where we did with our plant, to preserve the scenic beauty of Niagara Falls—the same reason advanced by Senator Burton and by the association which was represented here last night by Mr. Watrous, the American Civic Association. Now, I have a picture here.

Mr. Difenderfer. Wait a moment.

Mr. Lovelace. I am going to answer your question.

Mr. Difenderfer. Let me finish my question.

Mr. Lovelace. Yes.

Mr. Difenderfer. You certainly must have felt justified in selling to the paper company a sufficient amount to run their business out of your allotment, did you not?

Mr. Lovelace. Yes, sir; that was sold to them in 1894, long before allotments. It was the very first customer that we had for power.

Mr. Difenderfer. But now you come back and want part of this 4,400 cubic feet per second after disposing of enough to run their business?

Mr. Lovelace. Oh, that was disposed of long before the Burton law, and was a regular sale of power, but not electric.

Mr. Difenderfer. It does not make any difference whether it was disposed of long ago. You had your plant built.

Mr. Lovelace. That is exactly what it was built for. Most of us thought that plants would all be like the paper company, and great engineers said that those were the only kinds of industries that could be built there, because they could use the power on the spot. That is what the paper company is doing.

Mr. Difenderfer. Then, do you not think that the Government itself might as well have given it to the paper company?

Mr. Lovelace. I do think to-day that that was the proper method; that we should have taken advantage of it. The Burton law contains a provision that no one company shall apply for a permit in excess of 8,600 cubic feet of water per second. Now, instead of making the International Paper Co. a part of ourselves, that company should have gone to the Secretary of War and made application for its 800 cubic feet. We could have then applied for the full limit of 8,600 cubic feet for our own electrical development.

Mr. Difenderfer. But you made a profit out of it?

Mr. Lovelace. Out of which? We were glad to get the International Paper Co. as a tenant. Our development had to be financed and could not finance itself. Local men tried to finance it not only in this country, but in Europe; but it was only the men of undaunted courage and faith that finally were able to build the plants and patiently hold through until the success of the enterprise—years afterwards—was apparent. I believe that if anybody else but these particular men got hold of it it would not have been a success. Of course, the world would have come to it in time, but not as soon as they did. Now, this is why we went up the stream [referring to maps and pictures]. Do you see all those streams coming down here? That is the Falls there. That is the upper steel-arch bridge. You see those mills right there in front of the Falls. Now, gentlemen, this same agitation as is now made was in the air at the time this development began.

Power development at Niagara started back in the fifties, and they had put up the flour mills and other mills in front of the Falls and defaced and commercialized the Falls, but the men who had our enterprise in hand were men of broad views and they determined for the very purpose of preserving the scenic beauty of the Falls to go a mile and a half up the river and there they obtained a river frontage and constructed their plant. Now, gentlemen, by doing this, by their attempt at that early day to preserve the Falls, they lost some head, but even then the head developed was the greatest that had ever been used by any company before on a turbine wheel for power purposes.

My second request is in respect of the limitation of transmission of power from Canada. The arguments on that subject need not be repeated, but I would ask you to remove your limits. Trust Canada. She has contracted with the United States to limit her diversion of water to a certain amount, and she is certainly going to make that diversion; but it seems to me that the comity of nations requires that we should trust her to live up to her part of the treaty. If you are going to limit it at all, it has been suggested before in these hearings you should not limit it to less than one-half of the power produced by the 36,000 cubic feet treaty allowance to Canada. The actual figures are upward of 500,000 horsepower which can be produced in Canada by 36,000 cubic feet of water, possibly more if they get greater efficiency. But they are going to produce their 500,000 horsepower from this 36,000 feet.

Mr. DIFENDERFER. Do you not think it would be well for this Government to encourage the transmission of power into this country for this reason—that we would be encouraging enterprise on this side rather than on the other side?

Mr. LOVELACE. There is absolutely no doubt in my mind on that, and the only sensible way and the only polite way is to trust Canada herself to put into effect this solemn obligation on her part.

Mr. DIFENDERFER. Would there not be a possibility of collusion to prevent transmission—a gentlemen's agreement?

Mr. LOVELACE. Now, I want to answer that. There have been various references to " power trusts," " interlocking boards," and " gentlemen's agreements." I want to say that there is no place in the world where there is more active competition in electric power than at Niagara Falls. All of the four interests engaged there in the production of electric power are absolutely separate, unallied, and independent, and in active competition each with the other.

Mr. DIFENDERFER. How about the MacKenzie-Mann people? Has there been any effort to restrain those people from bringing power into this country?

Mr. LOVELACE. No, sir; they have a permit for 46,000——

Mr. DIFENDERFER (interposing). I believe the testimony here is 40,000?

Mr. LOVELACE. No; it is 46,000.

Mr. DIFENDERFER. And they bring it to the center of the river?

Mr. LOVELACE. They have never constructed a plant for transmitting any part of it into the United States. They own the Electric Light Co. in Toronto and the railways radiating out from Toronto. and they applied to the Secretary of War under the Burton Act and received a permit.

Mr. DIFENDERFER. Did they buy a gas plant at Niagara Falls?

Mr. LOVELACE. Yes, sir: and if you ask me if they have any intention of coming into the United States I will say that I believe they have. I will give you the facts if you will give me the time. They have themselves transmitted no power under the Burton law. The Niagara Falls Power Co. has an insistent power demand made on it at Niagara Falls and at Buffalo; all of Buffalo is dependent on our company not because there is no competition but because the other companies are not willing to undertake to supply Buffalo on account of the great investment which would have to be made. Take the Niagara, Lockport & Ontario Power Co.—they could not do it now because they are sold up, but before that they were unwilling to supply that city because of the burden of the expenditure required to construct a distributing plant and facilities and underground distribution. So Buffalo is solely dependent on us for her power, and we have a very large market there, and we have a very large market at Niagara Falls.

Under our permit for the transmission of power from Canada and for the production of power on the American side we are unable to supply all of the demands that are made on us. and we either must take power from somebody at Niagara Falls, who needs it badly, or take it from Buffalo, which is dependent on us for its public utilities. In that state of affairs, not being able to get our power from Canada: where we have ample, our subcompany has gone to the Toronto Power Co. and contracted with them to purchase 25,000 horsepower: and they are taking that power and distributing it in Buffalo, while at the same time we are compelled by the limitation of our transmission permit to let an equal amount of installation in our Canadian plant lie idle. That is the fact as regards utilization of the transmission permit of the Toronto Power Co.

Mr. CLINE. Do you not think it is better to make definite the amount of power that is to be brought over. for the reason that if it is left as you say it would involve the Government to a very large extent in controversy with the people getting the power as to whether they were getting more than they ought to have?

Mr. LOVELACE. I say "yes" to that. but I qualify it. I believe that if you are going to put any limit on it at all that the limit should be definite, but I do not think there should be any limit. If there is to be a limit I believe that it should be 250,000 horsepower. which is nearer one-half than 200,000. and it is less than one-half if you count the power used at De Cew Falls, only 10 miles farther over in Canada.

Now, gentlemen. this brings me to what is really on my mind. the third point, which is in respect of efficiency, as you have called it. Now, gentlemen, nobody can quarrel with you on the logic of that requirement as an academic proposition. But I want to say that, placed in this definite manner, which would absolutely require, within five years, the "scrapping" of our plant and very likely all present power developments at Niagara Falls, it is fraught with great danger. It may be—I will not say that it is. but it may be—a commercial, a physical, and a legal impossibility to do what you ask, and I will advance some of the reasons why it may be. The distinguished lawyer, Mr. J. Boardman Scovell, certainly a distinguished lawyer in that particular branch of the law. last night said that our company did not have the power to go down there and build a plant where we would be obliged to place it to fully comply with this provision——

Mr. GARNER (interposing). What do you mean by "power"?

Mr. LOVELACE. He referred to our State charter. I know some of the fundamentals of constitutional law as applied in the State of New York that I am sure of.

The CHAIRMAN. Why not answer his question?

Mr. GARNER. He said he did not have it in his charter.

Mr. LOVELACE. We might get the permit from the Secretary of War, but it is another question to have the power to utilize it.

Mr. GARNER. Haven't you a general incorporation act of the State of New York for the purpose of furnishing power to the public?

Mr. LOVELACE. Yes, sir.

Mr. GARNER. Could not you incorporate under that law and ask for a new permit?

Mr. LOVELACE. That would be a new company. I am talking about the powers of the present company.

The CHAIRMAN. And he was, too.

Mr. LOVELACE. But let me show you some of the difficulties that are apparent to me. It is a fundamental principle upon which you will all agree with me, I think, that in the State of New York there are certain rights—I will not name the rights that have been argued before you—but there are certain admitted rights that belong to riparian owners. They may not have the right to divert water for power purposes, but they have at least the right to have the water flow by their shores, and no company can divert water, take it around the lower riparian owner, and return it below without impairing the latter's rights. I am certain that we have not the power to condemn certain of these rights, because some of them are being used already for public purposes, for railway purposes, and could we condemn a public use, if we had the power, for our own use? That is the legal obstacle in our way. In addition to acquiring such riparian rights along several miles of river front we would also, of course, have to condemn a right of way from the source of intake to the point of discharge of tail waters, a distance of several miles. So there may be legal objections and there may be commercial objections which may be insurmountable, and the physical objection is the ice question.

Now, that has not been brought up here; but, gentlemen, I am sure that a canal 7 miles long in which only 8,600 cubic feet of water per second is to be conducted, and necessarily to preserve the head built at not a very great pitch, would be very likely to so fill itself up with ice in winter as not to be a practical proposition, a practical operating proposition. Now, the Hydraulic Power Co. found itself in that position many years ago, and until they deepened and widened their canal beyond the limits fixed by the State legislature, every winter they were locked up in ice, although the canal is only about 1-mile in length. The ice proposition is a very serious question in that climate, and the great public utilities depending on us for their power can not stand interruptions. The city of Syracuse to-day, in spite of all the money the Niagara, Lockport & Ontario Power Co. has spent to get its power down to Syracuse, is full of complaints of citizens about the service in that city. To the cities of Buffalo and Tonawanda we have eight independent lines extending from three separate plants, which can be switched together in any way, and we are thereby enabled to give them a pretty fair service.

Now we come to what I believe to be the real solution. I believe that such an absolute, definite requirement is fraught with grave danger; but, as I said before, I can not quarrel with you over the logic of the requirement. There is no doubt that by the provision which you have already put into the law, limiting the amount of water that may be used for power purposes, you will thereby compel us, who have already found the market, to make the most efficient use of the water that is practicable, feasible, and possible.

Now, these three requests I am urging. I believe, irrespective of my interest in the subject——

Mr. GARNER (interposing). You are a lawyer?

Mr. LOVELACE. I was admitted to practice law, but I found it more in keeping with my ability and my tastes and temperament to settle down as an officer of this corporation and draft its contracts; but I am not——

Mr. GARNER (interposing). Then you do not care to express an opinion as to the constitutionality of this provision or as to the power of your State legislature to force you to do the same thing?

Mr. LOVELACE. No; I do not care to go into a discussion of the cases. But I have already said to this committee that, having listened with great interest to the learned arguments that have been made to you, I am still of the opinion that your subcommittee has prepared a measure which is absolutely practicable in its administrative features.

The Burton law has been in operation for years without the slightest friction between the Secretary of War and the companies and has been found to be a practical measure for the control of the waters of the Niagara River. The only matter of complaint that I have is the matter of the two unnecessarily narrow limits which you have set and a requirement for efficiency of a kind that is probably impracticable and physically impossible. Now, as regards that question of efficiency. I do not know that I have it here, but I talked with the engineers who made the report upon which the table of efficiency is based, and those gentlemen said to me that they did not mean that table to be exact; that it was merely a comparison of the relative locations and operating conditions of the various companies at Niagara; and that the 100 per cent was not intended as a standard of required or desired efficiency, and that from the viewpoint of the

Burton law there were other more important features in respect of the relative operations of the several power companies.

Mr. CLINE. In all the discussion before this committee by constitutional lawyers and other lawyers the question of the power of the Federal Government or the State government to require this efficiency has not been raised by anyone.

Mr. KENDALL. I understood Judge O'Gorman to state——

Mr. GARNER (interposing). He said the Federal Government had no power. He was only discussing the Federal Government; he did not say anything about the State power.

Mr. LOVELACE. If Congress has the right to provide for the issuing of permits for the diversion of water from the Niagara River—and every gentleman who has spoken before you except, perhaps, Senator O'Gorman, certainly Gen. Carmody, did admit that right—if you have that right, then it seems to me that you can regulate the conditions under which the permits shall be given and exercised.

Mr. KENDALL. What is your objection to the substitute here—the proposed substitute? You read that, I suppose?

Mr. LOVELACE. The substitute of the Conservation Commission?

Mr. KENDALL. No, sir; of the subcommittee.

Mr. LOVELACE. I have already stated it.

Mr. KENDALL. I know, but does it substantially meet with your approval?

Mr. LOVELACE. Yes, sir; I believe it is an absolutely workable bill, except in that it contains that one condition which I have indicated may be legally as well as commercially and physically impossible.

Mr. KENDALL. If your three suggestions are adopted?

Mr. LOVELACE. Yes, sir; if you comply with the three requests made by me I believe the bill will be the best that can be passed. I would not object at all to your inserting the amendment asked for by the Conservation Commission, which is fair, if it would not encumber your bill, but I want to say that I am sure the Public Service Commission of the State of New York has the power to regulate the rates of our generating company, and they can very easily acquire the power to regulate the rates of the other company. The Hydraulic Power Co. since the institution of the public service commission has separated itself into two separate bodies. It has one body which is producing hydraulic power and it sells to its other self that mechanical power thus produced, and its other self turns that into electrical power and distributes it. Congressman Smith said that their hydraulic part, not being an electrical corporation, has refused to comply with the regulations of the public service commission, and the reason is this: The public service commission law of the State of New York contains a provision that its requirements and provisions shall apply to electrical corporations. The Hydraulic Co. is an hydraulic corporation, and therefore, perhaps, not now under the commission's jurisdiction. A very slight amendment of the statute will bring them in. As a matter of fact, my company has turned itself inside out, voluntarily and gladly, for the benefit of the Public Service Commission of the State of New York.

Let me say this in respect of Judge Hammond's argument before you a year ago: Judge Hammond has since that time tried the case——

The CHAIRMAN (interposing). Is that the corporation counsel of the city of Buffalo?

Mr. LOVELACE. Yes, sir. He made complaint to the public-service commission that the rates in Buffalo were unfair, and that case has been tried at great length, and there is no doubt in my mind that it will be settled before the 1st of February, when the term of the chairman of that commission expires.

The CHAIRMAN. That is merely speculation?

Mr. LOVELACE. Well, it certainly will be decided at an early date, and you will find, gentlemen, that the public-service commission has duly asserted its power absolutely to regulate rates in the city of Buffalo.

Mr. HARRISON. You have a live Canadian company there and the Niagara Falls Power Co.?

Mr. LOVELACE. Yes, sir.

Mr. HARRISON. Which charges the higher rates, the Ontario Power Co. or the Niagara Falls Power Co.?

Mr. LOVELACE. I do not understand there is much difference, except that the glut of the market in Canada and the extreme famine on the American side has reduced comparative power rates in Canada.

Mr. HARRISON. Notwithstanding the fact that the Canadian company pays rentals to the Canadian Government?

Mr. LOVELACE. They pay very much less than we do.

Mr. HARRISON. You have more of a monopoly on this side?

Mr. LOVELACE. Oh, no; there are two competing generating companies on this side, and in addition to that two of the other companies competing on the other side bring their power into the United States, and I am asking for an enlargement of that right in order that there may be greater competition. I would be very glad to give Mr. Bowen what he wants, so long as you do not destroy Niagara Falls.

Mr. KENDALL. Have you any objection to Mr. Bowen's proposition?

Mr. LOVELACE. Not the slightest, nor to any other prospective competitor.

Mr. CURLEY. What is the real value tax per thousand in Canada?

Mr. LOVELACE. It is very small.

Mr. CURLEY. Is it $8 a thousand?

Mr. LOVELACE. All the taxes put together will not amount to that, but the real thing about it is that the assessments are low.

Mr. CURLEY. What is the rate in Buffalo?

Mr. LOVELACE. The aggregate of the rates is about $25 or $26.

Mr. CURLEY. Then the tax rate is about three times as great as on the Canadian side?

Mr. LOVELACE. Oh, yes. We paid in taxes on our American plant last year about $3 per horsepower and approximately a dollar more per horsepower for municipal assessments for public improvements.

Mr. CURLEY. What did you pay the Canadian Government?

Mr. LOVELACE. It is a sliding scale, beginning at a dollar for 10,000 horsepower and running to 50 cents for all above 30,000 horsepower.

Mr. DIFENDERFER (interposing). That goes into the park improvement commission fund, does it not?

Mr. LOVELACE. Yes, sir; it is paid as " park rental," the plants being located in the park on Government lands.

Mr. CURLEY. So that, as a matter of fact, it is twice as expensive on this side as on the other side?

Mr. LOVELACE. It is very much more expensive. I thank you very much, and I hope you do not think that because I have raised my voice I have anything but an earnest interest in the subject.

Mr. KENDALL. You have a general counsel, however?

Mr. LOVELACE. I do not know that we have. I am the attorney for the company as well as the secretary. Our board of directors contains three lawyers considered among the most eminent lawyers of our State, if not of the country. They have not been formally designated as counsel and have never charged for their services.

Mr. KENDALL. This bill may require your company to transfer its plant?

Mr. LOVELACE. Yes; in its present form.

Mr. KENDALL. Now, there may be legal difficulties in the way of doing that; that is, that your New York charter may not be comprehensive enough to permit it?

Mr. LOVELACE. That may be one of the difficulties.

Mr. KENDALL. I want to know what your legal department thought about that proposition, whether you could junk your plant, start below, and get increased head.

Mr. LOVELACE. There is no doubt that under the constitutional law of the State of New York we have not the power of eminent domain sufficient to condemn other public uses. For instance, there is this Gorge Railroad, which was before you last night. We would be obliged to condemn their rights and also the rights of the Hydraulic Power Co., their riparian rights, in order to get by them, because both of these companies are owners of extensive riparian lands and riparian rights between our point of water diversion and the place where you would compel us to return the water to the river.

Mr. CURLEY. I believe Mr. Scovell or somebody else raised the contention last night that this committee had no power to compel you to take power from below the Falls and that the only body that had the power was the public utilities commission or the public service commission.

Mr. LOVELACE. The joint high commission alone has jurisdiction of the waters of the river below the Falls.

The CHAIRMAN. The treaty gives the jurisdiction over that to the joint high commission.

Mr. LOVELACE. I really think that is right. Of course, you have the treaty before you.

With the permission of the chairman, I would like printed as a part of my statement this clipping from a recent number of one of the most reliable technical journals.

The CHAIRMAN. Now, gentlemen, that ends the hearings on the bill.

––––––––

GLORIOUS HISTORY OF ELECTROCHEMISTRY AT NIAGARA.

[From Metallurgical and Chemical Engineering in a discussion on the position of electro-chemistry.]

When the story of the industrial evolution of the United States will be written by some future historian who must be both a philosopher and an engineer, one of his brightest chapters will deal with the glorious history of electrochemistry at Niagara Falls. August 26, 1895, the Niagara works of the Pittsburgh Reduction Co. started the manufacture of aluminum. On October 19 of the same year the current was turned on at the works of the Carborundum Co. In quick succession came calcium carbide, artificial graphite, phosphorus, ferroalloys made in the electric furnace and metallic sodium, caustic and chlorine, chlorates, made by electrolysis. In the span of 15 years these pioneer electrochemical industries and others that followed have become so firmly established in the industrial world that their products are well-nigh indispensable in present civilization. We have forgotten that not so long ago aluminum, carborundum, and calcium carbide were unknown.

The revolutionary features of the early inventions are gone. What remains are splendidly flourishing industries developing along logical lines into ever-extending fields of usefulness. We have almost learned to look at the pioneer Niagara works as the older generation of electrochemical industries. This is said in a spirit of filial pride. For if Germany may be justly proud of having nursed and raised the coal-tar chemical industries, the United States can claim applied electrochemistry as distinctly American. The bulk of these electrochemical industries was not imported; it was made, born, nursed, and raised at Niagara by such pioneers as Acheson and Hall and by those who worked with them or followed them. They represent the most distinctly American phase in the history of applied chemistry.

X

INTERNATIONAL JOINT COMMISSION (WATERWAYS)

HEARINGS

BEFORE THE

COMMITTEE ON FOREIGN AFFAIRS

HOUSE OF REPRESENTATIVES

FEBRUARY 24, 1913

ON

H. R. 28607

STATEMENTS OF

HON. JAMES A. TAWNEY
DR. ALLAN J. McLAUGHLIN

WASHINGTON
GOVERNMENT PRINTING OFFICE
1913

COMMITTEE ON FOREIGN AFFAIRS.

HOUSE OF REPRESENTATIVES.

[Committee room, gallery floor, west corridor. Telephone 230. Meets on call.]

HENRY D. FLOOD, Virginia, *Chairman.*

JOHN N. GARNER, Texas.
WILLIAM G. SHARP, Ohio.
CYRUS CLINE, Indiana.
JEFFERSON M. LEVY, New York.
JAMES M. CURLEY, Massachusetts.
J. CHAS. LINTHICUM, Maryland.
ROBERT E. DIFENDERFER, Pennsylvania.
WILLIAM S. GOODWIN, Arkansas.
CHARLES M. STEDMAN, North Carolina.
EDWARD W. TOWNSEND, New Jersey.

BYRON P. HARRISON, Mississippi.
CHARLES B. SMITH, New York.
WILLIAM B. McKINLEY, Illinois.
HENRY A. COOPER, Wisconsin.
IRA W. WOOD, New Jersey.
RICHARD BARTHOLDT, Missouri.
GEORGE W. FAIRCHILD, New York.
N. E. KENDALL, Iowa.
J. HAMPTON MOORE, Pennsylvania.

B. F. ODEN, *Clerk.*

2

INTERNATIONAL JOINT COMMISSION (WATERWAYS).

COMMITTEE ON FOREIGN AFFAIRS,
HOUSE OF REPRESENTATIVES,
February 24, 1913.

The committee met at 10.30 o'clock a. m., Hon. Henry D. Flood (chairman) presiding.

STATEMENT OF HON. JAMES A. TAWNEY, CHAIRMAN INTERNATIONAL JOINT COMMISSION.

Mr. TAWNEY. Mr. Chairman, it may be profitable to all concerned, before discussing the character and the extent of the work of the International Joint Commission since its organization a year ago, to briefly state the general scope of the jurisdiction and purpose of this international tribunal and some of the provisions of the treaty under which it has been created.

In some respects this treaty marks an advance with respect to the peaceable settlement of international controversies and the peaceable settlement of controversies between the inhabitants of two countries living under separate governmental jurisdictions far beyond anything thus far attained in the matter of creating and maintaining cordial relations between two independent Governments and their inhabitants.

The treaty dates from the day of the exchange of ratifications, which was May 5, 1910. The purposes of the treaty, as expressed in its first paragraph, are:

To prevent disputes regarding the use of boundary waters and to settle all questions which are now pending between the United States and the Dominion of Canada involving the rights, obligations, or interests of either in relation to the other or to the inhabitants of the other along their common frontier, and to make provision for the adjustment and settlement of all such questions as may hereafter arise.

Boundary waters are defined in the very beginning of the treaty as—

The waters from main shore to main shore of the lakes and rivers and connecting waterways or the portions thereof along which the international boundary between the United States and the Dominion of Canada passes, including all bays, arms, and inlets thereof, but not including tributary waters which in their natural channels would flow into such lakes, rivers, and waterways, or waters flowing from such lakes, rivers, or waterways or of the waters of rivers flowing across the boundary.

Article I of the treaty declares:

That the navigation of all navigable boundary waters shall forever continue free and open for the purposes of commerce to the inhabitants and to the ships, vessels, and boats of both countries equally, subject, however, to any laws and

3

regulations of either country within its own territory not inconsistent with such privilege of free navigation and applying equally without discrimination to the inhabitants, ships, vessels, and boats of both countries.

Article III provides:

In addition to the uses, obstructions, and diversions heretofore permitted or hereafter provided for by special agreement between the parties hereto, no further or other uses or obstructions or diversions, whether temporary or permanent, of boundary waters on either side of the line, affecting the natural level or flow of boundary waters on the other side of the line, shall be made except by authority of the United States or the Dominion of Canada within their respective jurisdictions and with the approval, as hereinafter provided, of a joint commission, to be known as the International Joint Commission.

Article IV provides that—

Except in cases provided for by special agreement between them [the high contracting parties] will not permit the construction or maintenance on their respective sides of the boundary of any remedial or protective works or any dams or other obstructions in waters flowing from boundary waters or in waters at a lower level than the boundary in rivers flowing across the boundary, the effect of which is to raise the natural level of waters on the other side of the boundary unless the construction or maintenance thereof is approved by the aforesaid International Joint Commission.

It is further agreed that the waters herein defined as boundary waters and waters flowing across the boundary shall not be polluted on either side to the injury of health or property on the other.

Article VIII of the treaty defines the jurisdiction of the International Joint Commission, as follows:

This International Joint Commission shall have jurisdiction over and shall pass upon all cases involving the use or obstruction or diversion of the waters with respect to which, under Articles III and IV of this treaty, the approval of this commission is required, and in passing upon such cases the commission shall be governed by the following rules or principles which are adopted by the high contracting parties for this purpose:

The high contracting parties shall have, each on its own side of the boundary, equal and similar rights in the use of the waters hereinbefore defined as boundary waters.

The following order of precedence shall be observed among the various uses enumerated hereinafter for these waters, and no use shall be permitted which tends materially to conflict with or restrain any other use which is given preference over it in this order of precedence.

(1) Uses for domestic and sanitary purposes.
(2) Uses for navigation, including the service of canals for the purposes of navigation.
(3) Uses for power and for irrigation purposes.

The foregoing provisions shall not apply to or disturb any existing uses of boundary waters on either side of the boundary.

The commission is also given, under Article VIII of the treaty, the power, as a condition to its approval, to require that suitable and adequate provision provided by it be made for the protection and indemnity for all interests on either side of the line which may be injured by reason of the elevation of the natural level of the waters on either side of the line as the result of the construction or maintenance on the other side of remedial or protective works or dams or other obstructions in boundary waters or in waters flowing therefrom, or in waters below the boundary in rivers flowing across the boundary.

Article VIII also provides that—

The majority of the commissioners shall have power to render a decision. In case the commission is evenly divided upon any question or matter presented to it for decision, separate reports shall be made by the commissioners on each side to their own Government. The high contracting parties shall thereupon endeavor to agree upon an adjustment of the question or matter of difference, and if an agreement is reached between them, it shall be reduced to writing in the form of a protocol and shall be communicated to the commissioners, who shall take such further proceedings as may be necessary to carry out such agreement.

It will be seen, therefore, that Articles III, IV, and VIII clothe this commission with final jurisdiction in the matter of the approval of any use, obstruction, or diversion, whether temporary or permanent, of boundary waters on either side of the line affecting the natural level or flow of boundary waters on the other side of the line. Also the commission is given final jurisdiction, "except in cases provided for by special agreement between the high contracting parties" over the approval of the construction or maintenance on either side of the boundary of any remedial or protective works or any dams or other obstructions in waters flowing from boundary waters or in waters at a lower level than the boundary in rivers flowing across the boundary, the effect of which obstructions would be to raise the natural level of the waters on the other side of the boundary. The decision of the commission in all cases arising under Articles III and IV is final, binding not only upon the inhabitants of the two countries, but upon the two Governments themselves.

Article X of the treaty clothes the commission with final jurisdiction over any question or matter of difference arising between the United States and the Dominion of Canada involving the rights, obligations, or interests of either country or in relation to their respective inhabitants. Under this article the questions or matters of difference over which the commission has jurisdiction when such questions or matters of difference are referred to it in accordance either national or individual interests; they may even involve so-called national honor or vital interest. If in the consideration of questions referred under this article a majority of the commission is unable to agree upon a decision, it is then made the duty of the commissioners to make a joint report to both Governments or a separate report to their respective Governments showing the different conclusions arrived at with regard to the matters or questions so referred. In that case the questions or matters are thereupon to be referred for decision to an umpire chosen in accordance with the proceedings prescribed in the fourth, fifth, and sixth paragraphs of Article XLV of The Hague convention for the pacific settlement of international disputes. "Such umpire shall have power to render a final decision with respect to those matters and questions so referred on which the commission failed to agree."

It will be seen, therefore, that the functions of this commission under the articles above quoted are entirely judicial, and that its jurisdiction in all matters brought before it, either by the two Governments or at the instance of the inhabitants of the two countries, under these articles, is a final jurisdiction.

In view of this fact, and recognizing the necessity for rules of procedure under which this jurisdiction of the commission might be invoked, Article XII of the treaty directs the commission to—

meet and organize at Washington promptly after the members thereof are appointed, and when organized the commission may fix such times and places for its meetings as may be necessary, subject at all times to special call or direction by the two Governments.

This article further provides that—

The commission may adopt such rules of procedure as shall be in accordance with justice and equity.

In addition to the final jurisdiction with which the commission is clothed under Articles III, IV, VIII, and X, Article IX clothes the commission with investigative jurisdiction. In this article the high contracting parties agree:

That any other questions or matters of difference arising between them involving the rights, obligations, or interests of either in relation to the other or to the inhabitants of the other, along the common frontier between the United States and the Dominion of Canada, shall be referred from time to time to the International Joint Commission for examination and report.

Upon any and all such references the commission is authorized to examine into and report upon the facts and circumstances of the particular questions and matters referred, together with such conclusions and recommendations as may be appropriate, subject, however, to any restrictions or exceptions which may be imposed with respect thereto by the terms of the reference. It is also provided by this article that the reports of the commission on questions thus referred—

shall not be regarded as decisions of the questions or matters so submitted either on the facts or the law, and shall in no way have the character of an arbitral award.

This, Mr. Chairman, is a brief outline of the functions, the power, and the jurisdiction of this commission as defined by the treaty.

Article XII of the treaty also provides that—

The United States and Canadian sections of the commission may each appoint a secretary, and these shall act as joint secretaries of the commission at its joint sessions, and the commission may employ engineers and clerical assistants from time to time as it may deem advisable. The salaries and personal expenses of the commission and of the secretaries shall be paid by their respective Governments, and all reasonable and necessary joint expenses of the commission, incurred by it, shall be paid in equal moieties by the high contracting parties.

All of the expense, therefore, incident to the carrying on and conduct of the work of the commission, outside of the salaries and personal expenses of the commission and of the secretaries, constitutes a joint expense under the treaty, which joint expense the two Governments have agreed to pay in equal moieties.

Owing to the delay in the appointment of the Canadian members of the commission, it was impossible for the commission to meet and organize until January 10, 1912, the Canadian members of the commission not being appointed until November 10, 1911. At the first meeting of the commission, held in the city of Washington, in accordance with the directions of the treaty, the commission organized and immediately proceeded to the consideration and preparation of its rules of procedure, required by Article XII of the treaty. These rules were finally adopted February 2, 1912. Under the treaty and under the rules of procedure, business before the commission can be initiated only by the two Governments or by the inhabitants of the two countries, acting through their respective Governments. Thus far the principal work of the commission has been initiated by the United States and the Dominion of Canada, under the provisions of Article IX of the treaty. It is manifest, therefore, that the work of this commission could not begin until the two Governments, or the inhabitants thereof, had submitted to the commission for its consideration, and either determination or report, questions or matters of difference for which the commission was created to decide or investigate and report upon. The commission can not itself initiate work for it to do any more than can a court of justice initiate litigation or other proceedings within its jurisdiction.

This commission has not been created to perform any temporary specific work. Its duty under the treaty is to transact the business which the two Governments or their inhabitants give to it growing out of the use of a common property.

The first question submitted by the two Governments was submitted under Article IX of the treaty—the investigation of the Lake of the Woods controversy. The next question referred for investigation and report under the same article was the proposed improvement of the Livingstone Channel, in the Detroit River, and the third question referred for investigation and report was the pollution of boundary waters.

Mr. DIFENDERFER. Properly speaking, then, this is a court?

Mr. TAWNEY. It is a court with final jurisdiction. The first four months of this fiscal year the commission did not incur any joint expenses under Article IX of the treaty. You understand that the work of the commission, or the cost of the work of the commission, is, under the treaty, a joint expense, so that our joint expenditures did not begin until after the first four months of this fiscal year had expired.

At the rate of expenditure at the present time, our joint expenses, together with our fixed charges, aggregate between $9,000 and $10,000 a month. One of the most important questions which the two Governments have submitted to us we have not yet commenced to investigate, because it was not finally submitted to us until the 19th of November. This reference involved a great deal of time and labor in organizing and preparing the plan for the investigation. That investigation is the pollution of boundary waters and how to prevent such pollution.

At the rate of expenditure at the present time we would have, at the end of this fiscal year, from $25,000 to $30,000 of an unexpended balance. If Congress does not intend that the work shall be performed which the two Governments have submitted to the commission to do, the commission will have money enough to pay its fixed charges during the next fiscal year, but its work will have to be suspended for the want of necessary funds to pay our one-half of the expense.

The CHAIRMAN. There is no statute on the subject, is there?

Mr. TAWNEY. Nothing but the treaty.

The CHAIRMAN. The point is: How are we going to meet the present situation? The Senate committee added $25,000 to the bill that we sent from the House, but when the bill reached the floor of the Senate it was stricken out and the bill passed the Senate just as it passed the House with reference to this item. Mr. Tawney took up the matter with some of the members of the Appropriation Committee of the Senate, and it was suggested that this committee meet——

Mr. KENDALL. The bill as passed the House, with reference to this item, was not amended in the Senate?

The CHAIRMAN. No.

Mr. KENDALL. Then, of course, there is not anything in conference on that item.

The CHAIRMAN. No.

Mr. TAWNEY. There were one or two unimportant amendments, one that the expenditure should be made under the direction of the Secretary of the State, the same as the former appropriation, and they also inserted an item for the expense of printing. But there is nothing in conference with respect to the amount of the appropriation.

The CHAIRMAN. The suggestion is to have the Senate Committee on Appropriations put the appropriation in the sundry civil bill and that this committee hold this hearing for the purpose of hearing arguments in favor of the appropriation and determining whether, when it came before the House, the committee acquiesce in it and help it along or not, the understanding being that hereafter the appropriation be carried in this bill.

Mr. TAWNEY. I want to say that it is entirely immaterial to the commission in which bill the appropriation is carried, and I also want it understood that I am not here for the purpose of asking the appropriation for any personal reason, because the unexpended balance, if Congress sees fit to appropriate no more, will be sufficient to meet the salaries of the commission, although I do not care to serve on a commission which where the members have no other duty than to draw the salary they are entitled to under the law. But, Mr. Chairman, I want this committee to understand the nature of the work the two Governments are requiring the commission to perform, and that in order to do that work our share of the joint expenses will involve the expenditure of a large sum of money during the next fiscal year, and that unless this money is appropriated the work can not be done.

Mr. KENDALL. What fixed charges has the joint commission?

Mr. TAWNEY. There are none. The fixed charges relate only to the expenses of the sections of the commission on each side of the line.

Mr. KENDALL. The charge that will have to be liquidated jointly will be the charge incurred in the prosecution of these investigations that are now going forward.

Mr. TAWNEY. Not only that charge, Mr. Kendall, but under Articles III, IV, VIII, and X the commission has final jurisdiction over a great many important questions involving the use of boundary waters. Now, under the first three of these articles and under the rules of the commission the inhabitants of both Governments may invoke this jurisdiction and initiate proceedings before the commission for its approval of contemplated projects for the use of these boundary waters. The expense incident to these proceedings would also be a joint expense to be paid in equal parts by both Governments.

Mr. KENDALL. That is where the commission is acting in a quasi judicial capacity?

Mr. TAWNEY. Yes.

Mr. KENDALL. As I remember it, there is no appeal from the final decision of the tribunal.

Mr. TAWNEY. No.

Mr. KENDALL. There are three on a side.

Mr. TAWNEY. Yes, sir.

Mr. KENDALL. Suppose the commission should be equally divided in its opinion: what then would transpire?

Mr. TAWNEY. The last paragraph of Article VIII answers your question. The treaty provides that each section will then report its conclusions to their respective Governments, and the question will then be taken up by the high contracting parties, who will endeavor to agree upon an adjustment of the question or matter in difference. If an agreement is reached it is then communicated to the commission for the purpose of carrying out the agreement. As to the joint expenses [reading]:

The United States and Canadian sections of the commission—

This is from Article XII—

may each appoint a secretary, and these shall act as joint secretaries of the commission at its joint sessions, and the commission may employ engineers and clerical assistants from time to time as it may deem advisable. The salaries and personal expenses of the commission and of the secretaries shall be paid by their respective Governments, and all reasonable and necessary joint expenses of the commission, incurred by it, shall be paid in equal moities by the high contracting parties.

So that all other expenses incurred by the commission, except the salaries of the commissioners and the personal expenses of the commission and the secretaries, are to be treated as joint expenses, and nobody can tell now or a year in advance what the joint expenses will be, because the joint expense will depend upon the amount of work the commission will have to do.

Mr. SHARP. Is there any agreement or obligation between the two countries that would make it embarrassing if the full amount asked was not appropriated at this time?

Mr. TAWNEY. It would be rather embarrassing to the United States if the State Department had to notify the Dominion of Canada that the work of the commission will have to cease because we have not the money with which to pay our share of the expenses incurred in doing the work.

Mr. SHARP. Would the work have to cease on that account?

Mr. TAWNEY. It would have to cease, because we have in this country statutes that absolutely prohibit the creation of any obligation or the incurrence of any expense for which appropriations have not been made.

Mr. SHARP. I understand that; but I had reference to the unexpended balance. Would that take it over long enough so it would relieve any embarrassment on our part in meeting the joint obligations?

Mr. TAWNEY. It would not, because if the work continued until the end of this fiscal year there would not then be a sufficient amount to meet the expenses of the American section of the commission during the next fiscal year.

I have here a copy of the first hearings that were taken in the Lake of the Woods investigation, and you will see in the front part of this volume of testimony the interests that are involved and were represented. The Lake of the Woods investigation was referred by the high contracting parties, and the investigation was instituted last September. Very shortly after the reference was made in this investigation, it became necessary for the commission to employ two engineers for the purpose of collecting engineering data and working out the engineering problems that will have to be solved in order to answer the questions submitted. You will find the questions submitted on the second or third page of the transcript. As Mr. Levy has the book before him I will ask him to read those questions, so the committee will know what the nature of this inquiry is.

Mr. LEVY (reading):

1. In order to secure the most advantageous use of the waters of the Lake of the Woods and of the waters flowing into and from that lake on each side of the boundary for domestic and sanitary purposes, for navigation and transportation purposes, and also in order to secure the most advantageous use of the shores and harbors of the lake and of the waters flowing into and from the lake, is it practicable and desirable to maintain the surface of the lake during the different seasons of the year at a certain stated level; and if so, at what level?

2. If a certain stated level is recommended in answer to question 1, and if such level is higher than the normal or natural level of the lake, to what extent, if at all, would the lake, when maintained at such level, overflow the lowlands upon its southern border, or elsewhere on its border, and what is the value of the lands which would be submerged?

Mr. TAWNEY. Now, gentlemen, the answer to that question necessarily involves a great many engineering problems. Let me say for the information of the members of the committee who are not familiar with that part of our country that the Lake of the Woods is 1,400 square miles in area, 200 square miles larger than the State of Rhode Island. The drainage area of the Lake of the Woods and its tributary waters is 26,000 square miles, as great in area as the whole of New England exclusive of Maine. That section of our country has never been topographically surveyed on either side of the line. I have here a tentative map, which our engineers have prepared, that will give you some idea of the magnitude of that area. That is the Lake of the Woods out there, and here is Rainy Lake [indicating on map].

Mr. KENDALL. Are they exclusively in the United States?

Mr. TAWNEY. No; on both sides.

Mr. KENDALL. Where is the boundary?

Mr. TAWNEY. Just follow that green line, Mr. Kendall [indicating].

Mr. KENDALL. The line I am following now?

Mr. TAWNEY. Yes.

Mr. LEVY. Where is Rainy Lake?

Mr. TAWNEY. I will show you in a minute.

Mr. DIFENDERFER. That is the drainage area through here [indicating].

Mr. TAWNEY. Yes, sir.

Mr. KENDALL. I suppose this red line [indicating] shows the drainage area?

Mr. TAWNEY. Yes, sir; of that whole lake system. What the two Governments want to know is what is the normal level of the Lake of the Woods and what level should be established that will best serve all of the interests on both sides of the line. And I might say that here on Rainy Lake and Rainy River, on both sides of the line, over $75,000,000 is invested in the lumber industry alone. At International Falls is one of the largest paper mills in the United States, and there is also a paper mill owned by the same company in course of construction on the Canadian side. The falls here [indicating] are 23 feet, and the falls out here at Kenora [indicating] are 26 feet.

This controversy between the United States and Canada and between the inhabitants of the two countries has existed for 17 years, and two years ago almost led to bloodshed here at Fort Francis and International Falls, because the parties who claimed their lands were being injured by the level of Rainy Lake maintained by this dam threatened to dynamite the dam. The controversy has become very acute.

Mr. SHARP. Does this line [indicating] show the international boundary line?

Mr. TAWNEY. Yes, sir; that green line.

Mr. LEVY. We got the best part of it.

Mr. TAWNEY. Yes; the best part of the lake. In the lower portion of the lake a rise of 2 feet in the Lake of the Woods will throw that water out over these agricultural lands from a half mile to 2 miles, and submerge the agricultural lands of Minnesota and eastern Manitoba as well, because on the south and west shore of the lake the water and land meet on a level. When they built this dam it had the effect as we are informed, of raising the level of the lake and submerging the agricultural lands on the south shore of the lake, owned by the Government of the United States, the State of Minnesota, and by private parties.

The CHAIRMAN. Please point out where that dam is located.

Mr. TAWNEY. Right here [indicating on map].

Mr. KENDALL. That was built by private parties?

Mr. TAWNEY. Yes; but under the authority of the Provincial Government of Ontario. There are hundreds of thousands of acres of land in Minnesota that are at times submerged. Forty miles of the southern boundary of the Lake of the Woods is in northern Minnesota. When we were there last fall, as you will see from the testimony, one farmer testified that he planted his farm in the spring, or the greater part of the farm, when all of the land was tillable, but when we were there in September, he testified that two-thirds of it was under water as the result of the construction and manipulation of this dam out here [indicating]. They raise or lower the level of the lake by putting in or taking out stop-logs intended for that purpose, and that is what has led to this controversy.

Mr. TOWNSEND. What is the nature of the navigation on the lake?

Mr. TAWNEY. Principally lumber.

Mr. TOWNSEND. You mean that they float logs?

Mr. TAWNEY. Yes.

Mr. TOWNSEND. Is there navigation in the sense that there is navigation on the Great Lakes?

Mr. TAWNEY. Yes. I have here a report giving the names and number of steamers plying on the lake and Rainy River. I think there are something like 20 steamers with an aggregate tonnage of about a thousand tons.

Mr. SHARP. Have you found any evidences of mineral lands up in there?

Mr. TAWNEY. No, sir.

Mr. LEVY. Does the Government own any of the lands there?

Mr. TAWNEY. Yes. The Chippewa Reservation is in here, and there are a great many acres owned by the Government that are submerged. An American citizen who finds his farm flooded and believes it is because some private interest has erected a dam over here [indicating] has heretofore had no other recourse than through the State Department, and for 17 years the farmers of northern Minnesota have been working through the State Department to have their rights adjudicated and damages collected, but without success, and that is one of the things——

Mr. TOWNSEND (interposing). That is the fault of the State Department, is it not?

Mr. TAWNEY. No. The State Department has never had, nor has Canada, the data on which to make a comprehensive agreement covering this controversy, because these waters are all connected or interlocked. This whole territory is connected with a chain of lakes and to determine the natural level of the Lake of the Woods or to establish a fixed level is largely an engineering and not a diplomatic problem.

Mr. TOWNSEND. Ordinarily, if the State Department lacked data upon which to propose an adjustment with the Canadian Government, would it not go to the Army engineers and ask a report to Congress of such data as was required?

Mr. TAWNEY. Of course, that could have been done.

Mr. TOWNSEND. And the Army engineers are competent to handle the matter?

Mr. TAWNEY. Certainly they are; we have taken one of them to act as our engineer in working out these engineering problems.

Mr. TOWNSEND. Does he receive extra compensation?

Mr. TAWNEY. No, sir; he does not; he receives no extra compensation from the Government.

Mr. TOWNSEND. And he will act in the same capacity as though the Secretary of State had received his services through the Secretary of War?

Mr. TAWNEY. Certainly. But he is acting under the direction of this International Joint Commission in conjunction with a Canadian engineer. They are both working from the same datum and must therefore reach the same conclusion. This will insure an agreement between the commission and the Governments on the engineering problems involved.

But this is only one of a great many questions of difference between the Dominion of Canada and the United States. The two Governments have negotiated this treaty to create a court, an international tribunal, calling it the International Joint Commission, and they have clothed this tribunal with power to finally determine all questions arising under Articles III and IV of the treaty between the inhabitants of the two countries or between the two Governments themselves. And let me say here that this is the only tribunal in the world that has been clothed by the countries creating it with power to compel the inhabitants of both countries to appear before it for the adjudication and determination of the rights of their respective inhabitants.

I may say that the boundary between the United States and Canada, extending from the Atlantic to the Pacific, is almost 4.000 miles in extent, and as I have said before almost 2,000 miles of that boundary is marked by navigable and nonnavigable waters. These waters are the common property of the inhabitants of the two countries; they enjoy the right to use these waters in common, and it is in the exercise of these rights that these controversies have arisen in the past and will continue to arise in the future. So that the two Governments have agreed by this treaty that these waters shall not be obstructed on either side of the boundary so as to affect their level or flow on the other side without the approval of this international tribunal before whom the inhabitants of both countries have the right to appear and be heard. In these waters are some of the most valuable water powers on the continent. As I have said, they are valuable for domestic and sanitary purposes, for navigation, and for irrigation, as well as for power purposes. Their importance in the industrial development of the country on both sides of the line is just beginning to be appreciated. There are now about 6,000,000 people living on these boundary waters between the United States and Canada, east of Duluth, and, of course, for industrial purposes the utilization of these waters is becoming more and more valuable all the time.

Let me again read Article III, for I want to impress on the committee the importance of the agreement of the countries in respect to the rights of the inhabitants of the two countries to obstruct these boundary waters on either side of the line:

That in addition to the uses, obstructions, and diversions heretofore permitted or hereafter provided for by special agreement between the parties hereto, no further or other uses or obstructions or diversions, whether temporary or permanent, of boundary waters on either side of the line, affecting the natural level or flow of boundary waters on the other side of the line, shall be made except by authority of the United States or the Dominion of Canada within their respective jurisdictions and with the approval, as hereinafter provided, of a joint commission, to be known as the International Joint Commission. The foregoing provisions are not intended to limit or interfere with the existing rights of the Government of the United States on the one side and the Government of the Dominion of Canada on the other to undertake and carry on governmental works in boundary waters for the deepening of channels, the construction of breakwaters, the improvement of harbors, and other governmental works for the benefit of commerce and navigation, provided that such works are wholly on its own side of the line and do not materially affect the level or flow of the boundary waters on the other, nor are such provisions intended to interfere with the ordinary use of such waters for domestic and sanitary purposes.

Then, in Article IV:

The high contracting parties agree that, except in cases provided for by special agreement between them, they will not permit the construction or maintenance on their respective sides of the boundary of any remedial or protective works or any dams or other obstructions in waters flowing from boundary waters or in waters at a lower level than the boundary in rivers flowing across the boundary the effect of which is to raise the natural level of waters on the other side of the boundary unless the construction or maintenance thereof is approved by the aforesaid International Joint Commission.

It is further agreed that the waters herein defined as boundary waters and waters flowing across the boundary shall not be polluted on either side to the injury of health or property on the other.

Under this latter provision the two Governments have submitted another question for investigation by the commission, which is the pollution of the boundary waters, and that question was finally referred to the commission on the 19th of November. From the reading of the questions you will get some idea of the scope and magnitude of the investigation:

To what extent and by what causes and in what localities have the boundary waters between the United States and Canada been polluted so as to be injurious to the public health and unfit for domestic or other uses?

In what way or manner, whether by the construction and operation of suitable drainage canals or plants at convenient points or otherwise, is it possible and advisable to remedy or prevent the pollution of these waters, and by what means or arrangements can the proper construction or operation of remedial or preventive works, or a system or method of rendering these wates sanitary and suitable for domestic and other uses, be best secured and maintained in order to insure the adequate protection and development of all interests involved on both sides of the boundary, and to fulfill the obligations undertaken in article 4 of the waterways treaty of January 11, 1909, between the United States and Great Britain, in which it is agreed that the waters therein defined as boundary waters and waters flowing across the boundary shall not be polluted on either side to the injury of health or property on the other?

It is claimed at certain places by the inhabitants on both sides of the line that this provision of the treaty is being violated in that the pollution of these boundary waters is being permitted to the injury of health and property on the other side of the line. For the purpose of accurately and definitely ascertaining the fact the two Governments have referred this question for investigation to the commission, and they also require the commission to investigate and recommend remedies for such pollution wherever it is found to exist.

Mr. TOWNSEND. During the testimony of another witness I understood it had been found that a United States engineer had made a very exhaustive report on the subject of that pollution.

Mr. TAWNEY. No; not an engineer, but a sanitary expert—an employee of the Public Health Service of the United States.

Mr. TOWNSEND. Oh, that was it.

Mr. TAWNEY. Dr. McLaughlin, who is here, and who has been employed by the commission jointly for the purpose of acting as sanitary expert in this investigation, has been given leave of absence for the time being, or while he is engaged in this work for the commission. Dr. McLaughlin's investigation, as he will tell you, was limited to the shore line on our side, and did not go into the question of whether or not the pollution extended beyond the boundary line in violation of this provision of the treaty. There is not much doubt about the fact of pollution at certain places. For example, the sewage of about 600,000 people at Detroit is being dumped into the Detroit River, and on the other side of the line the sewage of about 40,000 or 45,000 people is disposed of by being run into the Detroit River. The same condition of affairs exists in the Niagara River and at the lower end of Lake Erie, where the city of Buffalo, with a very large population—I think about 400,000 or 500,000—disposes of its sewage by dumping it into the Niagara River. So it is at Tonawanda and North Tonawanda and at Niagara Falls City. It all goes down the Niagara River, and it is claimed that it spreads there to both sides of Lake Ontario. Then, at Kingston, at Poughkeepsie, and at Ogdensburg and other places on the St. Lawrence, before the St. Lawrence leaves the boundary line, it is claimed, pollution exists to a great extent. The fact is, and it is shown by Dr. McLaughlin's report, that the death rate from typhoid fever in the cities adjacent the boundary waters between Canada and the United States is greater than in any other cities of the United States or of Canada, showing that there must be some real cause for that condition.

Mr. TOWNSEND. Mr. Tawney, with the permission of the chairman—and I am asking these questions in no spirit of criticism——

Mr. TAWNEY (interposing). I am here to answer any questions or to answer any criticisms.

Mr. TOWNSEND. But you read the second paragraph of Article III. Let me read it again and ask you a question:

> The foregoing provisions are not intended to limit or interfere with the existing rights of the Government of the United States on the one side and the Government of the Dominion of Canada on the other to undertake and carry on governmental works in boundary waters for the deepening of channels, the construction of breakwaters, the improvement of harbors, and other governmental works for the benefit of commerce and navigation, provided that such works are wholly on its own side of the line and do not materially affect the level or flow of the boundary waters on the other.

Now, that limits the matters that you may take up to practically governmental works, and would you claim, for instance, that if the engineers discovered that the sewage system of Detroit was tending to pollute the Detroit River and Lake Erie that any action that you could take would affect the municipal business of Detroit?

Mr. TAWNEY. No, sir; the only thing——

Mr. TOWNSEND (interposing). Then you could not take any action?

Mr. TAWNEY. Let me call your attention to the fact that this reference for the investigation of polluted waters is under Article IX of the treaty, and under Article IX the commission has only investigative jurisdiction; it has no final jurisdiction under Article IX. We would make our recommendation to the two Governments, after a careful investigation and study of the whole subject, as to how to remedy this pollution and thereby observe and fulfill the obligations which our Government has entered into with Great Britain; that is, that we will not permit the pollution of these boundary waters. It will then be for the two Governments to determine whether or not the recommendation of the commission should be carried out by agreement between them or otherwise.

Mr. TOWNSEND. Would you not be likely to get Congress into a peck of trouble if you made any recommendation that would suggest to Detroit that she was not properly carrying on her municipal public works?

Mr. TAWNEY. No; I do not see how it would get Congress in any trouble at all.

Mr. TOWNSEND. Under what authority could you go to Detroit and tell Detroit that her sewage system had to be remedied?

Mr. TAWNEY. The treaty.

Mr. LINTHICUM. Is Detroit properly carrying out her municipal works if she permits the pollution of the Detroit River?

Mr. TOWNSEND. Well, if she is not, can Congress tell her so?

Mr. LINTHICUM. I think if it is an international question Congress could do so.

Mr. DIFENDERFER. This pollution might extend to the Canadian side.

Mr. TAWNEY. If it did not extend to the Canadian side, of course we have no jurisdiction over it; but if it does extend beyond the boundary to the injury of health and property on the other side of the line, then clearly that is in violation of this treaty, and it would be the duty of the Government to put a stop to it in some way.

Mr. TOWNSEND. If Canada found that the people of Windsor were suffering from typhoid fever and claimed that it was caused by the sewage of the city of Detroit, would not representations be made to our State Department?

Mr. TAWNEY. Representations have been made to the State Department, and that is the reason why the two Governments have referred this question to the commission for investigation and a report, so that the two Governments can then take the subject up and arrange some mutual agreement between them by which such conditions will be remedied.

Mr. TOWNSEND. If we had an efficient State Department, this question as to the level of the Lake of the Woods and the pollution of international waters would have been settled without the intervention of the International Joint Commission.

Mr. TAWNEY. I do not say that we have had an inefficient State Department. This Lake of the Woods question involves a great deal of investigation, and during the 17 years that this controversy has existed we have had a State Department which, I think, has been very efficient.

Mr. TOWNSEND. It seems to me that might be so.

Mr. TAWNEY. But changing administrations every four years, of course, necessarily causes a great deal of delay in the consideration of a matter involving physical conditions, especially where we have had no official topographic survey or surveys of any kind to enable the State Department to determine what proceedings should be taken and what is necessary to be done to protect the rights and interests of the people on our side of the line.

Mr. SHARP. This question occurred to me when you were reading the articles as to the extent of the authority that has been conferred upon your commission: Does not the treaty practically constitute you a court and make your court or commission, whatever it may be styled, almost perpetual in its character?

Mr. TAWNEY. All the powers of this commission are judicial except those under Article IX, and to a certain extent they are judicial powers and therefore to all intents and purposes the commission is an international court.

Mr. SHARP. Does it not contemplate a very long duration of existence?

Mr. TAWNEY. Let me answer that question in this way: As I have heretofore said, almost 2,000 miles of the boundary between Canada and the United States is marked by navigable and nonnavigable waters. These waters are the common property of the people on both sides of the line. This property is valuable, too. It is valuable for domestic and sanitary purposes, for irrigation and navigation, for power purposes, and it is rapidly becoming a most important factor in the industrial development of the country on both sides of the boundary. The right to use this common property for all or any of these purposes is a right enjoyed in common by the inhabitants of both countries. Controversies have arisen in the past, and will necessarily arise in the future, with respect to the exercise by the people of this common right. There is no way whereby these controversies can be determined, for the people are living under separate and distinct governmental jurisdictions. Recognizing that fact, Great Britain and the United States have created this tribunal for the purpose of affording to both Governments and to the inhabitants of both countries an opportunity for the peaceable settlement of all such controversies. To render this tribunal efficient the high contracting parties have clothed it with final jurisdiction and with power to finally adjudicate and determine the rights of the respective inhabitants on both sides of the line in regard to the use of this property thus owned by them in common. As the country settles up along these boundary waters the demand for the use of these waters will continue to increase, and no doubt give rise to differences between the inhabitants as well as between the two Governments, so that as long as the Governments of Great Britain and the United States continue their policy of a century of settling their differences peaceably, either this tribunal or some other tribunal with equal power and jurisdiction will exist for that purpose.

Answering your question, therefore, directly, I should say that the life of this commission or of some similar body created for the same purpose will necessarily be of long duration.

If you will take the trouble to examine the rules of procedure which the commission prepared in accordance with Article XII, you will observe that provision is made for the initiation of proceedings before the commission both by the Governments and by the inhabitants on either side of the line. Rule 6 reads:

In all cases to be submitted to the commission under Articles III, IV, and VIII of the treaty the method of bringing such cases to the attention of the commission and invoking its action shall be as follows:

(a) Where one or the other of the Governments on it own initiative seeks the approval of the commission for the use, obstruction, or diversion of waters with respect to which, under Articles III and IV of the treaty, the approval of the commission is required, it shall file with the commission an application setting forth as fully as may be necessary for the information of the commission the facts upon which the application is based and the nature of the order of approval desired.

(b) Where any private person seeks the approval of the commission for the use, obstruction, or diversion of such waters, he shall first make written application to the Government within whose jurisdiction the privilege desired is to be exercised, to grant such privilege, and upon such Government, or the proper department thereof, transmitting such application to the commission, with the request that it take appropriate action thereon, the same shall be filed and be proceeded with by the commission in the same manner as an application on behalf of one or the other of the Governments. All applications by private persons should conform, as to their contents, to the requirements of subdivision (a) of this rule.

In preparing these rules the commission endeavored to make the procedure for invoking its jurisdiction as simple as possible.

Mr. TOWNSEND. To present a concrete case which will illuminate my nonlegal mind: Your secretary spoke the other day about some complaint that was made about a little harbor on the St. Clair Flats, through which a ship channel has been dug and defined by dikes. Now, suppose the case of this little harbor on the Canadian side, the St. Clair Flats, should be presented to you and the evidence proved to the commission that it was because of the construction of this ship channel that the water had been injuriously lowered in that little harbor over there, could you provide a remedy, even if you had determined that the ship channel was too deep or the dikes too high?

Mr. TAWNEY. We would have no jurisdiction over that whatever.

Mr. TOWNSEND. It was presented to the committee by your secretary.

81495—13——2

Mr. TANWNEY. We would have no jurisdiction, because it existed prior to the making of this treaty, and there is a provision that expressly provides that no existing work shall be interfered with.

Mr. TOWNSEND. Well, then, he was in error in presenting that as a concrete case that might be presented to you.

Mr. TAWNEY. I never heard of the ship channel through the St. Clair Flats in that connection, and have you not confounded that with the construction of the Livingston Channel in the Detroit River?

Mr. TOWNSEND. No; I am very familiar with all that country.

Mr. TAWNEY. I do not know anything about that.

Mr. TOWNSEND. But he suggested that to us as a concrete case that might be presented to you.

Mr. TAWNEY. If it is in regard to a work that was in existence when this treaty went into effect, then that is treated as having been settled and we have no jurisdiction.

Mr. TOWNSEND. I am not positive, but I think the other members of the committee will verify my statement that your secretary said that there was a little harbor on the Canadian side about which there was some complaint, to the effect that the ship channel through the St. Clair Flats had injuriously lowered the water of the harbor, and that that was one of the important cases presented to you.

Mr. TAWNEY. No, sir; there is no case of that kind; he was mistaken or else you misunderstood him, because there is no case of that kind before us at all.

Now, gentlemen, I want to have Dr. McLaughlin explain to you the plan that the commission adopted last week as its meeting in Detroit for the investigation of the pollution of the boundary waters, so that you may get a comprehensive idea of the work involved in that investigation. The doctor has several maps here which he will exhibit to you. But before the doctor proceeds I want to say that this question was finally referred to us on the 19th of November and that on the 17th of December a special meeting of the commission was called at Buffalo for the purpose of meeting with the health authorities of the States and Provinces bordering on boundary waters, with a view of ascertaining to what extent the States and Provinces would cooperate with us. I realized that this investigation would not only involve a great deal of time and expense but that the States and Provinces bordering on the boundary waters would be benefited as much by the results of the investigations as the two Governments and I thought it might be possible for us to get the States and Provinces to bear a part of the expense and cooperate with us.

Mr. SHARP. That pertained to all of the States on the border?

Mr. TAWNEY. Yes; bordering on the Great Lakes. And we called a special meeting of the commission and notified the representatives of the public health departments of these States to meet with us for that purpose. Here are the names of those who appeared:

Dr. Frederick Montizambert. I. O. S., director general of public health, Dominion of Canada, Ottawa, Canada.

Dr. Charles A. Hodgetts, medical adviser, commission of conservation, Ottawa, Canada.

Prof. John A. Amyot, director of laboratory of Provincial Board of Health of Ontario, Toronto, Canada.

Dr. John W. McCullough, chief health officer for Ontario, Toronto, Canada.

Mr. F. A. Dallyn, engineer, provincial board of health, Toronto, Canada.

Mr. Theo. J. Lafreniere, sanitary engineer, board of health, Province of Quebec, Montreal, Canada.

Dr. Allan J. McLaughlin, United States Public Health Service, Washington, D. C.

Dr. A. H. Seymour, State department of health, Albany, N. Y.

Mr. Theodore Horton, State department of health, Albany, N. Y.

Dr. Edward Clark, medical health officer, State board of health, Buffalo, N. Y.

Mr. George H. Horton, deputy engineer commissioner, department of public works, Buffalo, N. Y.

Dr. Francis E. Fronczak, health commissioner, Buffalo, N. Y.

Dr. H. A. Whittaker, assistant director, laboratory division, Minnesota State State Board of Health, St. Paul, Minn.

Prof. Edward Bartow, director State water survey, Urbana, Ill.

Mr. W. M. Mills, president Niagara Frontier Pure Water Conference, North Tonawanda, N. Y.

Mr. W. G. Palmer, member of the Niagara Frontier Pure Water Conference, North Tonawanda, N. Y.

Mr. Irving L. Pruyn, Oneonta, N. Y.

Mr. John W. Hill, member of the State Board of Health of Ohio, Cincinnati, Ohio.

We submitted a series of questions. The first question was:

At what points in the lakes and connecting tributary waters and other boundary waters will it be necessary to have investigations made?

These questions were submitted to them to get their judgment and because they are familiar with the localities as well as the local conditions. They answered that question in this way:

In reply to this question, we beg to state that the points of investigation of international boundary waters as to pollution by sewage should include the Rainy River, St. Marys River, Lake St. Clair, River St. Clair, Detroit River, Niagara River, St. Lawrence River, following this latter into Canadian territory as far as may be necessary; together with investigations into the water in the vicinity of Port Arthur, Fort William, and Duluth, on Lake Superior, the Saginaw Bay on Lake Huron, and the lower end of Lake Huron in the vicinity of Sarnia and Port Huron; the lake in the vicinity of Port Stanley, Cleveland, and the bay at the western end of Lake Erie; Rochester, Toronto, and the eastern and western ends of Lake Ontario; and that other international points on the boundaries outside of the Great Lakes system above described be investigated if subsequently deemed advisable.

Question No. 2. What in general will be the nature of the investigation at the several points, and how much time will probably be required to make the investigation complete?

Answer. This investigation will include a bacteriological examination of samples taken, including the bacteria count and the qualitative and quantitative estimation of *B. coli* according to the standard methods, and such chemical examination and hydrographic studies as may be subsequently deemed necessary.

An interim report could be submitted by November 1, 1913. From this report it could be judged what further investigation might be required.

Question No. 3. What steps should the commission take to commence and carry the investigation to its conclusion?

As to question No. 3 the following resolution was adopted:

We the undersigned representatives signify our willingness to cooperate in the investigation to be made by the International Joint Commission, in so far as this may be done consistent with State laws and appropriations available.

Question No. 4. Having in view the last question, can the commission be aided in its investigation by the cooperation of health authorities on each side?

Answer. Yes.

Question No. 4 (continued). Can it safely remit any part of its investigation to such health authorities alone?

Answer. We think so.

The following resolution was also adopted by the conference:

We recommend to the commission that a joint appropriation of $50,000 be secured to carry out this preliminary work.

The conference requests that copies of the questions and answers be sent to the representatives of the States and Provinces and that the members of the conference have an opportunity to make further suggestions in regard to them, after giving them some study, as a number of the representatives have not had an opportunity to consider them carefully.

That gives you some idea, gentlemen, of the extent to which this investigation goes and the effort the commission is making to have the work of the commission conducted as economically as possible for the Governments of the United States and Canada. I will now ask Dr. McLaughlin to make a statement to you.

STATEMENT OF DR. ALLAN J. McLAUGHLIN, PASSED ASSISTANT SURGEON, UNITED STATES PUBLIC HEALTH SERVICE.

Dr. McLAUGHLIN. In making an investigation of sewage pollution of international streams, the vital thing to be ascertained is the extent of pollution in relation to the international boundary. To get this data we must make cross sections above and below the gross sources of pollution. For instance, at the city of Detroit we will make a cross section above the city, where the water is comparatively pure, coming from Lake St. Clair, and then immediately below the maximum pollution, from Detroit to Windsor. Now, instead of making a cross section examination of the whole stream, midstream samples are taken at intervals. After 1 or 2 miles of stream flow, it will not be necessary to make these cross-section examinations, because a mixture between the water and the sewage has been effected, and in that case, after we get down a few miles, the cross-section examination may be supplanted by midstream samples. However, we will be careful to see that the mixture has taken place before we do away with the cross-section examination, and the cross-section work will show conclusively whether the pollution has crossed the international boundary or not. The mouths of the rivers are important in regard to pollution, because as the stream enters the lake the velocity becomes less and the pollution diffuses like a fan, so that investigation must be made on radiating lines from a central point, in order to show the extent of the pollution in relation to the international boundary. It will be necessary also to see whether the pollution from the Maumee River extends as far as the boundary, and in order to be conclusive the investigation must extend over quite a considerable period of time.

Mr. TAWNEY. The provision of the treaty under which this reference has been made to us is as follows:

The high contracting parties further agree that any other questions or matters of difference arising between them involving the rights, obligations, or interests of either in relation to the other or to the inhabitants of the other, along the common frontier between the United States and the Dominion of Canada, shall be referred from time to time to the International Joint Commission for examination and report, whenever either the Government of the United States or the Government of the Dominion of Canada shall request that such questions or matters of difference be so referred.

Now, it is claimed that this provision of the treaty is being violated, and for the purpose of ascertaining whether it is and to remedy it in the future the Governments have referred the questions to us for investigation, and this is the plan of investigation which the commission adopted at Detroit last week.

Dr. McLaughlin. In the eastern end of Lake Erie we have comparatively pure water, and we will have to run a cross section from Buffalo, reaching out into the lake, to ascertain whether the pollution reaches the international boundary there and whether it is then carried out across to the Canadian shore. The international boundary passes a little to the eastward of Waverly Shoal. Another cross section will be run from the mouth of the Buffalo River to the point from which Buffalo now takes its water supply, and from thence to the Canadian shore. Then, at Fort Erie, another cross section will be run from Buffalo to the city of Fort Erie, about on the line of the ferry, and another one below Squaw Island. Then, an important question to be determined is whether the Chippewa Channel is polluted, so we will have to take a cross section across it to determine in which channel the sewage of Buffalo is carried.

Mr. Cline. It is a notorious fact that the death rate of Buffalo from typhoid fever is greater than any other city in the United States.

Dr. McLaughlin. No; that is not strictly true, sir.

Mr. Cline. It may not be at the present time.

Dr. McLaughlin. Well, it is pretty bad.

Mr. Cline. I wanted to inquire whether it is not a fact that all the knowledge which could possibly be obtained by your examination has been obtained by the public health authorities of the city of Buffalo as to the extent of the infiltration of sewage, just the same as the city of Chicago made a complete and exhaustive examination as to the extent of the infiltration of Lake Michigan, for the purpose of getting far enough beyond any pollution to get good water—has not all of this subject matter been carefully gone over?

Dr. McLaughlin. No, sir.

Mr. Cline. Do you undertake to say that the health authorities so vitally interested in that subject matter have not made an exhaustive examination of those matters?

Dr. McLaughlin. Yes, sir; I do. They have made some inquiry, but have not extended their examination beyond their own local needs. My reason for saying that is that they consider that the intake in the Emerald Channel gives them pure water at all times of the year, but it has been demonstrated that they are mistaken, because they had an epidemic last year, although the death rate has not been as great this past year. I do not want to be understood as criticizing Buffalo in any way, but what I mean is that their investigation would not serve to settle the question involved in reference to this commission. However, whatever work they may have done is available and the data will be turned over by Dr. Fronczak and Col. Ward, of the department of public works of Buffalo, for our use. But it is not comprehensive enough to answer this question. A few examinations were also made by the State of New York, and Mr. Theodore Horton, the chief engineer of the State department of health, has consented to make whatever data they have available for our work.

Mr. Curley. You have some knowledge of typhoid conditions at Niagara Falls?

Dr. McLaughlin. Yes.

Mr. Curley. How recently have you been there?

Dr. McLaughlin. I was there in 1910. Their typhoid fever death rate has been greatly reduced.

Mr. CURLEY. How recently were you there?

Dr. McLAUGHLIN. We were in Buffalo on the 17th of December in order to meet with the State health officials of the States bordering on the Lakes.

Mr. CURLEY. The representatives of that section have contended that since the new filtration plant has gone in the health of that community has materially improved.

Dr. McLAUGHLIN. Yes; that is quite right.

Mr. TAWNEY. But the conditions that resulted in the high death rate prior to the installation of the filtration plant, so far as those conditions were caused by the disposal of sewage in the river, exist below now just as much as they did before, and it is claimed that they extend across the boundary and that those conditions are therefore allowed to exist in violation of this provision of the treaty.

Dr. McLAUGHLIN. I think I might make it a little more clear by saying that the Buffalo investigations were directed solely toward ascertaining the conditions around the Emerald Channel in regard to the new intake; they had very little interest in what became of their sewage below and made no investigations of any kind as to the ultimate disposition of the Buffalo sewage in the Niagara River.

Mr. CURLEY. They did not consider the proposition of taking care of that sewage any more than it concerned them?

Mr. TAWNEY. No. Of course, the reference, as I said, was finally made only last November, and we can not take up the second question in this reference until we have ascertained the facts under the first one, because we may be shooting in the air. We do not know yet where the pollution exists beyond the boundary line and we do not know the source of such pollution on either side of the line. But when we ascertain where the point of pollution is and that it extends beyond the boundary line, then we will be in a position to take up the second question in the reference, investigate, and dispose of it.

The CHAIRMAN. You are working on this question:

To what extent and by what causes and in what localities have the boundary waters between the United States and Canada been polluted so as to be injurious to the public health and unfit for domestic or other uses?

Mr. TAWNEY. Yes, sir.

The CHAIRMAN. How long do you anticipate it will take to come to a conclusion on that?

Mr. TAWNEY. The sanitary experts with whom we met in Buffalo on the 17th of December estimated that an interim report could possibly be made about November 1 next. I do not know whether you were here, Mr. Chairman, when I read their report. We invited, as I said before, the representatives of all the boards of health of all the States bordering on the boundary waters from the St. Lawrence clear through to Duluth, Minn. Nearly all the States were represented, and we submitted to them a series of questions. The first one was:

At what points in the Lakes and connecting tributary waters and other boundary waters will it be necessary to have investigations made?

Then they answered that by saying:

We beg to state that the points of investigation of international boundary waters as to pollution by sewage should include the Rainy River, St. Marys River, Lake St. Clair, River St. Clair, Detroit River, Niagara River, St. Lawrence River, following this latter into Canadian territory as far as may be necessary, together with investigations into the water in the vicinity of Port

Arthur, Fort William, and Duluth, on Lake Superior; the Saginaw Bay on Lake Huron and the lower end of Lake Huron in the vicinity of Sarnia and Port Huron; the lake in the vicinity of Port Stanley, Cleveland, and the bay at the western end of Lake Erie; Rochester, Toronto, and the eastern and western ends of Lake Ontario; and that other international points on the boundaries outside of the Great Lakes system above described be investigated if subsequently deemed advisable.

Question No. 2. What in general will be the nature of the investigation at the several points, and how much time will probably be required to make the investigation complete?

Answer. This investigation will include a bacteriological examination of samples taken, including the bacteria count and the qualitative and quantitative estimation of *B. Coli* according to the standard methods, and such chemical examination and hydrographic studies as may be subsequently deemed necessary.

An interim report could be submitted by November 1, 1913. From this report it could be judged what further investigation might be required.

Question No. 3. What steps should the commission take to commence and carry the investigation to its conclusion?

As to question No. 3, the following resolution was adopted:

We, the undersigned representatives, signify our willingness to cooperate in the investigation to be made by the International Joint Commission, in so far as this may be done consistent with State laws and appropriations available.

Question No. 4. Having in view the last question, can the commission be aided in its investigation by the cooperation of health authorities on each side?

Answer. Yes.

Question No. 4 (continued). Can it safely remit any part of its investigation to such health authorities alone?

Answer. We think so.

The following resolution was also adopted by the conference:

We recommend to the commission that a joint appropriation of $50,000 be secured to carry out this preliminary work.

The conference requests that copies of the questions and answers be sent to the representatives of the States and Provinces and that the members of the conference have an opportunity to make further suggestions in regard to them after giving them some study, as a number of the representatives have not had an opportunity to consider them carefully.

The CHAIRMAN. Who else besides Dr. McLaughlin is engaged in this work?

Mr. TAWNEY. The Canadian section of the commission has not named anybody as yet, but Dr. McLaughlin has been employed by the commission to have charge of the field work on both sides. Because of his experience and knowledge of the subject the commission has given to him the authority to supervise and control the field work on both sides of the line. They have in contemplation the expenditure of the same amount of money on the other side in the employment of, possibly, three sanitary experts for consultation purposes, but Dr. McLaughlin, by the unanimous action of the full commission, has been given full authority over all the field work on both sides of the line.

The CHAIRMAN. Dr. McLaughlin and his assistants have cost the commission how much?

Mr. TAWNEY. Dr. McLaughlin's compensation, as fixed by the commission at the joint meeting of the commission, was $7,000 a year.

The CHAIRMAN. And what other expenses in addition to that?

Mr. TAWNEY. Only his traveling expenses.

The CHAIRMAN. Has he no assistants at all?

Mr. TAWNEY. No; not on our side of the line at all. And in fixing that compensation I will say that the commission took into consideration the compensation paid to other members of the Health Service who have been loaned to cities for similar purposes. In the city of Chicago they have one to whom they are paying $10,000 a year, I believe.

Dr. McLAUGHLIN. No; $8,000.

The CHAIRMAN. In the work of the Lake of the Woods what engineering force have you?

Mr. TAWNEY. Two engineers, one on each side; and their compensation has been fixed at not to exceed $500 a month.

The CHAIRMAN. For the two, $12,000 a year?

Mr. TAWNEY. Yes; the two together.

The CHAIRMAN. Those are the only two questions you have taken up as yet?

Mr. TAWNEY. We have the Livingstone Channel investigation under way. We met at Detroit last week on that investigation. We sat there four days and had three sessions a day, one in the forenoon, one in the afternoon, and one in the evening. To show you how the work of this commission is regarded on the other side of the line I call your attention to the fact that Canada had seven able lawyers representing every interest involved in the Livingstone Channel investigation. The Dominion Government had two members of the Kings Council representing the Dominion Government; the Province of Ontario had Mr. Staunton, who is also a member of the Kings Council, and every interest from the Dominion Government down to the township opposite Detroit was represented before the commission in the investigation of that one subject. Our side of the case was presented very ably by one representative from the Department of Justice.

The CHAIRMAN. In this Livingstone Channel matter have you employed any engineers?

Mr. TAWNEY. No, sir; and I don't think we will have to do so. The Livingstone Channel matter is an altogether different proposition. The Government of the United States has authorized and appropriated money for the construction of the Livingstone Channel. We have expended about $11,000,000 on the project. That channel was excavated partly on Canadian territory with the consent of the Canadian Government. Our engineers anticipated that the deepening of this channel across the Limekiln Crossing, which was a barrier prior to that time, from 8 feet to 22 feet would necessarily increase the flow of water from Lake St. Clair and lower the level of the Lake and the waters above the entrance to Livingstone Channel. They also anticipated cross currents at the lower end of the cofferdam which was erected for the purpose of dredging in the dry; that is, blasting or quarrying out this Limekiln Crossing. Congress therefore was requested to authorize an investigation of what compensatory works would be necessary to compensate for the increased discharge through the Livingstone Channel and also protect navigation from these cross currents in the channel. A board of engineers was appointed to make the investigation, and they made their report to the standing board, and the standing board of engineers, which has general jurisdiction of river and harbor improvements, approved the report of the board of engineers in favor of the construction of a dike for that purpose. I do not know whether the Livingstone Channel map is here or not.

Dr. McLaughlin. Yes; it is here.

Mr. Tawney. However, they reported in favor of the construction of a dike.

Mr. Sharp. I know the currents down that channel are something terrific.

Mr. Tawney. Yes. This is downstream [indicating on map]; this is Amherstburg Channel, the old channel [indicating]. This shows where the cross currents are which the engineers anticipated would be in this channel [indicating], and so they recommended the construction of a dike about 3,000 feet long, extending from the lower end of the cofferdam to the upper end of Bois Blanc Island. Two-thirds of that dike would be on Canadian territory and one-third of it on American territory. On the recommendation of the engineers, Congress authorized the construction of that dike and appropriated the money for that purpose, but the people of Canada, locally, protested against the construction of the dike, because, they claim, it will increase the flow of water on their side, increase the flow of ice, and interfere with the use of their docks at Amherstburg, and that it will also increase the flow of polluted waters from Detroit. So the two Governments have submitted the two questions to us, as to whether or not this dike should be built or whether compensatory works could be built elsewhere, etc.

Mr. Sharp (interposing). Did they bear a proportion of that expense?

Mr. Tawney. None whatever.

Mr. Sharp. Why should not the Canadian Government have borne some of that expense?

Mr. Tawney. That is not a matter for the commission to pass upon.

The Chairman. You have had submitted to the joint commission three very important questions, or propositions?

Mr. Tawney. Yes, sir.

The Chairman. As to two of which you had to employ experts or scientists to aid you.

Mr. Tawney. Yes, sir.

The Chairman. And as I understand, from what you say, the cost of these experts and scientists was $12,000 a year for the Lake of the Woods proposition and $7,000 for the sanitary investigation?

Mr. Tawney. Yes, sir.

The Chairman. Making $19,000 a year, of which this Government is to provide one half and the Canadian Government the other half?

Mr. Tawney. Yes, sir.

The Chairman. Now, is that all the expenses outside of the fixed charges?

Mr. Tawney. Oh, no. Let me call your attention to the fact that there has never been a topographic survey of this section here [indicating on map], and the engineers can not work out these engineering problems in the Lake of the Woods investigation without surveys. We have one surveying party in the field now at an expense of $900 a month, and as soon as the weather conditions will permit we will have to make a survey of the Lake of the Woods, because we are called upon to report to the two Governments how much agricultural lands will be submerged at any certain stated level and the value of such lands; and we will have.another surveying party in there for probably four or five months at $900. The estimate is that the two parties will cost about $900 a month each.

The CHAIRMAN. For how long?

Mr. TAWNEY. For there or four months. This party here [indicating on map] will be in the field for nearly six months, and it is estimated that the party surveying the Lake of the Woods can get through their work possibly in four months. Then we have stream gaugers and other employees.

The CHAIRMAN. The engineering parties, then, will not cost over $8,000?

Mr. TAWNEY. Probably not. Then we must collect data regarding precipitation within the drainage area of 26,000 square miles. The engineers must get the run-off from all these lakes and rivers and ascertain the storage capacity in Rainy Lake and the other waters tributary to the Lake of the Woods, for the purpose of determining what level can be maintained in the Lake of the Woods. That is one of the questions the two Governments have asked us to report upon.

The CHAIRMAN. That would have to be done later, would it not?

Mr. TAWNEY. No; it is being done now.

The CHAIRMAN. Is that done by a separate engineering party?

Mr. TAWNEY. No; we have men stationed at certain places who read these gauges. Of course, the expense of gauge reading is not so very great. I do not know what these bills will amount to. I have here, Mr. Flood, a blank form which will give you an idea of how our accounts are kept and what the items of expense are. This is a form on which the vouchers are made by the engineers on the Lake of the Woods proposition.

The CHAIRMAN. What I was trying to get at was the exact amount of money that would be spent in caring for these two propositions on which you had to employ an expert force.

Mr. TAWNEY. I may say that before the question of the investigation of the pollution of the boundary waters was referred to the commission I made as close an estimate as I could without any reference to any additional business that might be referred to us; there are questions which are on the way now and may come before us, and no doubt will come before us, before the end of the fiscal year; but without any reference to them at all I estimated that $100,000 would be absolutely essential to carry on the work of the commission during the next fiscal year, and when we asked these sanitary experts as to the probable expense of their work they said they thought an independent appropriation of $50,000 should be made. Of course, we can't make a joint appropriation, so that would be $25,000 for our side.

Mr. McKINLEY. Let me ask a question which will, perhaps, clear this a little. For instance, there is an investigation being made at Buffalo, and you were asked if all the expense that was being incurred there was the doctor's salary of $7,000, and you said yes.

Mr. TAWNEY. I misunderstood that question. Let the doctor explain the number of employees that we will need in that work.

Dr. McLaughlin. This pollution work would take eight laboratories, four on each side. The United States Public Health Service has authority by act of Congress to investigate pollution of navigable streams and lakes and they would furnish us with the use of men and laboratories. We could count on four laboratories from the United States, but as the States are willing to help, instead of four we will use two from the Public Health Service, one from the State of New York, one from the State of Michigan, and, if necessary, we can use one from the State of Ohio. The persons in charge of these laboratories will be paid by the States to which they belong or by the Federal Government, but we can not ask them to spend money for us, so that in collecting samples we must hire the men to do the work. The men who gather the samples must have a great deal of expert knowledge and they must be absolutely reliable. The men best adapted to the work are young engineering students or young graduates, and we will have to pay those men about $5 a day.

The Chairman. In prosecuting that work what expense do you anticipate?

Dr. McLaughlin. One big expense will be the sample collectors and another big expense will be the tug hire, the hiring of tugs and boats. So that there will be an expense of, perhaps, $3,000 a month while the investigation is going on.

Mr. Sharp. Where are they going to take most of the samples from this coming year?

Dr. McLaughlin. Where?

Mr. Sharp. Yes; from what waters?

Dr. McLaughlin. The investigation was narrowed down, after consultation with the experts at Buffalo, to work on the St. Marys River, the St. Clair River, Lake St. Clair, the Detroit River, the Niagara River, and the St. Lawrence River, and the contiguous ends of the Lakes.

The Chairman. How many months do you expect to work this year?

Dr. McLaughlin. Well, we propose to make a report by the 1st of November.

Mr. Tawney. And that will be an interim report.

Mr. Sharp. I have gone up and down on those great steamers, freighters, and passenger boats, and there is a tremendous traffic there, and I would like to ask whether you consider that any considerable portion of this pollution comes from those steamers?

Dr. McLaughlin. Certainly. We have provided for that in this plan. We are going to make a plan for that investigation, and it will be made by the men of the Public Health Service stationed at Detroit, Buffalo, Cleveland, Chicago, and Milwaukee, where they can practically catch every steamer that plies on these waterways, and they will see whether any retaining devices are on board the vessels to hold the waste, or whether it is discharged into the lakes.

Mr. Tawney. Let me state that the statistics show the steamboat population on the Lakes during the navigation season to be from 15,000,000 to 17,000,000 people each season, and we consider that to be one of the great sources of pollution. That is claimed by people on both sides of the line.

The CHAIRMAN. Mr. Tawney, could you, within the next day or two, give us something in the nature of an itemized statement of what the expenses will be?

Mr. TAWNEY. Certainly; and I will be very glad to do so. We have a statement here that has been filed with the committee as to the expenditures——

The CHAIRMAN (interposing). You mean the fixed charges?

Mr. TAWNEY. Yes.

The CHAIRMAN. Well, we know what they are.

Mr. DIFENDERFER. Mr. Tawney, can you tell us how far the lake is navigable from its mouth?

Mr. TAWNEY. It is navigable clear up to International Falls.

Mr. DIFENDERFER. It is not navigable from there for the reason that there is a private dam built at that point?

Mr. TAWNEY. No; there is a natural dam there. There is a fall of 23 feet.

Mr. DIFENDERFER. When that grant was made to these private parties it was stipulated, as I understand it, that they at some time might be compelled to build locks which would permit vessels to pass that particular point?

Mr. TAWNEY. Yes, sir.

Mr. DIFENDERFER. Has this commission any power to compel that work to be done?

Mr. TAWNEY. No; and the commission does not need to have that power.

Mr. DIFENDERFER. That is within the power of the Canadian Government?

Mr. TAWNEY. Yes; that is within the power of the Province of Ontario, because they have so stipulated, as I am informed. I understand the condition is that upon the demand of the provincial government they will be required to put in a lock there, and they have built the dam with that end in view, in anticipation of being called upon at some future time to build that lock.

Mr. DIFENDERFER. East of that dam the waters, of course, are navigable?

Mr. TAWNEY. Yes.

Mr. DIFENDERFER. If those lakes——

Mr. TAWNEY (interposing). They are navigable for a considerable distance, and they might possibly be made so to Pigeon River.

Mr. DIFENDERFER. If that point could be passed by vessels, it would inure to the benefit of a very large class of people east of those falls, would it not?

Mr. TAWNEY. Well, a great many people do not inhabit that particular section.

Mr. DIFENDERFER. It looks as though there might be a considerable number.

Mr. TAWNEY. Oh, yes; in that section to which you are pointing on the map, up in the northern part of St. Louis County.

Mr. DIFENDERFER. And that is timber country?

Mr. TAWNEY. Yes, sir; and when you get down in here [indicating] you find iron.

Mr. CLINE. The judicial authority involved by virtue of this treaty extends to finding the ultimate fact, but not to passing judgment?

Mr. TAWNEY. Under article 9 you are right, but under articles 3 and 4 and article 10 our determination is final on all questions.

Mr. CLINE. It is final as to the ultimate fact?

Mr. TAWNEY. No; it is final and binds both Governments. Let me read you article 8.

Mr. CLINE. It is not provided in the treaty that you have authority to execute your judgment, is it?

Mr. TAWNEY. No; that is up to the Governments, the enforcement.

Mr. CLINE. That is what I say; it is in the nature of the finding of the ultimate fact as by a chancery court?

Mr. TAWNEY. Yes; and it must be enforced by the Governments.

Mr. CLINE. That is my understanding.

Mr. SHARP. It is like the decree of a court?

Mr. TAWNEY. Yes. The last paragraph of article 8 provides:

The majority of the commissioners shall have power to render a decision. In case the commission is evenly divided upon any question or matter presented to it for decision, separate reports shall be made by the commissioners on each side to their own Government. The high contracting parties shall thereupon endeavor to agree upon an adjustment of the question or matter of difference, and if an agreement is reached between them, it shall be reduced to writing in the form of a protocol and shall be communicated to the commissioners, who shall take such further proceedings as may be necessary to carry out such agreement.

Now, it is a fact that is not generally understood, either by Congress or by the public, that under Article X, with the consent of the Senate and with the consent of the Governor General of Canada, any question may be submitted to this commission, even questions of so-called vital interests or the national honor, if the Senate consents and the Governor General of Canada consents, and the decision of the commission is final. In cases, however, under Article X it is expressly provided that if the commission does not agree, then we make reports to our respective Governments, and an umpire is chosen, under the rules of The Hague conference for the selection of umpires, and the umpire takes the reports of the two sections of the commission and he decides, and his decision is, by this treaty, made final. So that, under Article X and Articles III, IV, and VIII, the jurisdiction of the commission is final and the powers of the commission are judicial.

Mr. CLINE. Under section 10 your labors, then, are strictly in line with a commission appointed by the court of chancery, from which there can be no review?

Mr. TAWNEY. Yes, sir.

Mr. CLINE. And judgment is based upon your conclusions by the umpire?

Mr. TAWNEY. Yes, sir.

Mr. SHARP. You are really a perpetual commission from the very nature of your duties?

Mr. TAWNEY. From the very nature of the jurisdiction and from the nature and extent of the common property owned by the inhabitants of the two countries in common, over which we are given jurisdiction, it is an international court for the settlement of controversies arising out of the use of this common property by the inhabitants on either side or on both sides of the line.

Mr. SHARP. And to that extent it differs from the other commissions that are simply appointed to establish a boundary line and then their labors are at an end?

Mr. TAWNEY. Yes, sir. The difficulty about this thing is in the name; it is a mismomer to call it a commission. When you study the treaty and see the scope of its jurisdiction and the powers with which it has been clothed by the high contracting parties, you will see it is not a commission created for some single and temporary purpose but that it is a judicial tribunal, the extent and character of whose jurisdiction is such as to make it, or the existence of some similar body, essential in the administration of international justice between a people as closely related in their commercial and industrial life as are the people of the United States and Canada.

Mr. CLINE. That depends upon the questions you are considering. If you are considering purely legal questions then you are a court, but if you are considering a question in which you find the ultimate fact then you are a commission.

Mr. TAWNEY. Article IX is the only one under which our jurisdiction is investigative. I will give you a concrete case. Here is Richelieu River, the outlet of Lake Champlain. Canada has granted a franchise to a private corporation for the construction of a dam and locks on the Richelieu River. This dam and the locks are to be located wholly in Canada territory and not within the jurisdiction of the United States at all, but the effect of the construction of that dam and the locks will be to raise the level of the lake and submerge the lands on our side.

The CHAIRMAN. Just the same as the Lake of the Woods?

Mr. TAWNEY. Yes. Now, the corporation to whom the franchise has been granted can not go on with that structure, although it has the authority of the Government in whose jurisdiction the dam and locks are to be erected—they can not go on with it until they have first made application to this commission under its rules of procedure, because the two Governments have expressly provided by this treaty that they will not permit the obstruction of boundary waters on either side of the line which affect the level or flow of these waters on the other side without the approval of this international tribunal. Under our rules, when an application is made for our approval of a project which would obstruct the water on one side and raise the level on the other side, the application must be made in the form prescribed by our rules, and then by the rules we provide for the giving of notice to everybody interested and the fixing of a time for a hearing. And that hearing is just the same as a trial in court; the witnesses are sworn and the procedure is entirely judicial.

Mr. DIFENDERFER. Is there not a local situation involved in this dam [indicating on map], the claim being that it has caused the overflow of acres of land?

Mr. TAWNEY. Yes, sir.

Mr. DIFENDERFER. Is that held up for the same reason?

The CHAIRMAN. That dam has been built—it was built 18 years ago.

Mr. DIFENDERFER. But the people who have constructed that dam are overflowing thousands of acres here on our American territory [indicating].

Mr. TAWNEY. Yes; in Minnesota.

Mr. DIFENDERFER. Can that be remedied?

Mr. TAWNEY. Yes. Now, let me tell you; the two Governments have submitted this whole question to us, and in addition to the question of what level should be established, they ask us to report and recommend as to what control should be exercised by the two Governments over the outlets of both of these lakes, which means that these two dams will be, or may be—I do not say they will be, because we have not reached any conclusion as yet—it may be that the two Governments will place both of these dams under international control, so that they will not be manipulated by the owners of the power to the detriment of the financial or industrial interests on either side of the line.

Mr. DIFENDERFER. In the event of a disagreement relative to this matter referred to in the Lake of the Woods and The Hague referee should render a decision that decision would be absolute, would it not?

Mr. TAWNEY. No; you are confounding our jurisdiction under Article X with our jurisdiction under Article IX. We are making this investigation under Article IX, and if you will study Article IX——

Mr. DIFENDERFER (interposing). I have paid no attention to it until this morning.

Mr. TAWNEY (continuing). You will see it expressly provides that our conclusions and findings shall not have the character of an arbitral award. We make our report and recommendations to the Governments under Article IX. It is intended, no doubt, that our report will afford the two Governments all the data upon which a final settlement of the question referred can be brought about through the ordinary diplomatic channels.

Mr. CLINE. And that is essentially so from the fact that your finding may involve interests over which you have no control?

Mr. TAWNEY. Certainly. Our findings may involve a great many things over which we have no control. In the case of the Lake of the Woods it will necessarily involve the international control of both the outlet of the Lake of the Woods and the outlet of Rainy Lake, which empties into the Lake of the Woods and is tributary to the Lake of the Woods.

Now, in regard to the status of the appropriation, I conferred with Mr. Flood on Saturday and with members of the Senate Committee on Appropriations. I am confident that neither House of Congress would knowingly withhold the money necessary to pay our Government's share of the expense incident to the doing of the work the two Governments require. When I presented the matter to members of the Committee on Appropriations of the Senate they suggested that the best way out of the difficulty now would be to offer an amendment to the sundry civil appropriation bill in the Senate and then for me to appear before the Committee on Foreign Affairs and explain the character and extent of the work of the commission and the necessity for the appropriation. The subcommittee considered the proposed amendment yesterday, as I am informed, and will put it in the sundry civil bill. I wanted the Committee on Foreign Affairs to understand the nature and extent of our work and what the commission has accomplished. I want to say that it is immaterial to me on which bill the appropriation is carried, but under existirg circumstances I do not know of any other way that the money can be appropriated at this session except upon the sundry civil bill.

Mr. DIFENDERFER. Have you submitted to the Senate committee the amount necessary, in your judgment?

Mr. TAWNEY. Yes; the State Department estimate of $100,000 is carried in the proposed amendment.

Mr. DIFENDERFER. In order to prosecute this immediately it will be necessary for us to have, as soon as possible, an estimate of the amount necessary so that our committee may pass upon it.

Mr. TAWNEY. It will come over in the sundry civil bill and be in conference.

The CHAIRMAN. What he wants is a detailed statement.

Mr. TAWNEY. I will make up an estimate as soon as I can. Of course, you understand this tribunal is like any other court; it is open to the two Governments to bring business before it at any time and all the work we have up to this time under Article IX has been submitted within the last eight months, and what amount of work may be submitted to us during the fiscal year 1914 I do not know. So I will give you as close an estimate as I can. I do not want to ask for any more than is necessary; at the same time I would not like to be compelled to say to our Canadian associates on the commission that we can not go on with this work because we have not the money with which to pay our share of the expenses. That would be rather humiliating to the American section of the commission and also to our Government.

The CHAIRMAN. We are very much obliged to you, Mr. Tawney.

Thereupon the committee adjourned.

CPSIA information can be obtained at www.ICGtesting.com
Printed in the USA
BVOW01s1126040115

381791BV00003B/28/P

9 781272 959968